BECOMING A LAWYER

DEDICATION

Michael dedicates this book to his inspiration—his gorgeous and intelligent daughters Giselle and Georgia.

David dedicates this book to his darling wife and best friend Mary-Anne and to his daughters and mates Millie and Prue.

'You complete me'

Stolen from:

Tom Cruise as Jerry Maguire in *Jerry Maguire*

Heath Ledger as the Joker in *The Dark Knight*

Keyshia Cole singing 'You Complete Me'

Mike Myers as Dr Evil in *Austin Powers: The Spy Who Shagged Me*

BECOMING A LAWYER

SUCCESS AT LAW SCHOOL

THIRD EDITION

Michael Brogan
David Spencer

OXFORD
UNIVERSITY PRESS
AUSTRALIA & NEW ZEALAND

OXFORD
UNIVERSITY PRESS

Oxford University Press is a department of the University of Oxford.

It furthers the University's objective of excellence in research, scholarship, and education by publishing worldwide. Oxford is a registered trademark of Oxford University Press in the UK and in certain other countries.

Published in Australia by Oxford University Press
253 Normanby Road, South Melbourne, Victoria 3205, Australia

First published as *Surviving Law School* 2004
Second edition published 2008
Published as *Becoming a Lawyer* 2014
Reprinted 2016(D)

National Library of Australia Cataloguing-in-Publication entry
Author: Brogan, Michael C., 1966– author.
Title: Becoming a lawyer : success at law school / Michael Brogan; David Spencer.
Edition: 3rd edition.
ISBN: 9780195524062 (paperback)
Notes: Includes index.
Subjects: Law schools—Australia.
Law students—Australia—Handbooks, manuals, etc.
Other Authors/Contributors: Spencer, David, 1961– author.
Dewey Number: 340.071194.

Edited by Natasha Broadstock and Valina Rainer
Text design by Denise Lane
Typeset by diacriTech, India
Proofread by Roz Edmond
Indexed by Glenda Browne
Printed and bound in Australia by Ligare Book Printers, Pty Ltd

Contents

List of Figures and Tables

Preface

Welcome to this renamed and fresh edition of the book formerly known as *Surviving Law School*. The new title, coupled with updates to every chapter, not only reflects the most recent technological changes that affect learning and teaching in law schools, but our desire to emphasise part of the hidden curriculum of law school programs. We acknowledge that law school provides opportunities for a tremendous general education as well as an opportunity to develop a profession. However, the increasing emphasis on ethics in law schools, the growing incidence of professionally-inspired JD programs, and the increasing use of practical skills-development in assessment tasks, suggested a need to focus on the evolution of the legally-inexperienced student into an adept and competent individual who may seek admission to practice as a lawyer. In addition to referring to professional cultural practices and expectations we have made significant changes to our discussion regarding legal research, statutory interpretation, and professional ethics.

As always, we trust that this book provides you with the tools and advice to confidently complete your studies and become a lawyer.

We wish you the best of luck on your journey and we hope you find as much satisfaction and enjoyment at becoming a lawyer as we did.

Michael and David.

Acknowledgments

The author and the publisher wish to thank the following copyright holders for reproduction of their material.

Australian Research Council, for extract from www.arc.gov.au; AustLII, Faculty of Law, University of Technology, Sydney, for extract from www.austlii.edu.au; Department of Industry, Canberra for extracts from their websites; Department of Industry, Innovation, Climate Change, Science, Research and Tertiary Education for Threshold Learning Outcomes; Goodwin, K., Kennedy, G. & Vetere, F. (2010). Getting together out-of-class: Using technologies for informal interaction and learning. Acilite Sydney 2010; National Association of Community Legal Centres Inc. (NACLC) for extract from www.naclc.org.au; Penguin UK for Charles Leadbeater, 'Living on Thin Air: The New Economy' (London: Penguin, 2000); ©State of New South Wales through the Department of Attorney General and Justice for extracts reproduced with the approval of the Office of the Legal Services Commissioner; Supreme Court of Victoria for case extract; Thomson Reuters Australia Limited www.thomsonreuters.com for extracts from Commonwealth Law Reports.

Every effort has been made to trace the original source of copyright material contained in this book. The publisher will be pleased to hear from copyright holders to rectify any errors or omissions.

1

WHY AM I STUDYING LAW?

Law courses are usually very tough to enter and can involve a great deal of hard work ... Law is a terrific field because it offers the opportunity for intellectual absorption, as well as career preparation ... The increase in law students in recent years has caused the LLB to transform from a purely professional degree to a popular generalist qualification.

'The Good Universities Guide'[1]

---

1 Hobsons Pty Ltd, 'The Good Universities Guide 2013' (Melbourne: Hobsons Pty Ltd, 2012), at 165.

Introduction

Congratulations! You did it. You made it into law school. Now the hard work really begins! You are about to join an honourable profession that has dedicated itself to a number of ideals, such as: the pursuit of justice; equality before the law; the pursuit of truth; the pursuit of the maintenance of the 'rule of law' (a term to be discussed below); the pursuit of a satisfying career; the pursuit of intellectual stimulation; and, for some, the pursuit of a comfortable living.

Congratulations on making it to law school

You may have entered law school in search of one or more of the above ideals, but whatever the reason, getting there is only half the battle. Staying in law school, managing the enormous workload and meeting the challenge of understanding what are at times difficult concepts are the real challenges. The attrition rate in law is high—in some law schools, up to two-thirds of students who commence studies fail to graduate with the coveted Bachelor of Laws (LLB) or equivalent. While this book cannot increase your intellectual ability, it will provide many useful hints on how to deliver what a university law school demands. Simple things—such as being able to analyse cases and solve legal problems in a structured fashion that display a high level of analysis and synthesis—will allow you not only to succeed at the study of law, but also to maximise your potential.

Gaining entry to law school is only half the battle

The first thing to accept is that studying law is very different from other disciplines (a point to be discussed in more detail in Chapter 3). Second, most students enter a university law school to undertake a combined law degree straight from their final year of secondary school, and will soon find that, unlike school studies, the study of law at university in Australia does not rely on 'rote' learning; that is, memorising parts of judgments and statutes is relatively useless! Not even law firms look for that ability any more, at least not since the advent of sophisticated legal databases accessible through the World Wide Web. Within two hours of the High Court handing down a decision in Canberra, any lawyer around the country (and, indeed, overseas) can download the case, read it and apply it. Therefore, the ability to regurgitate judgments is a task now performed by machines.

Studying law is not about 'rote' learning

What does the study of law entail?

The study of law in Australia is about critical analysis and synthesis. When we say 'critical', we mean that you need to be able to consider the law and how it affects—and is in turn affected by—the society within which it operates. Put simply, law does not exist in a vacuum, so your 'critical' analysis requires you to consider the social, economic, historical, and philosophical implications of the law and its impact on the community it serves. When it comes to 'analysis' it is important to be able to identify the legal issue(s) and then cite the appropriate authorities, but then you must be able to analyse the fact pattern before you can argue the facts and law in a coherent manner that produces a well-reasoned conclusion. 'Synthesis' requires you to take your critical analysis and mount an argument that is informed by the current state of the law together with persuasive reasoning as to why a court should vary or overturn its previous decisions.

Studying law is about critical analysis and synthesis

Lawyers should know what the law is when they enter a courtroom. If they do not know the law, then by rights they should not be charging their clients fees for service! Every day, in courtrooms around Australia, lawyers seek to explore the difference in facts between their client's case and the case that is the current precedent ('precedent' meaning a court decision that states the current law in relation to the issue before the court). Every day, lawyers seek to exploit the grey area of facts that may allow a court to apply precedent, distinguish precedent (where precedent is not applied because some essential difference exists between it and the case before the court), or perhaps overturn precedent (where the court, considering a similar fact situation, decides that the precedent was wrong). The use of precedent will be discussed in Chapter 5. For the moment, all you need to appreciate is that in this process, lawyers rely on analysis and synthesis. They analyse the facts in a way that will allow the court to apply or distinguish the accepted precedent, or they find new law or a variation of existing law, and then they argue their point. The sooner you learn the intellectual skills of analysis and synthesis, the sooner you will start to 'think and act like a lawyer'. Thinking like a lawyer is a guarantee of good marks being achieved in assessed tasks at law school.

Learn the intellectual skill of legal analysis and synthesis; 'think and act like a lawyer'

What is law all about?

While different lawyers would answer the above question differently, from the community's perspective the law provides a set of rules within which it operates. The importance of law is that people know what they can and cannot do. Without laws, society would be disorganised. Even simple things such as travelling on the roads would be reduced to chaos, with people not knowing which side of the road to travel on and who to give way to at intersections. You can imagine raising the level of importance of this analogy to violence within our society and the need for laws to protect the defenceless in society.

The law provides a set of rules within which the community operates

So the law is about the development and the maintenance of the rules by which we live. But it is a bit more complex than that. In Chapter 8 we will explore the development of the law and embark on a historical journey that will help to explain further what law is all about, but first, let us look at the rule of law.

The rule of law

So while the question 'What is law all about?' can be answered simply by stating that it is about a set of rules, that is not a complete answer. A second concept to understand is a concept called 'the rule of law'. The rule of law is an English doctrine that essentially means that all people are equal before the law. It does not matter if a person is a government official, a police officer, a judge, or a bricklayer; all people will be treated the same before the law. A notable exception is the sovereign. The rule of law has three important components:

The rule of law essentially means that all people are equal before the law

i) the law is predominant, so the government has no arbitrary power over the citizen;
ii) the law administered by ordinary courts applies equally to all; and
iii) the citizen's personal freedoms are protected by the law rather than by any special constitutional guarantees that favour certain sections of the community.

The reason that the rule of law is important is because our courts are the guardians of the rule of law and the law itself serves to ensure the survival of the rule of law, thereby protecting all people equally. The preservation of the rule of law is, some would say, the most important answer to the question 'What is law all about?'

Careers in the law

According to the 2012 Australian Graduate Survey,[2] 70.1 per cent of law graduates are in full-time employment; 19.7 per cent are in further full-time study; 4.6 per cent are in part-time or casual employment; and 5.4 per cent are unavailable for full-time study or work. Of those available for full-time employment, 81.7 per cent are working in the law.

In addition, 'The Good Universities Guide 2013'[3] (based on collection results from 2012) states that about 83 per cent of law graduates gain employment upon graduating. Australia-wide, those law graduates gaining immediate employment end up in the following job areas:

- 55 per cent in private legal practice;
- 19 per cent in the public sector (government legal and non-legal departments);
- 23 per cent in private industry (in legal and non-legal roles); and
- 2 per cent in employment abroad.

Even though only just over half of all law graduates are employed in private law firms, law graduates are employed in a wide variety of law-related jobs. In fact, there is barely a job that can be performed that does not have legal ramifications. For example, those who supervise or manage employees in just about any capacity need to be aware of industrial relations and occupational health and safety laws. Likewise, when conducting business in Australia today, the governance of organisations is covered by a plethora of legislation, foremost of which are the complex requirements of the *Corporations Act 2001* (Cth) and the *Competition and Consumer Act 2012* (Cth). Both statutes have federal watchdogs—in the form of the Australian Securities and Investments Commission (ASIC) and the Australian Competition and Consumer Commission (ACCC) respectively—that enforce the aforementioned statutes governing trade and commerce in Australia. Outside of the corporate watchdogs, consumers have numerous pieces of consumer legislation protecting their rights. So the conduct of all types of business

There is barely a job that can be performed that does not have legal ramifications

2 http://www.graduatecareers.com.au/Research/GradJobsDollars/BachelorAll/Law/index.htm (accessed 5 April 2013).

3 Hobsons Pty Ltd, 'The Good Universities Guide 2013' (Melbourne: Hobsons Pty Ltd, 2012).

in Australia is intrinsically linked to law. Hence the value of a law degree in the conduct of just about any business in the country.

But let us get back to careers in the law. For those 55 per cent of law graduates who enter private legal practice, predominantly as solicitors, the areas of practice are many and varied. It is not uncommon to find most large commercial law firms having a number of practice areas, including the following non-exhaustive list:

- aviation
- banking and finance
- biotech and health
- capital markets
- communications media and technology
- competition law
- construction
- energy
- environment and planning
- family and child services
- financial services reform
- funds management—real estate and superannuation
- government regulation
- infrastructure
- insolvency and restructuring
- insurance
- intellectual property
- litigation and dispute resolution
- mergers and acquisitions
- native title
- patents and trade marks
- privacy
- product liability
- project finance
- real property
- resources

- securitisation
- tax
- workplace relations
- private practice.

All of the above means that there is something for everyone who wishes to enter the legal profession. The practice areas offered by the large firms are replicated in common practice clusters in medium and small firms. Small firms, or those commonly known as 'general practice' firms, tend to include criminal law as a practice area. Because of the high level of specialisation within the law, lawyers in large and medium firms tend to specialise in one or two areas of the above-listed areas of practice. Generally, law graduates in larger firms will be rotated through three different areas in their first 12–18 months as a solicitor, after which they will be settled in one area where they will continue to gain the necessary experience and skills of a specialist lawyer.

Public sector

Of the approximately 19 per cent of law graduates that end up working in the public sector, those that practise law will find themselves doing some specialist tasks. For example, lawyers may just be dealing with commercial leasing documents or with construction contracts frequently used by the government department they are employed by. Just like any organisation, the government—whether it is state, territory, or federal—has specific needs to satisfy when it comes to legal services. While only solicitors are generally employed by government departments (with the exception of state, territory, and federal criminal prosecution authorities), those solicitors will find themselves doing a variety of skill-based work within the specialist area they operate in. For example, interviewing, drafting, advice work, presentations, and briefing counsel are just some of the tasks government solicitors become involved with on a day-to-day basis.

> Lawyers working in the public sector will find themselves doing some specialist tasks

Generally, when the government is suing or being sued, it will brief a member (or members) of the independent bar in the state or territory they are being sued in or are taking action in. In this way, like privately run organisations, they do not have to go to the expense of actually employing barristers to act on those occasions when litigation is likely. There is one notable exception.

The offices of the various Directors of Public Prosecutions (state, territory, and federal) employ Crown Prosecutors to bring criminal prosecutions before the courts. These prosecutors are members of their respective state or territory bar associations and act as advocates on almost a daily basis for their respective directors.

Corporate counsel

Of the approximately 23 per cent of law graduates that work in private industry, those that practise law will find themselves doing a number of specialist tasks. For example, a common combination is to have specialist corporate or in-house counsel dealing with issues such as: industrial relations; contract drafting and maintenance; and matters relating to corporate governance and regulation. As with government departments, even though the areas of law may be specialised, lawyers will find themselves doing a wide variety of tasks. The areas of law that in-house counsel practise in is as wide ranging as the kinds of businesses found in Australia and its trading partners.

The areas of law that in-house counsel practise in is wide ranging

Solicitor or barrister?

Following admission to their respective state or territory Supreme Courts, lawyers have a choice as to whether they practise as a solicitor or a barrister. While in some states, for example Victoria, a firm of lawyers may describe themselves as 'barristers and solicitors', an individual lawyer may only hold a practising certificate as one or the other at any point in time. A practising certificate is the legal requirement of legal practitioners to practise and is administered by the respective law societies or institutes and bar associations in each state and territory. Practising certificates allow legal practitioners to call themselves either barristers or solicitors, and usually tell a client that the lawyer is covered by professional indemnity and trust account fraud insurance.

A lawyer may only hold a practising certificate as either a solicitor or a barrister at any one time

Solicitors make up the vast bulk of the legal profession and handle the sort of work described above, and more. They are often described as being those lawyers who conduct general aspects of giving legal advice, transaction-based law (such as the drafting of contracts), and the general requirements of the conduct of litigation. While solicitors handle the bulk of work generated in legal practice, in litigation they serve the purpose of: administering and managing the litigation; communicating with the client(s) and witness(es); assisting in the process of research and information gathering; and instructing the barrister(s) regarding the client's instructions.

Barristers are those lawyers that act as advocates for litigants in courts and tribunals. In addition, most barristers undertake the writing of opinions on specialist areas of the law. Barristers are specialists in advocating a client's case in court, and for this reason they are experts in the rules of evidence and the rules and procedures of court. It is important to understand that solicitors are not prevented from acting as advocates in any jurisdiction and that many solicitors spend most of their time in court acting as advocates in a variety of matters. However, depending on the type of matter, many solicitors will brief a barrister to appear as they are the expert section of the legal profession that specialises in court advocacy.

Judges and parliamentarians

Finally, it should be mentioned that two other high-profile jobs attract many lawyers. First, the judiciary, which is charged with the important task of judging cases that require adjudication. Judges are generally drawn from the senior ranks of barristers. This is logical because barristers are experts in advocating cases before judges sitting in courts. Therefore, barristers have an excellent knowledge of the rules of evidence and rules of court and are the obvious choice for elevation to the bench. However, some senior solicitors and academic lawyers have been known to take up positions on the bench. Second, many politicians in both state and territory parliaments as well as federal parliament have law degrees. Given that parliament is largely about making law, it is not surprising that many lawyers seek a career in local, state, or federal government.

Judges are generally drawn from the senior ranks of barristers

Why study law?

Intellectual stimulation

The study of law is in some respects no different to other academic disciplines in that it is intellectually challenging and very interesting. If you have a desire to study law to determine the way in which it affects different parts of the

Think about how the law could be changed to better serve our society

community, or how it could—or should—be changed to better serve our society, then you have picked the right discipline. Studying law gives you that opportunity.

There is no doubt that some professions or vocations are repetitive in the tasks that people have to perform, and law is no exception. Lawyers routinely undertake activities that are repetitive. However, depending on the area of law practised, lawyers generally find the job an intellectually stimulating one. It is not only the law that changes frequently, depending on what area you practise in, but also the rules of court that change, to allow for new methods of conducting the court's business. Certainly in the area of litigation, the court rules and procedures are dynamic and keep up to date with technological and other changes occurring in society. The courts issue practice notes to assist lawyers to understand the methods by which they manage their workload.

Despite the fact that some areas of the law move slowly because of settled principles, for example, contract law, other areas change frequently, such as taxation, industrial relations and immigration law. In recognition of the fact that the law and its administrative procedures change regularly, the various law societies, institutes, and bar associations in each state and territory require lawyers to achieve a certain level of continuing legal education for each year that they practise. Most law societies, institutes, and bar associations have similar systems of Mandatory Continuing Legal Education (MCLE) that may include the following features:

- The participant must undertake around 10 hours of MCLE per year prior to the renewal of each year's practising certificate.
- The activity qualifying the participant for MCLE must be of significant intellectual or practical content and must deal primarily with matters directly related to the practice of law.
- The activity qualifying the participant for MCLE must be conducted by persons who are qualified by practical or academic experience in the subject covered.
- The MCLE must be relevant to a legal practitioner's immediate or long-term needs in relation to the practitioner's professional development.
- Activities qualifying for MCLE can be a face-to-face activity, or an individual professional development activity such as teaching or training

others in the legal profession. There must usually be a minimum number of hours of face-to-face activities.

- Sometimes, the law society, institute, or bar association may prescribe certain authorised providers of MCLE activities.

The law offers almost constant intellectual stimulation and the limit of one's intellectual stimulation may ultimately depend on the type of matters presented to the lawyer by his or her clients. In this respect, members of the legal profession acting as solicitors are entitled to turn down a client if the area of law is not one that the lawyer is proficient in. This ensures that clients receive highly professional and competent legal representation. This serves the client well and it serves the court system—and therefore the community—well by ensuring the efficient and competent resolution of civil disputes and the prosecution of criminal matters.

Solicitors may turn down a client if they are not proficient in that area of law

Postgraduate studies

These days, most university law schools offer extensive postgraduate research degrees that can assist those lawyers wishing to continue learning and developing professionally. A vast array of specialisations are available in the various Master of Laws (LLM) programs at most university law schools. These degrees can be taken either by coursework or by thesis, usually the latter leading to a Master of Law with honours (LLM (Hons)). For those with a yearning for research, most university law schools offer Doctor of Philosophy (PhD) programs that enable research that will make an original contribution to the body of legal knowledge in Australia culminating in a thesis of about 80–100,000 words. Finally comes another degree that falls between a Masters and a PhD, called the Doctor of Juridical Science (SJD). The SJD usually requires a candidate to pass a component of coursework and to conduct some original research written up as a thesis (usually of about 50–80,000 words). While Masters degrees are common in the legal fraternity, the SJD and PhD are quite rare. An academic career generally requires a SJD or PhD, but a higher degree by research is not essential for the practice of law.

Most university law schools offer extensive postgraduate research degrees

Remuneration

Let us explode one of the great myths about law. Not all lawyers make six-figure salaries. In fact, very few lawyers make six-figure salaries and those who do usually work, or have worked, seven days a week and 12 hours a day to get to the point in their career where they can earn such a large salary.

Not all lawyers make six-figure salaries

According to the 'The Good Universities Guide 2013'[4] the average gross starting salary for law graduates nationally is $53,201 per annum. This represents one of the highest starting salaries of any profession and is certainly on par with other professions and vocations. However, salaries for lawyers tend to climb quicker with experience compared to many other professions, particularly in commercial law firms when senior lawyers become associates and partners who share the profits from the firm. But, as stated above, this is the exception not the rule. Given that many law graduates will end up in suburban practice,[5] the potential remuneration is limited by the number of hours that lawyers in a small practice can work and the limited financial resources of their clients. However, it is not unknown for suburban practitioners to be making large sums of money equivalent to—and sometimes outstripping—many lawyers in large city practices.

The average gross starting salary for law graduates nationally is $53,201 per annum

But a cautionary note is in order for all those seeking to enter the legal profession in a law firm regardless of size—no lawyer has an easy run when it comes to earning a living. It does not matter what size firm you work for, few lawyers would objectively state that they do not have to work hard for a large salary. The practice of law is hard work and the remuneration generally flows to those that work hard to earn it. What the law can deliver on is that the hard work is generally worth it—the job is usually satisfying and interesting, and under such conditions hard work is not such a bad element of the job!

The hard work is generally worth it—the job is usually satisfying and interesting

4 Hobsons Pty Ltd, 'The Good Universities Guide 2013' (Melbourne: Hobsons Pty Ltd, 2012).

5 Hobsons Pty Ltd, 'The Good Universities Guide 2013' (Melbourne: Hobsons Pty Ltd, 2012), at 165.

To help others

Given the importance of the law in our society, lawyers are uniquely placed to help others who need its protection. While most lawyers would argue that they help people along the way by simply performing their jobs, there are career directions for lawyers that more directly help others who cannot avail themselves of the protection of the law. The community encourages the notion of lawyers helping others by the funding of various bodies to assist those that cannot afford legal representation. Many lawyers work for the Legal Aid Commission, a state- or territory-based statutory authority that seeks to provide legal representation for those who need but cannot afford it. Legal aid serves a very important purpose by providing legal representation to many people who would 'fall through the cracks' of our system of justice. Unfortunately, because of the limited resource of legal aid, it is means-tested in all states and territories. This means that people above a certain income will not be granted access to legal aid. Also, some types of matters do not attract legal aid, for example, commercial matters involving trade and commerce.

Lawyers are uniquely placed to help those who need the protection of the law

Community legal centres are an important link between the community and the legal profession. One of the oldest community legal centres in Australia is the Redfern Legal Centre, located in the inner city of Sydney. According to the centre's website:[6]

> Redfern Legal Centre (RLC) is an independent, non-profit community centre dedicated to promoting social justice and human rights. We offer free legal advice, referral and casework to disadvantaged people living in the City of Sydney, Botany Bay and Leichhardt local government areas ...
>
> We also provide community legal education and advocate for the reform of inequalities in laws, the legal system, administrative practices and society as a whole. Our specialist areas of work are domestic violence, tenancy, credit and debt, employment, discrimination, and complaints about police and other government agencies.
>
> We also provide volunteer opportunities for lawyers and law students.

6 http://www.rlc.org.au (accessed 5 April 2013).

According to the National Association of Community Legal Centres website, there are approximately 200 community legal centres nationwide, operating in every state and territory of Australia:[7]

> Some CLCs offer specialist legal services in areas such as child support, credit and debt, environmental law, welfare rights, mental health, disability discrimination, tenancy, immigration, employment, the arts, etc. Some CLCs provide services targeted to particular groups, such as Aboriginal and Torres Strait Islander people, children and young people, women, older people, refugees, prisoners, and the homeless. There are around 200 CLCs across Australia.
>
> The clients of CLCs are those who face economic, social or cultural disadvantage, are often experiencing multiple inter-related problems, and frequently their legal problem may affect their and their family's entire life circumstances.
>
> ...
>
> CLCs are located throughout Australia in urban, regional and remote locations. They are part of their communities and respond flexibly to the changing needs of those communities, offering creative, effective and targeted solutions to legal problems. CLCs also consult and involve their communities in their operations and management, always striving to make their services accessible and appropriate, to listen to their communities about their understanding of their needs and the solutions they want. It is the relationship with their community that distinguishes CLCs from other legal services.
>
> While providing legal services to individuals, CLCs also work beyond the individual. CLCs undertake community development, community legal education, capacity building and law and policy reform projects that are based on people's needs, are preventative in outcome and strengthen and empower the community they serve.
>
> Some CLCs receive no or very little funding and are largely or entirely staffed by volunteers. All other CLCs receive funds from a variety of sources including state and federal governments and philanthropic organisations. The sector harnesses the energy and

7 National Association of Community Legal Centres Inc. (NACLC): http://www.naclc.org.au/cb_pages/clcs.php (accessed 5 April 2013).

> expertise of thousands of volunteers across the country. CLCs are committed to collaborating and working in partnership wherever possible, with government, legal aid and other publicly funded legal assistance service providers, pro bono contributors, the private legal profession, community services agencies and other community partners to ensure the best outcomes for their clients and prevent social exclusion.

According to the NACLC, in 2011/2012:

- 195,000 clients were assisted by CLCs (this is a count of all clients who had an active matter over the 2011–12 financial year)
- 230,695 matters were handled by CLCs (this is a count of all matters that had an active case or an advice during the 2001–12 financial year)
- 237,266 advices were provided
- there were 74,406[8] active cases.

Law students who can manage their study load and any paid work commitments should consider volunteering for work at a community legal centre. It is an excellent way to get some 'hands-on' experience of understanding the practice of law and, after a while, the chance to participate in preliminary client interviewing—an important skill for the effective lawyer to develop. Any opportunity to link the theoretical learning of the law, conducted at university, with the practical application of the law, conducted by volunteering at a community law centre, is a valuable experience that will not only deepen your learning experience, but also help you gain employment after graduation.

Law students should consider volunteering at a community legal centre

Because it goes with my other degree

A law degree for an undergraduate normally consists of a combined law degree program where the LLB is linked with another non-law degree. Given the interdisciplinary approach to tertiary education adopted by most universities today, there are numerous combined degrees on offer. Gone are the days when

8 These figures are for centres funded through the Commonwealth Community Legal Services Program only.

one could choose only between Arts/Law, Science/Law and Business/Law. Today, one may select Health Science, Policing, Aviation, International Studies, Music, Social Sciences, Languages—the list goes on and on! Not only are universities producing graduates with a greater understanding of the world around them, but they are also allowing students to follow interests that may extend beyond the law.

Combined law degrees produce graduates with a greater understanding of the world

Further, certain combinations may sit well with the law degree. For example, a person with a flair for languages who would like to travel may combine languages and law with a view to joining the Department of Foreign Affairs as a career diplomat. Statistically, the most popular combined law degree is a business or commerce degree combined with a law degree. The reason this is so is because in the business community today, rarely can a corporate decision be made without recourse to the law. The law affects: corporate governance; the raising of capital; the treatment of shareholders and directors; auditing and reporting mechanisms; the declaration of dividends; the quality of goods and services; and much more. In other words, every step a corporation makes is watched by a statutorily empowered corporate watchdog, most commonly the ASIC or the ACCC. Even businesses that are not corporate entities are regulated by a vast array of consumer regulation. Given such a climate, it is not surprising that many businesses and corporations seek to employ graduates with a legal education.

Rarely can a corporate decision be made without recourse to the law

Students should consider two important questions when choosing their combined law program: first, 'What would I like to do with my life and career?', and second, 'What are my interests?' If students can satisfy the answers to both questions with their choice of combined law degree, then they are probably on the right path. While most people would agree that employment is a means to an end—that is, a way to earn a living—the best possible option for employment is a job that you actually enjoy. As a tertiary student you have a very short period of time to ensure that your chosen career option will lead you to an enjoyable working life. Make sure you make the right decision!

The best possible option for employment is a job that you actually enjoy

But a word of advice—simply put, a law degree will never hurt your chances of employment. A law degree displays more than just knowledge of the law. It shows that you have committed yourself to a long course of difficult study and have succeeded. It shows that you have been able to grapple with difficult concepts and intelligently work your way through them. It shows that you should have developed good communication skills. It shows that you are able to analyse facts and issues, synthesise them into a plausible argument, and produce a solution. Further, given most law courses employ problem-based learning, it shows that you have the ability to problem-solve and this is a valuable skill in all manner of careers, particularly law. In summary, a law degree sends a message to an employer that you have:

A law degree displays more than just knowledge of the law

i) commitment
ii) application
iii) intelligence
iv) problem-solving skills
v) communication skills
vi) an understanding of the doctrinal foundation of law, and
vii) an appreciation of the place of law in the broader historical, social, cultural and economic contexts.

These skills, or most of them at least, are desirable for any job. That is why lawyers are sought after in the job market and have a very high rate of employment after graduation.

2

THE UNIVERSITY AND LAW PROGRAMS

This place is the Devil, or at least his principal residence, they call it University, but any other appellation would have suited it much better, for study is the last pursuit of the society; the Master eats, drinks, and sleeps, the Fellows drink, dispute and pun, the employments of undergraduates you will probably conjecture without my description.

Lord Byron 1805[1]

1 Lord Byron, in a letter describing Cambridge University, 23 November 1805.

The university structure

Universities are large bureaucracies that generally employ thousands of full-time and part-time teaching and administrative staff. They are complex by nature because they have to deal with balancing economic responsibilities with academic integrity. That means that universities have to make their budgets balance while at the same time ensuring that their degree programs are highly valued and respected in the employment market place. This seemingly simple task is challenging in today's economic climate, where government funds to universities are on the decline and fees to students are on the rise. Universities attempt to maintain the integrity of their academic programs by having leading researchers in their fields teach you, while at the same time keeping class sizes down to a level that provides you with a meaningful learning experience. These two ideals cost a lot of money. Therefore, generally today, universities are seeking external funding in the domestic and international market places from fee-paying undergraduate and postgraduate students, as well as research funds to supplement the decline in government funding.

Universities have to balance economic responsibilities with academic integrity

An example of the generic structure of a university is set out in diagrammatic form in Figure 2.1. Most universities have a university council or senate made up of eminent members of the community and members of the university's academic and general staff. Like a board of directors in a company, the university council or senate sets policy, as opposed to having responsibility for the day-to-day running of the university, which is dealt with at academic board level. The academic board is responsible for the operation of the university and sets down the management criteria that ensure the university runs efficiently and achieves its twin goals of high-quality research and teaching, as well as being financial sustainability.

The university council or senate sets policy

While the existence of a council or senate is quite common in universities, albeit under various different titles, from this level downwards universities may vary considerably. Notwithstanding this variation, there tend to be two common models that most universities follow.

First, they may follow the structure set out in Figure 2.1, where a college, division or faculty acts as an administrative and quality-control unit over various discipline-based schools or departments, one of which will be the law school. A school of law would commonly fall under a College/Division/Faculty of

FIGURE 2.1 A generic university structure

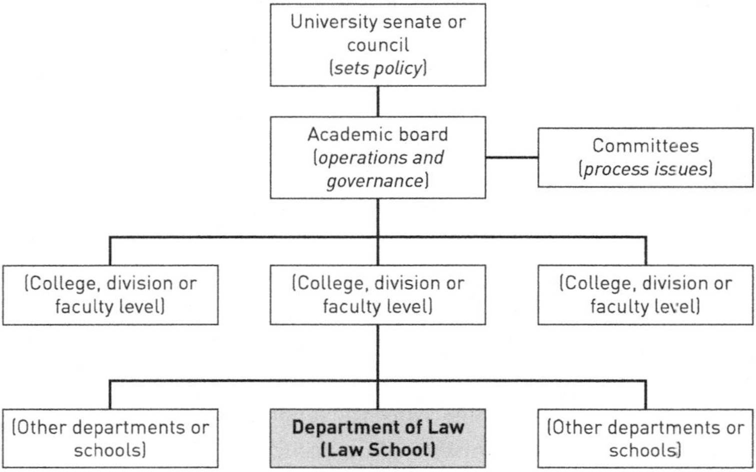

Law and Business or a College/Division/Faculty of Humanities. This model, sometimes called a 'super-faculty' model, is the more common model because it tends to be more cost effective for universities because there are fewer executive deans to employ, and reduced duplication of services. While schools of law are generally autonomous in relation to their own internal operating structure, issues such as budget approval, capital expenditure, and staffing levels are usually in the hands of the college/division/faculty managerial entity.

The second commonly found structure is the single-discipline faculty/school model that sees each discipline having its own faculty/school status. Once again, the autonomy of each faculty/school is (sometimes) limited to its operational structure, while major financial issues generally need approval further up the management structure.

No matter what structure a law school is, it is highly regulated by university policy and procedures. Notwithstanding the advent of combined degree programs, students should be subjected to the same sets of rules for both the degrees they are studying at the same university. This can only occur if the university is the administrator of major policy areas. For example, any one university would have a university-wide policy on grading. There would be one system that applies across the whole of the university that each faculty, college, division, school and department must comply with. This makes the awarding of marks consistent across the entire university, which in turn ensures some certainty when you are attempting to interpret your results at the end of each semester and employers are assessing graduates for prospective employment. This also ensures some element of consistency when it comes to the awarding of honours and the university medal for outstanding achievement.

One system applies across the whole of the university

The law school structure

Like the structure of universities, the structure of any given Australian law school can vary enormously. Figure 2.2 attempts to outline a common generic law school structure.

FIGURE 2.2 A generic law school structure

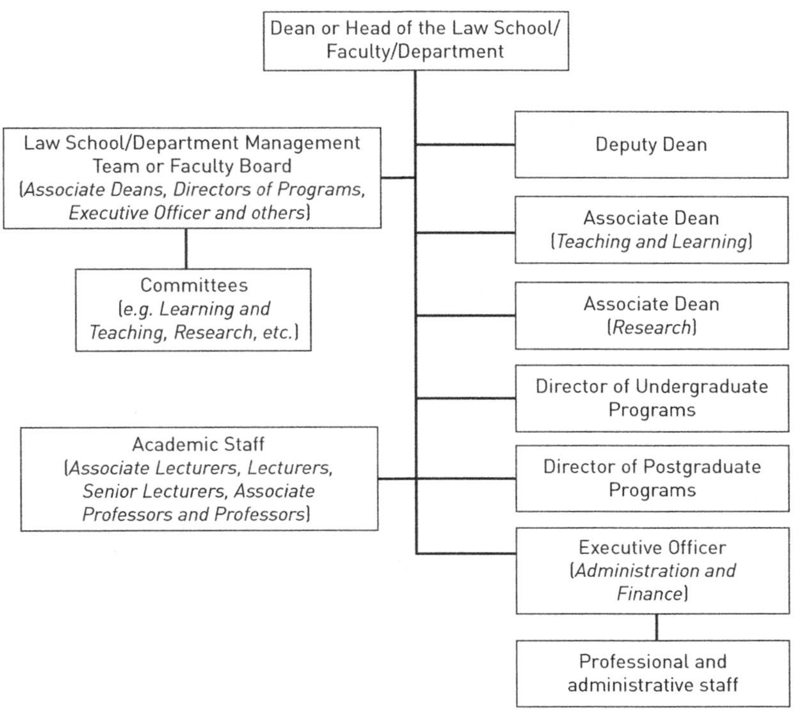

Dean or Head of Law School/Faculty/Department

In every law school, there is always a Dean or Head of School who is the managerial and administrative leader of the law school. The Dean will usually:

- be a senior academic who is a leader in her or his area of the law;
- hold, among other degrees, a Doctor of Philosophy (PhD) in Law;
- be the author or co-author of one or more leading texts in her or his field of speciality;
- be well respected in academic circles and throughout the legal profession; and
- have a strong network of professional contacts.

As well as being the manager, the Dean will be a mentor to the academic staff of the law school and will delegate certain managerial and administrative tasks to other members of the academic staff. For example, most law schools require lecturers to fulfil various administrative tasks, such as: advising students on their degree programs; being responsible for the approval of credit for study completed at other universities; or being responsible for the changing of subjects or units once semester has commenced. These and many other administrative tasks are essential for the smooth operation of the law school, but clearly cannot all be managed by the Dean. These tasks are essentially administrative, yet require academic knowledge—hence the need for lecturers to share the administrative and managerial burden of the law school.

As well as being the manager, the Dean is a mentor to the academic staff

The Dean usually sits on the senate/council and academic board, as well as several other high-level university committees, each dealing with policy and operational issues. The Dean will also chair a number of committees internal to the law school. Further, the Dean is in charge of running the law school, including the following non-exhaustive list of responsibilities:

- recruitment and retention of academic staff;
- recruitment and retention of senior administrative staff;
- formulation, implementation, and responsibility for the annual budget;
- achievement of research outcomes (publications and grants);
- chairing various intra-department meetings;
- overall management of the law school (including quality issues at academic and administrative levels);

- overall administration of the law school;
- operational issues surrounding the law school (such as: staff workload; honours requirements; appeals procedures; advanced standing; admission of students; disciplinary matters; morale of staff; mentoring programs; earned income centres etc);
- liaising with external accreditation bodies; and
- if the above allows, some teaching, research and writing and some family and social life!

The above list is undoubtedly incomplete, but its point is to prove that the Dean is a very busy person. Therefore, many second-tier administrative functions are delegated down to the various academics within the law school. Accordingly, if you are seeking advice on your degree program, then the chances are that you will not speak to the Dean about it. Find out which academic member of staff is responsible for the task and make an appointment to see that person.

Many of the Dean's second-tier administrative functions are delegated to various academics

Most Deans try to stay in touch with the student body in order to understand how well the law school is functioning. Many have an 'open door' policy towards students. However, keep in mind how busy a Dean is and only seek advice when you are sure that no other member of the academic or general staff can assist.

Executive Officer

An essential member of any law school team is a senior administrative officer, commonly called the Executive Officer, or the School/Faculty/Department Manager. This person runs the administrative side of the law school and deals with essential issues such as: resources; enrolment; timetables; leave; and administrative support for the academic staff. They are usually assisted by administrative staff, the number of which depends on the size and affluence of the law school.

Management team

Sometimes the academic and administrative staff are brought together on a management team that helps set operating rules and guidelines that interpret

The management team sets operating rules and guidelines that interpret the university's policies and rules

the university's policies and rules and ensure the law school can run smoothly. Depending on the university rules, the management team may also deal with disciplinary matters and manage quality-control issues relating to the degree programs offered. In most law schools there are also a number of committees that could cover such areas as:

- learning and teaching;
- research output (publications and grants);
- student progress and misconduct;
- staff sabbaticals;
- library resources;
- curriculum, new programs and subjects;
- staff workload; and
- appeal of grades.

These committees are important to the life of a law school as they set in place procedures to be followed, as well as initiatives to stimulate the various activities of a law school that are its life blood.

Law school personalities

Like any other organisation, law schools have an interesting array of personalities that make it work: a mixture of administrative, technical, and academic staff, as well as the student body itself. Negotiating with all or some of these people during your years at law school can be challenging. As in other parts of your life, you will find diverse attitudes to some issues where university policy does not dictate a singular view.

As in any organisation, sometimes your success within law school may depend on your people skills. By analogy, a fundamental rule of trial advocacy is not to be 'cross on cross', meaning that you should not adopt an 'American' television-style technique of aggressively cross-examining a witness in court. Generally, if you treat witnesses the same way that you would prefer to be treated, then you will get a lot more out of them than if you put them on their guard from the very first question. The same premise applies to dealing with the various personalities at a law school. Treat them the same way that you would wish to be treated and you will get a lot further with the help that you will, on occasions, need.

Treat people the same way that you would wish to be treated

Associate Deans/Directors of Programs

The Associate Deans manage the learning and teaching and research portfolios

The sorts of generic managerial functions delegated to academic staff include the positions of Associate Dean (Learning and Teaching) and Associate Dean (Research). These two roles serve two important functions. First, where there is no Deputy Dean, they deputise for the Dean when he or she is away from the law school on leave or university business. Second, they manage the learning and teaching and research portfolios by working to engage staff in both these important areas of law school life.

The Director of Undergraduate Programs (sometimes called Sub Dean or Associate Dean of Undergraduate Programs) usually advises students about their degree programs, and performs a number of administrative functions, such as change-of-course approvals, and approval for credit for subjects studied at other universities. The Director of Undergraduate Programs may also be responsible for the submission of final marks to the Registrar's office, change of grades, and approving applications to graduate.

Either the Director of Undergraduate Programs or another academic member of staff will usually be responsible for students who wish to withdraw from a subject after the university-imposed cut-off date. Universities have a cut-off date both for administrative reasons and for reasons of government funding (commonly known as the census date). If you decide to withdraw from a subject after these dates there are usually ramifications, such as a 'fail' appearing on your academic record and your incurring liability to pay Higher Education Contribution Scheme–Higher Education Loan Program (HECS-HELP). While the government may waive your HECS-HELP payments in extraordinary circumstances, the law school usually has the discretion to allow you to withdraw without penalty (avoiding the 'fail' grade appearing on your academic record). There usually needs to be exceptional circumstances for late withdrawal without penalty, and in this respect you should note key cut-off dates during each semester so that if you need to withdraw from a subject, you do not miss the cut-off date.

There must be exceptional circumstances for late withdrawal from a subject without penalty

The Director of Postgraduate Programs performs similar tasks to the Director of Undergraduate Programs, except that he or she deals only with postgraduate students; that is, those students who already have a Bachelor of Laws or equivalent and are seeking a Master of Laws or other postgraduate law degree.

Sometimes the roles of Associate Deans and Directors of Programs are amalgamated into one position depending on the size of the law school. In large law schools, sometimes both Associate Deans and Directors of Programs exist.

Academics

Academics at Australian universities are classified according to merit-based criteria. The ranking of full-time academics, in order of seniority, is as follows:

i) Professor
ii) Associate Professor
iii) Senior Lecturer
iv) Lecturer
v) Associate Lecturer.

Casual academic staff may include recognised experts in their field, who are generally awarded the honorary title of Adjunct Professor. Retiring eminent professorial staff are generally awarded the honorary title of Professor Emeritus, and such academics are usually invited to continue to take part in the life of the law school by delivering guest lecturers and attending social occasions. Other part-time academic staff may include tutors (usually Associate Lecturers or lawyers acting as casual teaching and clinical staff) who are generally charged with the responsibility of conducting tutorial sessions (small-group teaching), as opposed to subject coordination and the delivering of lectures to large groups of students.

Academic members of staff at most Australian law schools are selected based on eight basic criteria:

i) a bachelor's degree in law or equivalent;
ii) a higher degree in law or substantial completion of a higher degree in law;
iii) experience in teaching law at university level;
iv) a research profile or the development of a research profile;

v) a publication profile or the development of a publication profile;
vi) experience and/or the ability to contribute to the administration and management of the law school;
vii) ability to generate external research grants that assist in the funding of law school activities and facilities; and
viii) professional experience and/or community engagement activities.

It can be seen from the above list that academics have to cram a lot into a working week. The days of academics leading a leisurely lifestyle, just occasionally turning up to teach or write a few pages of a textbook, are gone (although one questions whether those sorts of days ever existed). The standard that academics have to achieve in each of these criteria is usually very high indeed. For example, simply being able to teach at tertiary level is not enough in today's law schools. The law school of the twenty-first century requires of its academics the ability to be able to teach in an engaging way, employing the latest in educational technologies, active learning techniques and delivery models that give students a choice over the type of engagement they will have with their learning. Gone are the days of delivering an entire subject via what has come to be known as the historical 'chalk and talk' (standing at a black/whiteboard, writing and talking at students). Further, because of financial constraints imposed by successive federal governments, a research profile means not only conducting empirical research of interest and relevance to the academic concerned, but also being able to embark upon the sort of research that will attract financial grants, most predominantly from the government-funded Australian Research Council (ARC).

Academics must be able to teach in an engaging way

With academic life being so busy in the twenty-first-century law school, it is not surprising that academics have their minds on other elements of their jobs outside of teaching. You should consider this when seeking advice on a range of issues that might arise in your life as a law student. In your first few years in legal practice, before walking into your supervising partner's office to ask a question, you should attempt to seek an answer yourself first. Similarly, only when you have 'hit a brick wall' should you knock on the door of an academic. Most academics have an 'open door' policy when it comes to students (as they should, given that without students there would be no academics), but you should at least show the academic that you have addressed your mind to the question and have tried to answer it before seeking advice. This will impress the academic and get you into a very good habit that will pay dividends in legal practice or other forms of work.

Professional and administrative staff

Professional and administrative staff at most law schools are 'hidden treasures'. They usually possess a wealth of information about the law school and its degree programs. They can advise on important issues such as: the structure of the degree program you are studying; what kinds of advanced standing or credit for previous study should be available; prerequisites; the process for graduating; submission of assessed tasks; postgraduate studies; which members of staff are teaching which subjects; and other important administrative information that makes life at a university law school easier to manage.

Professional and administrative staff at most law schools are 'hidden treasures'

The professional and administrative staff are usually overworked (mainly because of a large number of student enquiries and the ever-diminishing resources they have to do their job). Therefore, it is important to be polite and straight to the point when asking questions about various administrative issues, as administrative staff in a law school are constantly under pressure to complete certain administrative tasks and projects.

One of the frustrating things that students experience at a university is the time taken to complete administrative tasks. Because of the size of the average university, it is inevitable that paperwork will become lost or delayed, or that records will sometimes reflect incorrect information. Do not treat such instances as a conspiracy against you. Such administrative problems are simply a product of professional and administrative staff having to do more tasks with fewer resources. Therefore, when dealing with staff, again, treat them the way you yourself would wish to be treated. The smart student should recognise that experienced professional and administrative staff are a potential resource as you navigate yourself through law school.

Students

Probably the most important groups of people to recognise in the law school structure are your fellow students. You will spend more time with them over the period of your law school studies than most other people in your life.

Therefore, it is important to ensure you have a working relationship with them. Other students are an ideal resource in your studies; after all they share the same interests as you and probably the same or similar aspirations in life. Your fellow students can be a great source of social activity, but also an efficient study tool.

The first point should not be understated. While the law is interesting and challenging in an intellectual sense, generally speaking it should not become your entire life. Balancing your life is very important. Occasionally one still hears stories about lawyers (and other professionals) dying at their desks. Keep in mind the truism that nobody ever said on their death bed, 'Gee, I wish I had spent more time at the office!' You need to balance your life between career, family, friends, and your interests. In most cases, it is advisable not to make your career a substitute for a satisfying life. This is not to say that if you decide to make the law your 'life', you should not work hard at it. Just remember that law is a satisfying career, but rarely is it a substitute for other enjoyable things in life. It is a 'means to an end'; that is, it will supply you with a satisfying and intellectually stimulating career and hopefully a comfortable living!

While the law is interesting and challenging, it should not become your entire life

Try to discover things that you enjoy, and indulge yourself in them even at law school. If you do not, you risk burning yourself out at a time when you are still too young to be burnt out. Friends, law school, and the university can help you focus on important extracurricular activities such as sporting or drama groups. Most universities have an array of clubs to be involved in, and it is worthwhile exploring at least one or two extracurricular activities. You should also consider becoming involved in the various competitions and activities run by most Law Students Societies. Competitions include a variety of moots (legal debates presented like cases in court) on a range of topics covered in the core curriculum, as well as negotiation and client interviewing competitions. These are run at law school level and at national and international level. Activities such as organising the annual law ball, law review (law school law journal), or law revue (a stage production about life as a law student) can be fun, rewarding, and a worthy digression from studies. Many employers look favourably on graduates that have done more than 'just study'.

Indulge in things that you enjoy at law school, otherwise you risk burning yourself out

In relation to the second point—that fellow students can be a great study tool—at law school, students often form into study groups that share the workload by reading and writing up cases and drafting answers to legal problems for distribution among the group. There is no doubt that law school demands a huge time commitment from you. If you are a full-time student, you will usually take four subjects per semester. Each law subject requires around four hours' face-to-face teaching, plus another two hours for every face-to-face hour in preparation for lectures and tutorial classes. In this respect, friends can be helpful when it comes to dividing up the workload and a study group is a popular way to do this. A study group will often meet once a week in somebody's home or in one of the many informal learning spaces around campus. The study group will divide up the work, especially things such as reading cases and producing case notes (the latter to be discussed in Chapter 7). In this way, you still cover the material required of you, but you have shared the workload and had the opportunity to discuss concepts with fellow students—this often involves a valuable exchange of ideas that can lead to a greater understanding of difficult concepts and deeper learning of the foundations of the law. Just ensure that the quality of the work of the group is high and that you avoid any habits of plagiarism. While group research and discussion should be encouraged, students must present their own work in assessed tasks, unless otherwise specified. In this respect you should refer to the discussion on plagiarism in Chapter 12.

Study group discussions can lead to a greater understanding of difficult concepts

At the end of the day, law school should be a memorable part of your life. The friends you make should last a lifetime and you should avail yourself of the 'experience' of going to a university law school. It is surprising that even in a large city, the legal fraternity is still generally small and you will frequently bump into former university colleagues who can provide friendship and a source of advice at times when you need a 'second opinion'. Whether you become involved in university-wide student politics, or organising or participating in law school mooting competitions, or even just having coffee on a regular basis with a group of friends, try to enjoy your time at law school. Believe it or not, law school will go by quickly and it is a shame not to have some fond memories to take away from it.

How law schools are funded

In a curious set of circumstances brought about by virtue of the fact that Australia is a federation of states, universities are constituted by their respective state governments using state law, but are funded by the federal government.

Universities used to be funded using a formula that effectively put a price on the head of each student. For each student taught by the university, the federal government would pay an amount of money depending on the discipline the student was being taught. Usually, the university would then apportion part of the money per student to the law school to pay for: academic wages; wages of professional and administrative staff; the funding of (or contribution to the funding of) a law library; the building and maintenance of a moot court; student law societies; and other things important to the life of a law school. For example, let us say that the federal government would pay a university $7,000 per law student per year for an average full-time study load of eight subjects. The university in turn may allocate $2,000 per law student per year as the amount of money that ultimately funds the law school.

Universities are constituted by state governments, but funded by the federal government

One problem that developed under this funding model was due to the high attrition rate of law students and hence the potential to lose funds over the life of a cohort of law students. Let us say, for example, that 300 law students started out in year one. Attrition rates in some law schools translate into the loss of up to 100 of these students. If only 200 of the original 300 students did not complete their degree, then the law school would lose money. To counter this, universities would over-enrol students. For example, a university may enrol 400 students in its law program, knowing that 100 would drop out for various reasons over the life of the five-year combined or three-year law degree program. Adopting this strategy, the law school would not lose its continuing funding because it deliberately over-enrolled, thereby accounting for the natural attrition rate over the life cycle of each student. This was not a perfect system because over-enrolling meant spending more money on casual teaching staff, which in turn cut into the budget and generally led to overcrowded classrooms as law schools tried to maximise the funds available per student.

To counter the impact of student attrition, universities used to over-enrol students

In 2004 the federal government announced a major overhaul to the funding of universities that included a penalty for over-enrolment above approximately 10 per cent. Universities paid a fine to the federal government if they over-enrolled students in a degree program that carried an allocated number of government-funded places. Further, universities were allowed to charge their students up to 30 per cent more in fees on top of the existing HECS-HELP fees, and were allowed to offer full-fee-paying places across all university programs.

The Bradley Review

In 2011 the funding model changed again with the federal government implementing a de-regulated system pursuant to the findings of the 2008 'Review of Australian Higher Education Report' (the Bradley Review).[2] The federal government adopted the targets proposed in the Bradley Review that 40 per cent of all 25–34-year-olds should have attained at least a bachelor-level degree by the year 2025; and that by 2020, 20 per cent of higher education enrolments at undergraduate level should be people from low socio-economic status backgrounds. To facilitate this, the federal government lifted the ceiling on university places and allowed universities to accept any number of students they wished, providing the university was satisfied of the entry standard of the student. Every student gaining a place at university would be funded by the federal government. The result of this was an uptake of university places in 2011 and 2012, with a slight flattening of the number of commencing students in 2013, indicating that a natural ceiling had been met by the university sector.

As a result of the Bradley Review, the federal government lifted the ceiling on university places

Research funding

Research funding in Australia has seen two significant changes over the past decade.

In 2004 the federal government announced the introduction of the Research Quality Framework (RQF), which sought to reward high-quality research by assessing the research undertaken by university academics and then attributing funds for that research. Research produced by university academics was assessed by an expert panel using agreed criteria that required proof of quality and impact of the research. 'Quality of the research' meant assessing its intrinsic merit and academic impact. As regards 'impact, according to the 'Recommended RQF' report by the Development Advisory Group for the RQF, published in October 2006:[3]

The RQF assesses research undertaken by academics and attributes funds accordingly

2 http://www.innovation.gov.au/highereducation/ResourcesAndPublications/ReviewOfAustralianHigherEducation/Pages/ReviewOfAustralianHigherEducationReport.aspx (accessed 14 August 2013).

3 Dr Jim Peacock, 'Research Quality Framework: Assessing the Quality and Impact of Research in Australia—The Recommended RQF' (Canberra: Department of Education, Science and Training, 2006), at 10.

> Academic impact relates to the recognition of the originality of the research by peers and its impact on the development of the same or related discipline areas within the community of peers; and the impact or use of original research outside the peer community that will typically not be reported in traditional peer reviewed literature … Broader impact relates to the recognition by qualified end users that methodologically sound and rigorous research has been successfully applied to achieve social, economic, environmental and/or cultural outcomes.

In 2009 the federal government published 'Transforming Australia's Higher Education System'[4] and introduced the Excellence in Research for Australia (ERA) program to reward research excellence. According to 'ERA Facts 2012':[5]

> All universities submit comprehensive information to the ARC about their research activities, including details relating to staff, publications and other research outputs, awards, grants, income from industry and other research users, income from the commercialisation of research, and other applied measures such as patents. Submitted items can be coded to multiple fields of research, facilitating the capture of interdisciplinary activity.
>
> Committees of internationally-recognised researchers evaluate this material by discipline. Their expert judgments are informed by a range of summary indicators and quality assessments derived from the data submitted. The indicators used include measures of research application and recognition, as well as more traditional measures of quality, such as citation analysis or peer review.

ERA is focused on research outputs and the development of research strengths that allow Australian universities to compete internationally. Further, they are included in negotiations between the federal government and each university for mission-based compact agreements.

4 http://www.innovation.gov.au/highereducation/Documents/TransformingAusHigherED.pdf (accessed 14 August 2013).

5 http://www.arc.gov.au/pdf/era12/ERA%20Factsheet_Nov%202012.pdf (accessed 9 April 2013).

Mission-based compact agreements

Another important new development took place in 2010 with the federal government announcing that it no longer wished to fund universities based simply on benchmarking universities against each other. This recognised the reality that universities have slightly different student bodies. Regional universities are different to suburban universities, which are in turn different to sandstone universities (those older universities that were first created in each capital city). Also, although universities have a unique mission and strategic purpose, they also share some common elements as to their focus and intent. With these in mind, the new Mission-based Compact Scheme allows universities to negotiate individually with the federal government to assess their current levels of achievement and to estimate their future levels of achievement over the subsequent life of each agreement, currently set at three years. According to the 'Summary Report on Mission-based Compacts 2011–2013':[6]

Universities can negotiate individually with the federal government to assess their levels of achievement

> Each compact contains information on:
>
> - the university's mission;
> - government and university priorities for teaching and learning, research, research training and innovation;
> - the university's strategies for achieving its mission and contributing to government priorities; and
> - DIISRTE [Department of Industry, Innovation, Science, Research and Tertiary Education] funding inputs.[7]
>
> ...
>
> The principles under which Commonwealth funding for higher education is provided, as outlined in the compacts, are:
>
> - opportunity for all, especially for those students from groups under-represented in higher education;
> - access to university based on merit;

6 http://www.innovation.gov.au/Research/MissionBasedCompacts/Pages/default.aspx (accessed 9 April 2013).

7 Post the 2013 federal election the government portfolio responsible for universities is the Department of Education, Employment and Workplace Relations.

- world-class teaching and learning that advances the international standing of Australian education;
- world-class research and research training that advances knowledge, critical thinking and Australia's international standing;
- responsiveness to the economic and social needs of the community, region, state, nation and the international community;
- a sustainable higher-education sector; and
- academic freedom and institutional autonomy.

The federal government will fund universities to achieve outcomes agreed to in each individual mission-based compact agreement and will reward them for doing so. In other words, universities enter a contract with the federal government and agree upon certain academic and administrative outcomes that will determine additional funding.

Universities agree upon academic and administrative outcomes that will determine additional funding

The cost of higher education

It is apparent that successive federal governments want universities to be more self-funded, thereby reducing the burden of the cost of higher education on the taxpayers. This means that the government wants to shift the cost of higher education from the public purse to students who pay fees to attend university. However, federal governments of both political persuasions are sensitive to the need to ensure that the Australian university sector does not become as expensive as the American higher education sector, where students carry university fee debt for much of their working life.

The federal government wants to shift the cost of higher education from the public purse

In Australia, students taking up a government-funded place at a university will attract HECS-HELP fees. Students accrue these fees for every year they study until they graduate. Table 2.1 shows the fees charged for each discipline area per equivalent full-time student load (EFTSL), which means a full-time study pattern of up to eight subjects per year.

You will notice that law sits in the highest band of HECS-HELP fees charged to students. Using this table, a combined law and accounting degree could cost up to $48,960 in tuition fees for a five-year course. Add on your books and other resources and, if you are an Australian citizen, you are probably closer to $60,000 for a law and accounting degree in Australia on a government-funded place.

TABLE 2.1 2013 student contribution amounts per year of full-time study

Student contribution band	2012 Student contribution range (per EFTSL) per year of study
Band 3: Law, dentistry, medicine, veterinary science, accounting, administration, economics, commerce	\$0–\$9,792
Band 2: Computing, built environment, other health, allied health, engineering, surveying, agriculture, mathematics, statistics, science	\$0–\$8,363
Band 1: Humanities, behavioural science, social studies, education, clinical psychology, foreign languages, visual and performing arts, nursing	\$0–\$5,648

Source: 'Commonwealth Supported Places and HECS-HELP Information for 2013'[8]

You are not required to pay these fees up front in order to attend university, although you can if you wish to do so. The government treats HECS-HELP fees as a loan and, while you pay interest on your outstanding HECS-HELP debt, you only have to start paying it back once you start earning a wage. According to the booklet 'Commonwealth Supported Places and HECS-HELP Information for 2013':[9]

You only have to start paying back your HECS-HELP debt once you start earning a certain minimum wage

> You must start repaying your HELP debt when your repayment income is above the minimum repayment threshold for compulsory repayment, which is \$49,095 for the 2012–13 income year. Repayments made through the Australian taxation system are called compulsory repayments. Compulsory repayments continue until you have repaid your whole debt. The amount you repay each year is calculated as a percentage of your repayment income. The percentage increases as your income increases.

While you may think that the cost of a law degree is expensive in Australia, you should feel some sympathy for international students wanting an Australian law degree. According to 'The Good Universities Guide 2013', international

8 http://studyassist.gov.au/sites/StudyAssist/HelpfulResources/Documents/CSS%20and%20HECS-HELP%20information%20for%202013.pdf (accessed 9 April 2013), at 3.

9 http://studyassist.gov.au/sites/StudyAssist/HelpfulResources/Documents/CSS%20and%20HECS-HELP%20information%20for%202013.pdf (accessed 9 April 2013), at 15.

students can pay anything between $66,336 at Charles Darwin University and $180,453 at the University of Sydney for a (non-combined) law degree.[10]

Law programs

Bachelor of Laws

University law schools are quite similar when it comes to the type of law graduates they produce; that is, all Australian law schools produce 'generalists', or law graduates who can critically think about the law as well as practise in a general practice. This is a deliberate objective promulgated by the various admitting bodies in each state or territory (an admitting body being the administrative body that regulates who is admitted as a lawyer in the respective state or territory). The simple idea is that every law graduate should be able to work in a general practice that caters for a wide variety of clients with differing legal problems. Or more to the point, when lawyers seek to open their own practice, they should have the knowledge to take on a wide variety of work to ensure that clients are well served and that they can run a sustainable practice. This protects the public from lawyers who do not have an understanding of the issues raised in a general practice.

The idea is that every law graduate should be able to work in a general practice

Most general practices act for clients in the following types of matters:

- criminal law
- conveyancing transactions (sale and purchase of land)
- real property law (leases, mortgages, etc.)
- basic commercial transactions
- family law
- will drafting and applications for probate
- debt recovery
- personal injury.

However, the practice of law today involves a high level of specialisation. So how do generalists cope with high levels of specialisation within the profession?

10 Hobsons Pty Ltd, 'The Good Universities Guide 2013' (Melbourne: Hobsons Pty Ltd, 2012), at 167–8.

Even generalist practitioners have to make a decision as to what areas of the law they specialise in and combine those areas with other areas of practice where they have only generalist knowledge. For example, it would be practically impossible for a generalist practitioner to be a specialist in all the above-mentioned areas of law. So the generalist practitioner becomes a specialist in a few areas and relies on a general knowledge of other areas of the law when required. When a matter requires an assessment of the client's rights, generalist practitioners may call upon a barrister with experience in that area of the law to tender advice on the client's legal rights and their chances of success should clients wish to take the matter to court.

The generalist practitioner becomes a specialist in a few areas

In larger legal firms that have bigger client bases, and therefore more lawyers, law graduates are encouraged to specialise in one or two areas of the law. In this respect the law firm turns a generalist law graduate into a specialist lawyer. This is a job that the legal profession has been doing for many years and probably will continue to do for many more years.

So, law schools turn out law graduates armed with an understanding of the doctrinal (the basic principles of law) and contextual (the circumstances surrounding the law) foundation of law in a wide variety of areas of the law, while the profession turns law graduates into lawyers by teaching them the skills of a lawyer and turning them into specialist lawyers in one or more areas of the law.

Law graduates are armed with an understanding of the doctrinal and contextual foundation of law

The above describes the progression from generalist to specialist for solicitors. The same process tends to occur for barristers, although their main speciality is advocating a case in court—in other words, advocacy itself is a specialist skill. Again, because of the speciality of the law, even barristers—while they start out accepting briefs (cases) in different areas of the law while they gain experience—end up specialising in just a few different areas so that they may gain the skills of an expert advocate in a certain jurisdiction of the courts.

So how do law schools decide what collection of generalist legal knowledge law students should learn? Usually the law admissions consultative committees in the various states and territories set down what subject areas should be taught and the content of those subject areas. However, at the end of the day, all law students are basically taught the same compulsory subjects that produce the generalist law graduate.

All law students are basically taught the same compulsory subjects that produce the generalist law graduate

An externally accredited program

External accreditation is the process whereby once a law school and the university to which it belongs agrees that a law degree program passes certain internal standards for quality and academic rigour, that program must be examined by an outside body or agency that is an expert in the field. Other discipline areas such as accounting, nursing, and teaching have external accrediting bodies that tell universities whether their programs comply with external accreditation. In the case of law, the process of external accreditation means that the university degree is examined by either the state Supreme Court or a professional accrediting body. The court or accrediting body examines the degree in great detail and determines whether it is suitable for the education of professionals within its state or territory.

Accrediting bodies determine whether the degree is suitable for the education of professionals

Suitability is largely based upon the extent and depth of coverage of 'black-letter' topics (case law and legislation), in which the courts and accrediting bodies have a primary interest. A law school, and its university, may choose to teach a non-accredited law degree; however to do so would mean risking losing students, who usually want to know that at the end of their time at university they have the choice of whether to enter the legal profession or not. Non-accredited law degrees will not allow their graduates to be admitted as a lawyer in their respective state or territory. Thus, the profession has a strong influence over what is taught within each of the core (compulsory) units. Therefore law schools are required to attest that, at minimum, certain topics are covered throughout the degree.

The profession has a strong influence over what is taught within each of the core units

The Law Admissions Consultative Committee is a national body that consists of representatives of: the law admitting authority in each Australian state or territory; the Council of Australian Law Deans; the Australasian Professional Legal Education Council; and the Law Council of Australia (the national body representing lawyers). Its main role is to forge:[11]

> consensus between the bodies represented by its members on matters relating to the academic and Practical Legal Training requirements for admission to the Australian legal profession, the accreditation and appraisal of academic and Practical Legal Training institutions and courses, and other matters related to admission to the Australian legal profession.

11 http://www1.lawcouncil.asn.au/LACC/index.php (accessed 10 April 2013).

In 2008 the Law Admissions Consultative Committee drafted and had approved by the various stakeholders a set of Uniform Admission Rules;[12] however, admitting lawyers to practise is a matter for states and territories, and not a national responsibility, so while the state and territory admitting authorities largely comply with the principles set out in the Uniform Admission Rules, they do so in slightly different ways.

The admitting authorities adhere to a common set of subject areas: the Priestley 11

Throughout Australia, the various state and territory admitting authorities adhere to a common set of subject areas that go to make up an accredited law degree. The list of 11 subject areas, and topics within those subject areas, was developed by a committee of experts headed by Justice Priestley, and therefore the list is known as the 'Priestley 11'. Today, the list may be found in legislative form, for example, the Legal Profession Admission Rules 2005 (NSW), Schedule 5.

Table 2.2 provides you with the contents for each of the core subject areas (units) within each law degree. You should note that each law school offers its programs in different ways and therefore you might study a particular topic that is named differently from the names used below. Similarly, you might find that some parts of a Priestley subject area are taught in one subject in your law school, and other parts of the same Priestley subject area are taught in another. Note that law schools are compelled to teach either the specific defined topics in column 2, or topics of such breadth and depth as to satisfy the guidelines specified in column 3.

Electives exist for you to follow your interests in a variety of areas

While the Priestley 11 set out the core subject areas that must be studied in an accredited law degree, most law degree programs allow elective (non-compulsory) subjects to complement the suite of core subjects. These electives exist for you to follow your interests in a variety of areas and to link a number of subjects in the one area of interest. For example, if you have an interest in criminal, commercial, international, or family law, then the chances are that there is a group of elective subjects you can choose that will allow you to follow your interest. The number of electives available to you will depend on the law school and the structure of the degree program.

12 http://www1.lawcouncil.asn.au/LACC/images/pdfs/212390818_1_LACCUniformAdmissionRules2008.pdf (accessed 14 August 2013).

TABLE 2.2 The 'Priestley 11'

Unit name	Specific defined topics	Topics of such breadth and depth as to satisfy the following guidelines
Criminal Law and Procedure	1 The definition of crime. 2 Elements of crime. 3 Aims of the criminal law. 4 Homicide and defences. 5 Non-fatal offences against the person and defences. 6 Offences against property. 7 General doctrines. 8 Selected topics chosen from: — attempts — participation in crime — drunkenness — mistake — strict responsibility. 9 Elements of criminal procedure. Selected topics chosen from: — classification of offences — process to compel appearance — bail — preliminary examination — trial of indictable offences.	The topics should provide knowledge of the general doctrines of the criminal law and particular examination of both offences against the person and against property. Selective treatment should also be given to various defences and to elements of criminal procedure.
Torts	1 Negligence including defences. 2 A representative range of torts (other than negligence) and their defences. 3 Damages. 4 Concurrent liability. 5 Compensation schemes.	The potential compass of this area is so large that considerable variation might be anticipated. At the very least, there should be a study of negligence and of a representative range of torts, with some consideration of defences and damages, and of alternative methods of providing compensation for accidental injury. Examples of these topics are: concurrent liability, defamation, economic torts, nuisance, breach of statutory duty and compensation schemes.
Contracts	1 Formation, including capacity, formalities, privity and consideration. 2 Content and construction of contracts. 3 Vitiating factors. 4 Discharge. 5 Remedies. 6 Assignment.	Some variation may be expected in the breadth and detail of the topics. In general, however, knowledge of the formal requirements for concluding contracts, capacity, the content and interpretation of contracts, their performance and discharge, available remedies together with an understanding of the broad theoretical basis of contract would be expected.

(continued)

TABLE 2.2 The 'Priestley 11' (*continued*)

Unit name	Specific defined topics	Topics of such breadth and depth as to satisfy the following guidelines
Property	1 Meaning and purposes of the concept of property. 2 Possession, seisin and title. 3 Nature and type (i.e. fragmentation) of proprietary interests. 4 Creation and enforceability of proprietary interests. 5 Legal and equitable remedies. 6 Statutory schemes of registration. 7 Acquisition and disposal of proprietary interests. 8 Concurrent ownership. 9 Proprietary interests in land owned by another. 10 Mortgages.	The topics should include knowledge of the nature and type of various proprietary interests in chattels and land, and their creation and relative enforceability at law and in equity. Statutory schemes of registration for both general law land and Torrens land should be included. A variety of other topics might be included, e.g. fixtures, concurrent interests and more detailed treatment of such matters as sale of land, leases, mortgages, easements, restrictive covenants, etc.
Equity	1 (a) The nature of equity; (b) Equitable rights, titles and interests; (c) Equitable assignments; (d) Estoppel in equity; (e) Fiduciary obligations; (f) Unconscionable transactions; (g) Equitable remedies. 2 Trusts, with particular reference to the various types of trusts and the manner and form of their creation and variation. The duties, rights and powers of trustees should be included as should the consequences of breach of trust and the remedies available to, and respective rights of, beneficiaries. (It is expected that about half the course will be devoted to trusts).	The topics should cover the elements of trust law, equitable doctrines apart from those relating to trusts, and equitable remedies. The following aspects of trusts law should be dealt with: various kinds of trusts, the rights, duties, powers of trustees; the consequences of breach of trust, apart from trusts, the following equitable doctrines might be covered, for example, fiduciary obligations, equitable assignments, unconscionability and the confidential information. The remedies of specific performance, injunction, declaration and damages in equity should be included. (It is expected that about half the course will be devoted to trusts).

Unit name	Specific defined topics	Topics of such breadth and depth as to satisfy the following guidelines
Company Law	1 Corporate personality. 2 The incorporation process. 3 The corporate constitution. 4 Company contracts. 5 Administration of companies and management of the business of companies. 6 Duties and liabilities of directors and officers. 7 Share capital and membership. 8 Members' remedies. 9 Company credit and security arrangements. 10 Winding up of companies.	The topics should include an analysis of incorporation and its effects, management and control of a company, the various methods of financing by the issue of shares and by debt, and the processes of winding up a company.
Administrative Law	1 Organisation and structure of the administration. 2 Administrative law theory. 3 Common law and statutory avenues of judicial review at Commonwealth and State level. 4 Grounds of judicial review. 5 Remedies. 6 Crown immunity. 7 Administrative Appeals Tribunal. 8 Statutory review. 9 Freedom of information.	The topics should not only embrace traditional common law remedies concerning judicial review of administrative action, but should also cover the range of Commonwealth and State statutory regimes.
Federal and State Constitutional Law	1 State constitutions and constitutional systems. 2 The Commonwealth constitution and constitutional system. 3 The constitution and operation of the legislature, executive and judiciary. 4 The relationship between the different institutions of government and the separation of powers. 5 The relationship between the different levels of government.	The topics should include knowledge of the major principles of both the relevant State or Territory Constitution and the Commonwealth Constitution, including the relations between the different Commonwealth and State or Territory laws. A general knowledge of the scope of both State or Territory and Commonwealth Constitutions is required, although the topics will differ in the depth of treatment of specific heads of power, particularly in the Commonwealth sphere.

(*continued*)

TABLE 2.2 The 'Priestley 11' (*continued*)

Unit name	Specific defined topics	Topics of such breadth and depth as to satisfy the following guidelines
Civil Procedure	1 Court adjudication under an adversary system. 2 The cost of litigation and the use of costs to control litigation. 3 Service of originating process as foundation of jurisdiction, including service out of the relevant State or Territory and choice of forum. 4 Joinder of claims and parties including group proceedings and the defence of prior adjudication as instances of the public interest in avoiding a multiplicity of proceedings and inconsistent verdicts. 5 Defining the questions for trial pleadings, notices to admit and other devices. 6 Obtaining evidence, discovery of documents, interrogatories, subpoena and other devices. 7 Disposition without trial, including the compromise of litigation. 8 Extra judicial determination of issues arising in the course of litigation. 9 Judgment. 10 Appeal. 11 Enforcement.	The topics should embrace the general study of rules of civil procedure relevant in the State or Territory. Rules concerning jurisdiction, the initiation and service of process, the definition of issues through pleadings and judgment and enforcement should all be included.
Evidence	1 Introduction. 2 Competence and compellability. 3 Privilege. 4 The examination of witnesses. 5 Disposition and character. 6 Similar fact evidence. 7 The accused as a witness. 8 Burden and standard of proof. 9 Documentary evidence. 10 Opinion evidence and prior determination.	The topics should include examination of both the sources and acceptability of evidence, including rules concerning the burden and standard of proof and technical rules concerning such matters as hearsay, admissions and confessions, illegally obtained evidence and res gestae.

Unit name	Specific defined topics	Topics of such breadth and depth as to satisfy the following guidelines
Evidence (*cont.*)	11 Hearsay: — the exclusionary rule; — the common law and statutory exceptions. 12 Admissions and confessions in criminal cases. 13 Illegally obtained evidence and confirmation by subsequent fact. 14 Res gestae. 15 Corroboration.	
Professional Conduct (including basis Trust Accounting)	Professional and personal conduct in respect of practitioners' duty: (a) to the law; (b) to the Courts; (c) to clients, including a basic knowledge of the principles of trust accounting; and (d) to fellow practitioners.	The topics should include knowledge of the various pertinent rules concerning a practitioner's duty to the law, the Courts, clients and fellow practitioners and a basic knowledge of the principles of trust accounting. The aims of the trust account segment of Professional Conduct are: — to impart an understanding of the legal requirements on solicitors for dealing with trust property; — to help students obtain a level of competence in, and understanding of, the recording requirements for trust accounts and other trust dealings. Areas covered should include: — Provisions of the relevant State or Territory legislation governing the legal profession which relate to the handling of trust money and other trust property; — Legislative provisions which enable the proper identification of trust moneys; — The ramifications of breach of trust; — An overview of trust accounting systems; — Methods of maintaining trust account records. This includes class exercises in recording of receipts, payments and direct payments of trust moneys and of investments (including mortgage investments) by solicitors on behalf of their clients; — A detailed study of any relevant legislation, regulations or rules relating to trust accounting.

Practical legal training

In New South Wales, the Australian, Capital Territory, South Australia, and Tasmania, after completing a Bachelor of Laws or equivalent, students are required to fulfil a Practical Legal Training (PLT) course prior to being admitted by their respective state Supreme Courts. PLT is designed to teach law graduates the skills of a lawyer. Most importantly, it is designed to link the theory of law, taught at law school, with the practical skills of a lawyer. PLT courses will teach you the following non-exhaustive list of skills:

PLT is designed to link the theory of law with the practical skills of a lawyer

- client interviewing;
- basic advocacy;
- basic negotiation;
- basic litigation practice and procedure;
- how to administer files; and
- how to keep trust and general accounts records properly.

PLT is designed to replace the old 'articled clerk' system inherited from the British, which provided a period of time as a trainee in a law firm during which law graduates would learn the practical elements of practising law. All PLT courses do, however, require students to complete a certain number of hours' work experience in a law firm. Most PLT courses are around three to four months in duration, and offer both face-to-face and distance learning modes.

Most PLT courses are around three to four months in duration

In Victoria you have the choice of completing PLT or Supervised Workplace Training (SWT), which is a 12-month period of supervised training under a practising lawyer. SWT allows a law graduate to acquire an appropriate understanding of and competence in a number of practice areas. There are 220 performance criteria, which largely match the competencies acquired during PLT. According to the Victorian Council of Legal Education:[13]

> Most of these competencies can be completed through either internal or external training. The exceptions are Ethics and Professional Responsibility, which must be completed through an approved

---

13 http://www.lawadmissions.vic.gov.au/admission_requirements/supervised_workplace_training (accessed 10 April 2013).

> Practical Legal Training (PLT) provider, and Lawyers Skills together with the Risk Management element of Work Management and Business Skills, which must be completed through an approved PLT provider or another provider approved by the Board.

Queensland has a mandatory SWT-style system called a traineeship, which provides for a minimum of one year's training that meets the practical legal training standards specified in the current Supreme Court (Legal Practitioner Admission) Amendment Rule (No 2) 2005. In Western Australia and the Northern Territory you have a choice between an approved PLT course and a SWT/traineeship called articles of clerkship.

When it comes to completing PLT, students in most states and territories have a choice between providers. For example, in Victoria you have the choice of enrolling in a PLT course at the Leo Cussen Institute or the College of Law. In New South Wales the choices are the College of Law and some university providers, such as the University of Technology Sydney.

When it comes to completing PLT, students have a choice between providers

Transferring from one law school to another

If you are transferring from one university law school to another for a specific reason, such as because your partner or family are moving interstate, then you may not have much choice over moving law schools. However, if you have a choice over whether to move law schools or not, you must find out what sort of credit for previous study will be granted at your new law school before committing to the move. Some law schools give little credit and make it difficult to gain credit for core units in their LLB program. Most universities have a credit point limit on credit for previous study (called advanced standing), so that you may not get full credit for the units you studied at your old law school.

You must find out what credit for previous study will be granted at your new law school

Difficulties arise when curricula do not match up. For example, some law schools teach contract law over two semesters while most law schools only teach it over one semester. How do you get credit for all the study you have successfully completed in such circumstances? The common way around this problem if you are coming from the 'two-semester' law school is to grant you credit for

Difficulties arise when curricula do not match up

the compulsory one-semester contract law unit at the new law school, and then give you 'unspecified credit' towards your elective units in lieu of the second contract law unit studied. If you are going the other way, then depending on how the syllabus of each unit at each law school matches up, you may get credit for the first semester of contract law but then have to complete the second semester unit to satisfy the university and the accrediting body that you have completed a proper course of study in contract law. The task of granting credit involves comparing the syllabus of the units you are seeking specific credit for and matching it as closely as possible to any available credit in units taught by the new law school. Remember, law schools have to satisfy accreditation bodies in each state and territory, and their accreditation rests on ensuring that students have studied the accredited law degree as approved by the accrediting body.

Each law school has an academic member of staff who makes these decisions under delegated authority from the Dean or Head of the School/Faculty/Department. This person may be known as an Exemptions Officer, Advanced Standing Officer, Director of Undergraduate Programs, Sub Dean, or Associate Dean. Whatever their title is, make an appointment to see them or to speak to them by phone. Make sure you have information about your studies to date that will allow them to advise you on what sort of credit you are likely to gain if you transfer law schools. Information such as a comparison of the syllabus of units you are seeking credit for would help the responsible officer make a decision in your favour. If you can make out a case that the unit you are seeking credit for is substantially the same as the unit you have studied, then you will probably be successful in gaining credit for that unit. It is up to you to make the case, not the academic assessing your situation. Bring relevant information to assist that person to make a favourable decision. Similarly, do not try for credit in a unit that is not substantially the same as one you have already studied. This will annoy the responsible academic and will not help your case. You are better off going for 'general credit', which are credit points that go towards your elective units in your degree program. Depending on the university, there may be an appeals process if you think you have not been granted enough credit for previous study. You will need to enquire at the university's student centre or admissions office to make an application to appeal the granting of advanced standing or credit.

It is up to you to make the case, not the academic assessing your situation

Mutual recognition of lawyers from interstate and overseas

INTERSTATE MOBILITY

Prior to 1992, it was difficult for lawyers admitted in one state or territory to practise in another state or territory. In fact, state and territory admitting authorities set up barriers to lawyers practising in more than one jurisdiction. Since then, however, steps have been taken that mean legal practitioners can more easily practise in jurisdictions other than their original one. These include the Mutual Recognition Scheme and the Travelling Practising Certificate Scheme. According to the Office of the Legal Services Commissioner:[14]

> **Mutual Recognition scheme**
>
> In 1992 the Commonwealth passed a *Mutual Recognition Act 1992* (Cth) whose purpose is to enable a legal practitioner registered in one jurisdiction to be able to practise in another. The legislation has subsequently been adopted by all States and Territories.
>
> Under the Mutual Recognition scheme, legal practitioners are required to register with the second jurisdiction by applying to have their name entered on its Roll of Legal Practitioners and by obtaining a practising certificate for that jurisdiction (a 'local' practising certificate).
>
> **Travelling Practising Certificate scheme**
>
> In 1998, steps were taken to develop a national Travelling Practising Certificate scheme (also known as Interstate Practising Certificate regime) so that a legal practitioner with a practising certificate from one State/Territory could practise in another State/Territory *without* having to be admitted and obtain a second practising certificate.
>
> The scheme has now been adopted by the Australian Capital Territory, Northern Territory, New South Wales, Queensland, Victoria, South Australia, Tasmania and Western Australia.

---

14 http://www.olsc.nsw.gov.au/olsc/olsc_education/lsc_lawregulate/lsc_mobility.html (accessed 14 August 2013).

A move to develop a national legal profession began with the Law Council of Australia's 1994 response to the federal government's competition policy reform agenda. The Law Council's 'Blueprint for the Structure of the Legal Profession: A National Market for Legal Services' provided proposals for the regulation of the profession on a national basis, as well as bringing the profession into line with other professions, service providers, and industries. Specifically, the profession moved to remove restrictions on interstate practice and ensured that competition principles applied to the profession of law. In 2004 the National Legal Profession Model Bill, was published and endorsed by the states' and territories' attorneys-general. As amended in 2006 and 2007, the National Legal Profession Model Bill was adopted by all states and territories, except South Australia. In 2009 the federal government announced that its micro-economic reform agenda would include the legal profession. A taskforce and consultative group then developed model legislation that made fundamental changes to the regulation of the legal profession across the country. The revised draft was released 2011, and to date New South Wales and Victoria have signed on the model law.

As a result of the 2004 changes, every Australian legal practitioner has their 'home' jurisdiction. This 'home' jurisdiction is the only, or most recent, Australian jurisdiction in which the legal practitioner has been granted a practising certificate. The grant of a practising certificate in a jurisdiction results in the practitioner being known as a 'local legal practitioner'. A legal practitioner may only hold one Australian practising certificate at one time. An 'interstate legal practitioner' refers to a practitioner who is currently practising in another jurisdiction and holds a practising certificate in their home jurisdiction. For example, a practitioner whose home jurisdiction is Queensland but who is practising in Western Australia will be considered to be a 'interstate legal practitioner' in Western Australia, but a 'local legal practitioner' in Queensland.

TRANS-TASMAN AND INTERNATIONAL MOBILITY

Again according to the Office of the Legal Services Commissioner:[15]

> The *Trans-Tasman Mutual Recognition Act 1997* (Cth) recognises within Australia regulatory standards adopted in New Zealand

15 http://www.lawlink.nsw.gov.au/lawlink/olsc/ll_olsc.nsf/pages/lra_mobility (accessed 10 April 2013).

> regarding goods and occupations. The legislation is as contemplated by the Trans-Tasman Mutual Recognition Arrangement entered into in 1996 between Australia, New Zealand and the States and Territories of Australia. In all States and Territories, except Western Australia, New Zealand practitioners are not considered foreign legal practitioners, however, they still need to apply for registration under the Trans-Tasman Mutual Recognition Scheme.

Lawyers coming from countries outside of Australia and New Zealand may be granted rights to practise in Australia, but must apply to the state or territory in which they wish to practise to be assessed by that local authority. Often the state or territory authority will require the applicant to study non-award or 'one-off' subjects at an accredited law school in areas of Australian law such as: criminal law; constitutional law; ethics; evidence; trust accounting; and civil and criminal procedure.

What should I study at law school?

Because law school is quite competitive to enter, the subjects you study at school can sometimes have a great bearing on the marks you end up with. Our advice is to study those units that you most enjoy if they are ones that will assist you to maximise your result. Studying something you enjoy is much easier than studying something you do not enjoy. Having said that, it is obvious that reading, and lots of it, is essential to successfully completing law studies. Accordingly, there is real benefit in understanding English comprehensively.

If your first language is not English, particularly if you have recently arrived in Australia, we advise you to seek assessment of your English language skills. If your English language skills are not at a certain level you may find that the university of your choice may restrict your entry into programs where the English language is paramount. Most universities restrict entry based on successful completion of Australian high school English subjects or level of attainment in the International English Language Testing System (IELTS) examination. The level of English language proficiency required will differ between universities and between degree programs. While focused on a person who wishes to practise law, as opposed to merely study it, the Legal Profession Admission Board (NSW) requires the following standard of attainment in IELTS as shown in Table 2.3:

TABLE 2.3 Legal Profession Admission Board (NSW) requirements for IELTS attainment[16]

IELTS (Academic)	
Overall	**Section minimum score**
8	7 listening 7 reading 8 writing 7.5 speaking

While law schools will accept the brightest students based on their marks, it is also the case that some institutions will provide some enrolment benefits to those who have studied advanced English and Legal Studies. You should check with your prospective law school about their approach to high school studies.

16 Legal Profession Admission Board (NSW), http://www.lpab.lawlink.nsw.gov.au/lpab/legalprofession_overseas_practitioners/legalprofession_overseas_practitioners_english_req.html.

3

HOW IS LAW SCHOOL DIFFERENT FROM OTHER STUDIES?

Teachers open the door; you enter by yourself.

Chinese proverb[1]

If you wish to be a lawyer, attach no consequence to the place you are in, or the person you are with; but get books, sit down anywhere, and go to reading for yourself. That will make a lawyer of you quicker than any other way.

Abraham Lincoln[2]

1 'Chinese Proverbs from Olden Times' (Mt Vernon, NY: Peter Pauper Press, 1956).
2 Abraham Lincoln, letter to William H. Grigsby, 3 August 1858.

Introduction

Studying law is different from studying other disciplines at university, TAFE, or school. It is also different from learning law in the workplace. The aim of this chapter is to give you an idea about some of those differences.

The distinctions between law school and high school or TAFE

Studying at high school and TAFE is a highly regimented process. Teachers provide detailed class notes and activities, and while the school system and TAFE are focusing on more active learning, a lot of the learning revolves around the memorisation and use of large amounts of facts and figures. At advanced levels, students in schools are encouraged to engage in independent thinking in relation to certain projects, but as a general rule school and TAFE students are led through a lot of their learning by their teachers. The message students receive from their school studies and TAFE is largely that if you follow the learning template provided by teachers, you will do well.

At universities the learning process is very different. We explain this process in the next chapter, but to summarise here, university learning requires the student to take responsibility for their own learning and to be very active in ensuring that they know and understand the material. Knowing the material involves much more than simply memorising it and being able to regurgitate it in exams. Knowing the material requires you to be able to critically analyse and evaluate it, and hold an educated opinion about it, in addition to simply understanding the content. At law school this is placed in sharp relief in class discussions and assignments.

University learning means you must take responsibility for your own learning

The distinctions between law school and the workplace

Legal working environments aside, learning the law in the workplace is quite different from studying at law school. Most workplaces provide you with a set amount of tasks or duties to manage or do. Most workplaces also have constant or direct supervision of your activities, fixed working hours, a definite path for personal progress (if one exists), and a financial benefit for the time you invest in your work. Law school by comparison is a little different. You are considered to be a self-starter, whether you are one or not, and you will only be supervised when you are engaged in a formal class performance or undertaking a practically oriented assessment. Your hours of work are, besides class, up to you to determine. There is no defined path for you in your studies: you need to decide what sort of student you wish to be. It is up to you to determine how relaxed, successful, competitive, focused, or sociable you want to be. In contrast to receiving an immediate financial return for your efforts, you will be forced to spend thousands of dollars towards your student contribution for a Commonwealth-funded university position, your HECS-HELP loan, or your full-tuition fees, in addition to your university's student fees and textbooks, on-campus meals, and, perhaps, transport and housing costs.

You are considered to be a self-starter, whether you are one or not

The long-term financial return cannot be guaranteed either. As we discussed in Chapter 1 there are many different career paths in law and, contrary to popular views and government belief, not all of them involve six-figure salaries in large firms.

One of the few similarities between law school and the workplace is that there are specified bonuses for good performance and penalties for poor performance. That is, studying successfully at law school can mean you reap the intrinsic rewards of good grades and the extrinsic rewards of prizes, positions representing your law school in competitions, and general approbation. The ramifications of poor performance may be that you receive fail grades, generate less respect among your colleagues, or are forced to leave the law school because you have not completed enough units of study to continue your program.

Law students must take responsibility for their own learning

As a law student you must take responsibility for the standard and extent of your knowledge. This is not to say that you will not be given guidance about what to study and how to do it. What this means is that after you have been given that guidance, usually in the form of a unit learning guide, you must ensure you do what is required to achieve the aims and objectives of the unit.

Your university law school lecturers will not be constantly monitoring your performance and ensuring that you will pass your units. Your lecturer will be ensuring that you have the tools to learn the material, and thereby have the potential to pass the unit, but you are the one who, ultimately, has the responsibility to use the tools properly and ensure you get through the unit's requirements.

You are the one responsible for ensuring you get through the unit's requirements

There are a number of different approaches that may be taken to teaching and learning in law schools. We examine some of these in the next chapter. In our view, the best programs offer a variety of opportunities and approaches, and ensure that the agreed teaching and learning philosophy of the law school is adopted by all the staff and the students; that is, that there is a coordinated approach throughout the law degree. Most law schools espouse, or use, a philosophy that ensures that learners are forced to become independent adult thinkers. If you are in, or about to enter, law school it is important that you find out what the school's preferred teaching approaches are. If the school's teaching philosophy is difficult to find, or not articulated, then you should attempt to determine the approach that each of your lecturers uses. The different ways lecturers approach the marking of the same tasks, such as exams and essays, is sometimes quite diverse. It is unwise to assume that one approach that you have experienced—for example, by your legal studies teacher at school, or last semester's lecturer—is the one adopted by your lecturer this semester, or indeed those in later years.

Law schools attempt to develop independent thinkers

The distinctions between law school and other university studies

A difference quickly noted by students from other disciplines who come to the law is the large amounts of reading. This is particularly noticeable for students who move into law after having completed some studies in the sciences, computing, or business disciplines. While it is true that law requires you to read a lot, another crucial difference between law and other disciplines is the attention to detail required. In many other disciplines where one is required to read material, such as in the arts and humanities, the volume of material is sometimes equivalent,

There is a significant amount of reading in law school

but with respect to our colleagues in the non-law disciplines, our experience is that law students need to spend more time on the readings for law. This is for several reasons:

i) The readings are generally comprised of primary materials, as opposed to secondary sources or commentaries, and therefore are generally less easy to process quickly.
ii) The primary materials, such as cases and legislation, often use legal jargon, which may be unfamiliar to you.
iii) Many of the primary materials need to be linked, or cross-referred, to other primary materials.
iv) Much of what is being read is relevant and important and can prove crucial to your understanding of a topic; it is less easy to 'skim over' vast chunks of text in a case or statute, as one might do in a novel or textbook, and still retain essential meanings.

We talk more about the time demands of your law studies below, and more about the amount of reading you will be expected to do in Chapter 4.

Another key difference between law schools and other programs of study is the strong link between what you study and the profession of law. Disciplines such as medicine, accounting, nursing, and pharmacy, to name only a few, also have external accreditation requirements; however, when compared to generalist degrees such as arts, science, computing and the like, the study of law is much more rigidly regulated.

There is a strong link between a law program and the legal profession

While we take the time in the next chapter to show that law school is not simply about how to become a lawyer, it is true to say that all law schools must base their degree programs largely on the requirements of the legal profession. In the previous chapter we indicated how the legal profession has a significant role to play in determining what is taught in law school.

Professional responsibility and legal ethics

Another way in which law studies are different from many other disciplines is the centrality of professional and ethical concepts to the studies. While not always explicit in every unit you study, the combination of professional responsibility issues and the ethics of legal practice is imbued in most activities that you will undertake as a law student. If we classify professional responsibility and legal ethics to be the professional moral underpinnings of a lawyer's activities—the ethical parameters and restrictions on practice—then it is clear that where you are engaged in learning activities that simulate the theoretical or practical processes of legal reasoning and argument, you will be implicitly involved in ethical decision-making. This happens in most activities you will be engaged in at law school. Put more simply, when you are engaged in a task that requires you to provide advice to a client—say, as a result of a problem question in a tutorial, or where you are acting as an advocate in a dispute—you will, consciously or not, be making decisions of an ethical nature, or with an ethical undertone to them. The pervasiveness of legal ethics into most of what you read and do in law school is not always made expressly clear to you. Sometimes you need to have 'ethical issues' pointed out to you by lecturers in different units, by your colleagues, or you need to have done a unit entitled something 'Lawyers and Legal Ethics' before you realise the professional responsibility implications of what you are studying or considering. The point we wish to make here is that in all of your law studies you should recognise that the materials you are reading and the activities you are engaged in will almost always have a connection to ethical practice. Even if you do not wish to be a practitioner, knowing that your law studies have a strong connection to a professional moral dimension can assist in understanding why law is different from most other areas of intellectual enquiry.

Legal ethics is a central component to studying law

An example of how easy it is for ethical issues to arise in practice, and in your law studies, will best illustrate our point. A typical exercise encountered by most law students is the moot. This traditional form of instruction, a part of appellate advocacy, is discussed in more detail in Chapter 11. Briefly, a moot may be described as the submission of oral arguments about a legal issue, or problem, in a mock court setting, usually an appeal court. After having been instructed on the typical protocols applicable to advocates in a court setting, you will be required to make oral arguments or submissions for your client. These submissions are based upon your analysis of the legal principles applicable to the issue or problem. If a judge in your moot asks you a question about a case, or a fact, or how the law applies to a given fact scenario, but you do not know the answer, you might be tempted to 'fudge' your response by talking around the point, or making something up. This temptation may be based on your desire to appear in complete control of your arguments and not be embarrassed in front of your colleagues, or your lecturer, because you do not have all the answers required.

In some disciplines an ability to 'ad lib' and make something up, or to 'baffle and waffle', might be considered an acceptable action—consider for instance, certain forms of debating, or acting, or comedy. However, in law, a conscious decision to mislead the court in any way is simply unacceptable. It breaches the well-known and accepted ethical rule that a lawyer has a paramount duty to be candid with the court at all times. The simple response to a question for which you do not know the answer is to alert the court to your inability to help it. Your honest response—that you do not know the answer required—may be coupled with a request for a few moments to consider your file or case note, or to speak with counsel on your team, or ask for an adjournment. This reply may be uncomfortable as, by implication, you are acknowledging that you may be unprepared in some way. However, it is honest and entirely in keeping with the ethical standards of the legal profession. You may lose marks for not being as well prepared as you may have been expected to be, but you will be respected for your candour.

Your reputation as a student and future professional depends on your honesty

The high entry standard

A noticeable difference between law studies and those in other disciplines is that in order to enter law school, students generally need to be top performers at high school, or graduates of another university degree. This restriction on the entry into law programs has two bases. One is that law studies are very popular. Given the fact that there are a finite number of places in university law programs, the simple fact of supply and demand means that the significant and continuing interest in studying law causes the entry level to be much higher than that for most other disciplines. A second reason that law has a high standard for entry is because of the intellectual requirements to be a successful law student.

The amount and nature of the reading necessary to understand the law, and the analytical, speaking, and writing skills essential for assessment tasks, means that the student who is more academically able is generally better equipped to deal with law than those less able. A more academically advanced student will take less time reading, analysing, critiquing, and writing than a less advanced student. However, having acknowledged the need to be academically able, it is also our experience that a diligent and persevering performer is just as able to excel in law studies as a brilliant student. In fact, brilliant students rarely exist if they do not do the necessary preparation. Simply put, there is a large amount of reading and writing to undertake and those that do the work are those who typically find learning the law the easiest. The key to law studies is, primarily, a methodical and industrious approach to the large amount of work involved. Clearly most students who perform very well in their final years of high school are academically more gifted but are also hard workers, and this augurs well for the years at law school.

Law school rewards hard workers

Resources

The tools of the law are also different from the tools used in other disciplines. For law students, the resources that are most used are the primary materials of cases and statutes, coupled with secondary materials such as textbooks and journal articles. These reading materials are based on words, more words, and even more words. These words are analysed in explicit and minute detail. In summary, law students need to do lots of reading and be able to analyse and criticise the specific words, phrases, and concepts in those readings. In other disciplines there is also a need to use textbooks, but these are, generally, less focused on the meaning of individual words to the extent that law studies entail. In addition, some non-law disciplines use laboratories, or are heavily based on practice, and the readings are thus an adjunct to other types of learning. In law the central focus is on the words of the law and how they are interpreted and used by legal practitioners for the benefit of clients: people, organisations and governments.

The focus is on the words of the law and how they are interpreted and used

Study methods

Study methods across all disciplines require students to engage intellectually with the materials and make the effort to complete the tasks, such as readings or exercises. In law, the process you will need to adopt is one that is extremely methodical and requires you to really concentrate on every aspect of the readings you have been set. In Chapter 7 we speak more about study patterns. But, needless to say, a successful study pattern in law revolves around time management, a clear study plan, and becoming efficient in how you deal with the vast, but not always relevant, resources available to you.

Studying law requires an extremely methodical approach

Time demands

Make no mistake; the study of law is a demanding task. The amount of reading for each unit you study each week is anywhere from 30 to 100 pages of densely worded text. A typical comment from students who have completed studies in other disciplines is that there is a tremendous amount of reading in law compared to what they are used to. It would not be unreasonable to say that you will generally spend anywhere from one to four hours reading and preparing outside of class for every hour of class time you have for each unit. So if you are a full-time student and have, say, 12 hours of face-to-face classes each week, you could expect, depending on your interest and efficiency of study, to have somewhere between about 12 and 30 hours of preparing and reading associated with those classes. Our experience suggests that a total of somewhere between 25 and 40 hours work each week is the average for most students who are undertaking full-time studies. Please note that the upper amount of time is consistent with that required by a full-time occupation and, to some extent, provides an excellent grounding in the discipline required to perform well in professional life.

You will probably spend between 25 and 40 hours each week preparing, reading and being in class

Deadlines

Like courts of law and other places of work, law schools work to deadlines. Like courts of law, there is a penalty if you miss a deadline. In court the sanction for missing an appearance may be having your case struck out of the court list—a hard thing to explain to your client—as well as potentially earning an allegation of professional misconduct! At law school the sanction is not so devastating. If you miss a deadline in law school you will normally lose marks from your paper or

At law school, as in courts of law, there are sanctions for missing deadlines

assignment, and could possibly fail the task or the whole unit of study. If you are someone who wishes to achieve an Honours degree, the loss of marks can be disastrous; you may not achieve the necessary high standards, or you may incur a fail grade. The advice is short and simple—do not miss deadlines!

Looks can be deceiving. You may only see your lecturer for several hours each week, but as we saw in Chapter 2, behind the scenes academics are very busy people. Your lecturer will generally determine deadlines for assessed pieces of work based on a number of criteria:

i) to ensure you have a threshold of information under your belt before attempting the assessment task;
ii) to ensure as few clashes as possible with other pieces of assessed work in different units;
iii) where relevant, to allow you time to research the assessed piece of work in order to ensure a high standard of response;
iv) to fit in with the workload of the academic in question;
v) to ensure that assessed piece(s) of work can be returned to you prior to the final exam so that you have feedback about how you are understanding the materials in that unit (see Chapter 4 for more on this issue).

So generally, deadlines are not just randomly selected—the date is thought about and selected using some or all of the above criteria. Therefore, if you miss a deadline you are compromising one or more of these criteria and, the chances are that you are creating a problem for the academic charged with the responsibility for marking that piece of work. As well as this, you are putting yourself under pressure and may well compromise other deadlines for assessed work in other units.

Missing a deadline puts both you and the responsible academic under pressure

However, genuine difficulties can arise due to sickness or misadventure. In such cases an extension of the due date can usually be approved by the relevant unit coordinator. The first rule of thumb is to try and avoid ever putting yourself in the position of having to seek an extension. A good study plan will help avoid the need to request an extension—a topic that will be covered in the next chapter. These days it is common for students to work part time or full time to support themselves and pay their HECS-HELP debt to the government when it falls due to take the benefit of any early repayment discounts. However,

In cases of genuine illness or misadventure, an extension to a deadline may be granted

you should be aware that most universities will not accept work as an excuse for the late handing in of assignments. Most universities take the view that if you need to work full time, then you should enrol in a part-time program and not take up the place of a full-time student who can genuinely devote themself to full-time study. Nevertheless, students still tend to try to work long hours while studying full or part time. Some academics are sympathetic to work as a reason for late submission of assignments, but others are definitely not as sympathetic. You should check to see what reasons may be reasonably relied upon in order to seek an extension. This information will either be in the university undergraduate handbook or available from your lecturer in the unit learning guide. A word of warning—check *before* you make a request for an extension, not after!

If you are seeking an extension for medical reasons, you will need to supply proper original documentation to the unit coordinator in order to avail yourself of an extension. Again, be guided by the unit learning guide and the university rules as to what proof needs to be tendered. The general rule is for original medical certificates or other acceptable documentation to be provided. You may also find that a medical certificate is needed to indicate the severity of any medical condition and to verify that you are unable to attend class, or complete an assignment, due to that medical condition. Further, be aware that while a medical certificate may indicate that a person is genuinely ill on, or just before, the day of an assessment task, some lecturers will demand to see the work you have completed up to the point of the onset of the illness. If you have left your assignment to the last moment and then become ill, some lecturers will decide to reject the advice within the medical certificate.

If you are claiming illness or misadventure, you will need to produce original documentation

Many academics have experienced or heard of cases of fraudulent medical certificates, and the like. The proffering of any evidence that is untrue is regarded as serious misconduct on the part of a student, and such conduct may be the subject of formal misconduct proceedings at university level and beyond. As law students considering entering the legal profession, this type of behaviour is unacceptable. The ramifications of misconduct proceedings go far beyond possibly failing an assessment task or a unit. Such misconduct is a matter that must be explained to the relevant legal profession admission authority when the graduate student is seeking to become a legal practitioner.

The proffering of any evidence that is untrue is regarded as serious misconduct

So treat the academic staff the same way that you yourself would prefer to be treated—do not lie!

If you have to seek an extension on an assignment, try to hand it in ahead of the extended deadline. Academics view this sort of effort by a student very positively. There is nothing more impressive than seeing a student who, because of illness or misadventure, has managed to work extra hard to hand in an assignment earlier than the requested extension. Remember that giving an extension on an assignment will probably put the responsible academic marker out by increasing the amount of time it will take them to finalise all the marks. Also remember that an extension on an assignment is a privilege, not a right.

If you have received an extension, try to hand the work in ahead of the extended deadline

In all of the above discussion about missing deadlines, it is important to give the academic in charge of the unit as much notice as possible. There is usually little sympathy for a student who misses the deadline for an assessed piece of work and who contacts the unit coordinator a week later for an extension. In short, give academics as much notice as possible of problems you may be having; that way the academic will usually try to assist you to overcome the problems and keep you on track to hand in the assessed piece of work on or near to the deadline. Generally, academics will try to help you if you have a genuine problem. However, once deadlines have passed, it is very difficult to help you, and marks penalties will usually apply. You should treat your unit coordinator the same way you would wish to be treated if the roles were reversed; namely, with some consideration.

Give your lecturer as much notice as possible of your inability to meet a deadline

When it comes to formal exams, the situation is more serious. The majority of law schools run most of their exams for core (compulsory) units through the university's Exams Department, which interprets the rules strictly and enforces them vigorously, hence the term 'formal exam' (by contrast, an 'informal exam' is, for example, a take-home exam or one administered in class by your tutor). If you suffer illness or misadventure on the day of the exam, the best advice is not to sit the exam. You will not produce a result that truly reflects your ability—therefore, given the investment you have made by studying a whole semester (or year, if it is a year-long unit), do not risk a poor mark by sitting an exam you are not mentally or physically ready for. However, check the university rules, because the rules of most universities will state that if you should miss

If you miss a formal (sit-down) exam, contact the university immediately

a formal exam, you must contact the student centre or Exams Department within 24–48 hours of that scheduled exam. You will also have to furnish original documentation to prove the illness or misadventure. Some universities may only accept 'extreme' illness as a valid excuse for missing a formal exam. Once again, check the rules and make sure you comply with them should you consider missing a formal exam. Law schools may offer students a deferred exam if the formal exam is missed through illness or misadventure. These deferred exams are usually offered within a few weeks of the conclusion of the formal exam period at the end of each semester. Check the university rules for the procedure if you should miss the deferred exam. Sometimes the unit coordinator will have the discretion to provide a further examination—but again, do not expect this as a right.

Student learning responsibilities

Adult learning

Most academic members of staff understand that adults learn in different ways. Some adults like to learn by reading material and do not get as much out of face-to-face teaching as others. Some like to learn by 'doing', as opposed to listening. In this respect, academics usually seek to teach in a variety of media to ensure that there is some element of the teaching of a unit that appeals to everyone. Please consider that no one teaching style may necessarily satisfy your individual learning strengths. You should be flexible and understanding of the approach that your lecturers have to your preferences to learn. You should also respect that other students will favour other teaching methods and styles, and that academics seek to achieve the best for all learners. A more detailed look at teaching methods and styles will be discussed in Chapter 4.

Lecturers seek to teach in a variety of media or use varying teaching approaches to account for different learning styles

Nowadays it is recognised that students are not always ready to learn at the designated day and time set down in the university timetable. For example, if you have experienced illness, misadventure, or have significant employment or family commitments on the weekend, then the chances are that you are not going to be able to concentrate on a lecture at 9 o'clock on the following Monday morning. Because of this, most universities have developed flexible

Flexible delivery strategies mean you can learn at a time that suits you

delivery strategies to enable you to learn when you are intellectually and emotionally ready to learn. Flexible delivery may mean, for example, having learning materials available online so you may access those materials at any time of the day or night, via the World Wide Web. Also, materials may be provided in electronic form—such as some textbooks, learning guides, and research journals—allowing you to read and learn at a time that suits you. You should note that this flexible approach to learning is increasingly becoming a standard part of university delivery systems. You will thus need to be familiar with how to use the World Wide Web, how to access email and online learning programs, and how to submit assignments via university websites.

Personal responsibility

In the next chapter we discuss how law school is different to high school and other institutes of learning, both in the subject matter and the types of learning approaches used within them. In addition, another notable area where law school may differ from other institutions is that you are expected to take personal responsibility for achieving your own learning objectives. Law school (and most university degree programs) seek to provoke thought, not to provide it! In this respect, you need to find the answers to legal problems yourself. Your lecturers will help guide you to the answers and will be more than happy to discuss the answers that you have found, but generally, they do not see themselves as simply providing answers to problems or questions on a weekly basis. There is no doubt that one of the deeper and therefore more effective forms of learning is when you find the answer to a problem or question yourself. Therefore, at law school you are charged with the responsibility of taking personal responsibility for achieving your own learning objectives.

Studying (and practising) law is about finding the answers yourself, with the guidance of a mentor

The learning objectives for each unit can usually be found in the unit learning guide. While you are responsible for achieving the learning objectives, the your unit coordinator is responsible for setting the parameters of the unit in terms of topics and depth of topics, and setting the learning strategies that help you achieve your learning objectives. This symbiotic relationship enables you to have a deeper learning of material

You are responsible for achieving the learning objectives; academics are responsible for setting the parameters of those objectives

because you have confronted the problem, searched out the answer or answers, and considered and delivered an appropriate outcome.

The time demands of studying law are such that we have devoted a chapter to time management (Chapter 7).

Different law schools

Each law school has its own character, philosophy, and mission. These will have a significant impact on your studies. Proximity to home or work may be of benefit to you. Whether you know anyone studying at the institution, or whether it offers certain non-academic features such sporting or childcare facilities, may also be crucial to your ability to survive and flourish during the rigours of your study. We would argue that where these factors are not important to you, the number-one criterion in guiding you through your studies should be the stated teaching philosophy of the school. That is, what does your law school, in tandem with the university, state about its approach to the study of law? You can readily find out this information by consulting the websites of the institutions that offer law.[3]

Each law school has its own character, philosophy, and mission

Set out below is a list of Australian universities offering law programs:

- Australian Catholic University
- Australian National University
- Bond University
- Central Queensland University
- Charles Darwin University
- Curtin University
- Deakin University
- Edith Cowan University
- Flinders University
- Griffith University
- James Cook University
- LaTrobe University

3 A listing of websites for law schools can be found at http://cald.asn.au/slia (accessed 15 August 2013).

- Macquarie University
- Monash University
- Murdoch University
- Queensland University of Technology
- RMIT University
- Southern Cross University
- University of Adelaide
- University of Canberra
- University of Melbourne
- University of Newcastle
- University of New England
- University of New South Wales
- University of Notre Dame
- University of Queensland
- University of South Australia
- University of Southern Queensland
- University of the Sunshine Coast
- University of Sydney
- University of Tasmania
- University of Technology Sydney
- University of Western Australia
- University of Western Sydney
- University of Wollongong
- Victoria University of Technology

In addition to the universities listed above, the Legal Profession Admission Board of New South Wales, in conjunction with the Law Extension Committee of the University of Sydney, operates a non-degree, accredited diploma course within New South Wales (only).[4] The course is taught by practitioners and academics, and is geared towards part-time students who are working in a legal environment and who wish to be engaged in legal practice. This course is open to students from a variety of backgrounds.

4 See http://www.lpab.lawlink.nsw.gov.au/agdbasev7wr/lpab/documents/pdf/pathway_to_legal_practice_2010.pdf (accessed 15 August 2013).

4

LEARNING AND TEACHING IN LAW SCHOOL

The Socratic Method

Law professor's definition: 'The Socratic Method is the sword of knowledge. Through incisive questioning I am able to hurl the student down the path of wisdom to the mother lode of insight.'

Law student's definition: 'All the freakin' guy ever does is ask questions. He hasn't answered one all year. I'm clueless.'

Andrew McClurg 'The Law School Trip'[1]

1 Andrew McClurg, 'The Law School Trip' (Victoria, BC: Footnote Press, 2001), at 58.

Introduction

As we saw in the last chapter, university studies are different from learning at school or in the workplace. This is largely due to the fact that at university you have the primary responsibility for your learning: there is no one person, such as a teacher or employer, who is telling you what to learn and how to learn it. Yes, you have a lecturer or tutor—an expert, who instructs you or facilitates your developing knowledge base—but as a university student you have a greater responsibility for determining how much you wish to learn and the method by which you do so. We provide guidance about how to manage your time and develop a study plan in Chapter 7.

To make matters even more difficult for you, the learning of law is different again from other academic disciplines. This is due to the fact that reading and understanding the law requires a comprehension of certain rules (such as the use of precedent within the court system and techniques of statutory interpretation: see Chapter 9), and an appreciation of the adversarial nature of much law-making, with its consequent malleability.

This chapter will examine the nature of teaching and learning in universities and introduce the often unseen drivers of the law school curriculum. By understanding better why your degree program and units are conducted the way they are, you will be better able to fine-tune your learning approach and develop a deeper appreciation of the law under consideration. Skip this chapter at your peril!

We note that there are innumerable ways of running a law school and teaching a law unit. What we provide below is a personal view of teaching and learning in law, tempered by our observations of, research about, and discussion with university colleagues at home and internationally. Your individual law school, and the lecturers within it, may have a distinctly different view of teaching and learning to that which we hold. What is important about the following is that by understanding this chapter, you will be better able to understand what makes your law program (and lecturer) tick, and thus be better prepared to engage with that form of study.

A cautionary note about different law schools and lecturers

During the course of this chapter, certain terms will be used that may be new to you or may be called different things at your university. To simplify matters, the small set of definitions shown in Table 4.1 will allow you to understand what we mean when we use those words.

TABLE 4.1 Frequently used terms

Academic	The 'catch-all' name for your lecturers, tutors, seminar leaders, online mentors, and teachers, regardless of their position in the university hierarchy. We will use the term 'lecturer' for any academic staff member unless we have reason to use another term.
Aims	The broad statements of intention for the degree or unit.
Class	The generic term for any formal teaching situation. It includes lectures, seminars, workshops, and tutorials. For more information about different class types, see Chapter 6.
Coordinator	This term is usually applied to the person who has primary administrative and scholarly responsibility for a given unit.
Course	A term usually reserved for the degree or diploma you are studying; thus the 'course' that many readers of this book would be undertaking is the Bachelor of Laws, which is abbreviated to LLB, or Juris Doctor (JD).
Credit points	These, or variants such as 'unit weightings', are the ways in which the university assigns a notional value to the units (or subjects) you study for administrative purposes. If your degree is one that requires the attainment of, say, 100 credit points, then you will need to complete 10 units of 10 credit point value or 5 units of 20 credit point value, etc. Some universities, which use the modularised semester-length system for units taught, place the same value on all the units to be studied in a given degree program. Other institutions may give more weight to year-long units or core units, with the result that some units are deemed to be 'worth' more. The higher number of credit points attached to a unit does not necessarily reflect a greater degree of intellectual difficulty, but may result from increased length, staff involvement, or assessments.
Degree	The award you will obtain on graduation. Readers of this book will usually be interested, or enrolled, in an LLB or JD. Degrees are sometimes also referred to as your 'course' or 'program of study'.
Discipline	A term used by governments and university administrators to broadly define an area of study. Examples of disciplines include: law/legal studies, science, computing/technology studies, business/economics/commerce, and arts/humanities/social sciences.
Learning guide	The term we use to reflect the documentation provided by your unit coordinator to assist you in knowing exactly what you need to do in order to successfully complete the unit of study. Learning guides may be voluminous tomes that including all your weekly learning activities and readings, or less bulky documents that may be known as a 'subject guide', 'unit outline', 'course planner', or 'unit reader', among others.
Lecture	The class type that typically comprises large groups of student listening to, and observing, a single teacher. Lectures have typically been teacher-oriented, in that the teacher will speak and direct, and the students will listen and take notes. Today, many lectures are being given in a more interactive—and student-oriented—manner.
Lecturer	The person who typically conducts lectures and may also conduct one or more tutorials or seminars. Lecturers frequently also wear the hat of unit coordinator. Lecturers may be anyone from a casual staff member who runs a private legal practice to a visiting judge or even the Dean of your law school. Usually your lecturer will be a full-time member of staff within the law school.

(*continued*)

TABLE 4.1 Frequently used terms (*continued*)

Objectives	Statements about the nature and levels of understanding that should be achieved in relation to specific areas of content, or activities, or tasks. These are usually focused on achievable academic outcomes.
Practical sessions	Students engaged in science or information technology may be familiar with laboratory sessions and practical sessions. In law school a practical session may be attached to a variety of teaching methods and units, including: work experience, practical legal training, summer clerkships, advocacy exercises, and clinical placement units.
Professional staff	The term used in many universities to refer to non-teaching staff, including the staff located in areas such as student centres and central administration. The professional staff you will most often encounter are those who work in schools to support the work of the academic staff.
School	The term we use to refer to the organisational unit comprising the academics and professional staff (administrators) involved in teaching and running law degrees and associated programs. Your 'school' may also be known as a 'department', 'division', 'branch', or 'faculty'.
Seminars	These generally fit between lectures and tutorials in terms of student numbers and student–teacher interactions. A seminar will typically involve a bit of a lecture from the seminar leader followed by some student-led discussion akin to a tutorial. Of course, individual academics may use the seminar format in a different way again.
Subject	This term is often used interchangeably with 'unit' or 'course', with confusing consequences. While many universities use 'unit' to refer to a discrete area of study (see below), many use the term 'subject' in its place. In this book we use 'unit' to refer to the discrete area of study typically run over the course of one semester, e.g. Contract Law or Criminal Law.
Tutor	The person who runs any small-group, face-to-face teaching sessions, or tutorials. Your tutor may also be your lecturer, unit coordinator, or the Dean.
Tutorial	The smaller-group-teaching situation that may be distinguished from a lecture. While there are fine distinctions between the terms, we use 'tutorial' interchangeably with any small-group–teaching situation, such as: seminar, class, or workshop.
Unit	The series of classes on a related set of topics that you study over the course of a semester or year. Most degrees are arranged so that students will study between 20 and 30 different units. A typical example of a unit common to all law degrees is Criminal Law. A unit may be known as a 'subject' or 'course' in your law school.

Learning and teaching approaches

Why is this chapter entitled 'Learning and Teaching in Law School'? The answer is that learning and teaching are two different components of any educational experience involving a teacher. In simple terms, teaching is what the teacher does in the classroom and learning is what the student does during that class. However, as our later analyses of teaching and learning approaches will show, there is frequently a significant divergence from this simple definition.

One obvious example is that, while we recognise the importance of learning in the classroom, the most significant teaching and learning events often occur outside the formal classroom environment. This is particularly true given the increasing use of blended-learning models of learning and teaching. From a teaching perspective, speaking with your lecturers outside of class, during consultation times, about a particular topic can sometimes be more valuable than the discussion of the topic in the formal classroom environment. From a learning perspective, the reading that you do before and after class, coupled with your discussions with your student colleagues (see our discussion of study groups in Chapter 7) can similarly be significant relative to the discussions that arise in class.

Students learn; academics teach to assist learning

If the law program curriculum is carefully designed, the teaching approach adopted by your lecturer and the learning approaches recommended by your lecturer, plus those that students naturally utilise, will allow each and every student the opportunity to maximise their understanding of the discipline and achieve the planned outcomes for the unit and degree. If the teaching and learning approaches used are in conflict with each other, then it will be more difficult for students to achieve the stated outcomes of a particular unit or degree. Put another way, where a school or a lecturer designs their teaching so that learning activities accord with the stated degree or unit outcomes, and the learning approaches and opportunities used by their students are complementary, then the potential for increased student comprehension and understanding is optimised.

Well-designed teaching programs maximise opportunities for learning

Deep, surface, and lifelong learning

Before we move into a discussion of the different approaches that may be encountered in law school, it is important to understand the latest jargon or buzzwords used by researchers in academia and governments.

'Deep learning' is a form of learning that promotes a level of understanding that goes beyond mere memorisation or rote learning. Deep learning is characterised by the student endeavouring to make links between the material being considered and their world experience. In other words, deep learning approaches are adopted by those who seek not just a comprehensive understanding of concepts, but also an ability to consider those concepts in a broader context. Typically, a person adopting a deep

Deep learning develops links between materials

learning approach is someone who is better able to analyse and criticise materials and situations. These abilities are those most useful in the study of law.

'Surface learning' describes the methods whereby a student will learn the bare minimum in order to try to pass an assessment item or unit. Surface learning is typified by rote learning (simple memorisation) and reading the bare minimum of material required to (hopefully) gain a rudimentary understanding of a topic or idea. In law school this would probably mean reading 'nutshell'-type books instead of the primary law (cases and statutes). The danger with this form of approach is that the inter-linkages between important cases within an area of law, between different areas of law, and between law and the broader society are frequently lost.

Simple memorisation is a form of surface learning

Not understanding how the law you are studying fits into the broader context of the world means:

- You will continually need to revisit the same law when you are studying related topics or later or advanced units.
- You will markedly reduce your ability to develop critical thinking skills and thus be a less successful student and lawyer.
- You will be in grave danger of failing the unit.

We should note here that surface learning approaches are not always bad; for instance, you may need to memorise certain facts, such as a client's details, for the purpose of a mock discussion of a legal problem. What is important is that in order to properly advise a client, or present a powerful argument, or write a good paper, you will normally need to have done more than memorise the relevant law—you will need to have considered it carefully and sought to determine how facts, law, and broader issues associated with a problem interlink. As to the process of solving problems, see Chapter 5 where we discuss the problem-solving model in some detail.

Surface learning can be useful when you need to memorise certain facts

The Honourable Justice Jack Goldring, when writing as a law professor, noted:[2]

> Students who take a surface approach tend to learn by rote, not to question the assumptions that underpin the material nor relate it to

2 John Goldring, 'Coping with the Virtual Campus: Some Hints and Opportunities for Legal Education', *Legal Education Review*, 1995, vol. 6, no. 1, at 91–116.

> its context. Students with a deep approach examine the arguments critically, question the assumptions on which they are based and relate them to previous knowledge and understanding. Understanding of legal material, both from a perspective of internal consistency and structure, and of its relation to the social context, is essential to the making of sound professional judgments and evaluations.

'Lifelong learning' refers to a system of learning that promotes a deeper level of understanding of an area, like law, such that the learner is skilful enough to comprehend, assess, and respond to new and different facts, circumstances, or scenarios without the need, necessarily, for outside assistance or prompting. Lifelong learning is a form of deep learning, which we submit is the form of learning that most academics desire in their students.

Lifelong learners seek out answers for themselves

Lifelong learning has been defined by Cropley to:[3]

> last the whole life of the learner; lead to systematic acquisition, renewal, upgrading and completion of knowledge, skills, and attitudes made necessary by the constantly changing conditions in which people now live; have as its ultimate goal promotion of self-fulfilment of each individual; be dependent for its successful implementation on people's increasing ability and motivation to engage in self-directed learning activities; and acknowledge the contribution of all available educational influences, including formal, nonformal and informal.

The benefits of lifelong learning are based on providing the control for learning to the learner.

According to Candy, the advantages of using a learner-control model of learning include the following:[4]

> It responds to the apparent inflexibility of conventional education in the face of rapid change; it recognizes the way in which people generally, and adults in particular, habitually learn; it reflects the primacy of learning over teaching; it accommodates individual differences in learning; it leads to enhanced learning outcomes

3 Arthur John Cropley, 'Lifelong Education: A Stocktaking' (Hamburg: Pergamon, 1979).

4 Philip C. Candy, 'Self-direction for Lifelong Learning: A Comprehensive Guide to Theory and Practice' (San Francisco: Jossey-Bass, 1991).

> through increased motivation; it models democratic principles and develops skills of democratic participation; it inculcates habits of curiosity and self-initiated inquiry; and it encourages the development of self-determining individuals, capable both of undertaking learning on their own outside formal instructional settings and giving meaning and direction to their lives.

It sounds great, but unfortunately does not always happen. Lifelong learning appears to be something that all lecturers should be fostering in their students and all students should be actively engaging in; however, circumstances sometimes result in a less beneficial learning approach being adopted by students. Why does this happen? In large part, it is because surface learning is easy to do. If you are pushed for time because of multiple assignments, work commitments, or family and social matters, then surface learning, or what we think of as 'last-minute learning', is the only option. Additionally, surface learning by way of rote learning and regurgitation of facts has previously been a successful formula for learning in high schools—thankfully this situation is slowly changing. A final, and hopefully rare, reason that lifelong learning approaches are not always adopted is because your lecturer may adopt teaching and assessment methods that reward a less deep approach.

Circumstances do not always favour lifelong learning approaches

Personal strengths and weaknesses

Your personal learning style and dominant communication approach are strengths that you need to take advantage of during your time at law school. They are strengths in the sense that if you are in a learning situation where your learning style is being utilised and the mode of communication is within your dominant approach, then you will naturally find yourself interested and engaged in the process. The weaknesses come about when you do not understand your personal learning style and communication strengths and thus cannot explain to yourself why some tasks are less interesting to you. If you can recognise your learning and communication weaknesses then you are in a better position to work upon improving them and minimising their impact.

You must understand your learning strengths and weaknesses

There are a number of different ways in which learners can be categorised. One way that has been used by the Australasian Law Teachers' Association in its teaching workshops is based on the work of an American psychologist named David Kolb. Here learners' styles are divided into several broad groupings. The following summary is derived from Le Brun and Johnstone:[5]

- Accommodators are those who learn predominantly by using personal insight and feeling coupled with learning by doing.
- Assimilators are those who learn by thinking and reasoning about abstract ideas in conjunction with watching, listening, and considering different perspectives.
- Convergers learn by thinking and reasoning about abstract concepts coupled with practical learning by doing.
- Divergers use personal insight and feelings as well as watching and listening as their main modes of learning.

Le Brun and Johnstone observe that most, but not all, law teachers, and those interested in law, utilise the 'assimilators' learning style.

In terms of communication approaches there are three main ways of sending and receiving information. They are oral/auditory, visual/writing, and physical/tactile.

- A person who is predominantly an oral/auditory communicator is one who enjoys communicating by speaking and listening more than other modes of communication. Typically, a person with a dominant oral/auditory communication mode will enjoy listening to their lecturers and fellow students speaking about the law. They will also enjoy being involved in classroom debates and study groups where discussion is the norm, and will utilise these learning situations to maximise their learning development.
- A person who is predominantly a visual/writing communicator mostly enjoys reading and seeing things when they are learning. Such a person will be comfortable reading lecture notes and seeing their lecturers use flowcharts, diagrams and PowerPoint slides, when running classes. A person who is primarily a visual/writing communicator will normally enjoy making notes, writing essays, and clarifying issues by reference to the written word.
- A physical/tactile communicator is one who gains a lot of their learning from their surroundings. Thus, the lighting and temperature of the learning

---

5 Marlene Le Brun & Richard Johnstone, 'The Quiet Revolution' (Sydney: The Law Book Company Limited, 1994).

environment is an important component of their learning. A person who responds positively to the tactile will also be responsive to physically engaging in their learning; thus they will enjoy the activity associated with tasks such as mooting and client interviewing through to smaller tangible activities—from physically writing their class notes, working in small groups, and taking part in class role-plays, to simply feeling the texture of their books and materials.

Every individual is a combination of all three modes of communication, and depending on context you might be very happy communicating in all three ways. Law school emphasises reading, writing, and talking, however; therefore you will need to be a competent communicator in these modes, even if you are a particularly tactile person.

Most lecturers who are familiar with different learning styles and communication modes will attempt to cater to the needs of most of their students. They will do this by varying the nature of their communications and assessment tasks so that different learning approaches and communication modes are facilitated.

Most lecturers try to cater to the needs of all learning types

Different lecturers and their teaching approaches

All law schools have their own mission statements, philosophies, or policies that give a prospective student an idea about how that school expects learning to be undertaken. Some schools' approaches may be constrained by budgets, university structures, or personnel, but most will be seeking to ensure that their graduates are lifelong learners, with skills acceptable to the professional market place, and with the ability to engage in many forms of employment or social activity. The individual lecturers, entrusted with the production of the school's graduates, will usually be required to teach in accordance with the school's view of teaching and learning. Within those parameters, however, is a markedly different range of philosophies and techniques. Each lecturer has an individual teaching preference and style, and you must learn to adapt yourself to these different approaches in all the different units that you study within your law degree.

You must adapt to the different teaching approaches held by different lecturers

The approaches adopted by lecturers range from the 'authoritarian expert' who shares their knowledge with a passive class, through the 'Socratic interrogator' who fires questions at random to every member of the class, to the 'student-focused facilitator' who, with minimal input, forces students to find the answer to problems and issues by themselves. All of these approaches, including combinations and permutations not mentioned, can be effective teaching techniques in different contexts. What is important for you to understand is that you will generally be exposed to differing techniques from unit to unit and sometimes from tutorial to tutorial. Importantly, you will be more comfortable with some approaches than others, but to survive and succeed in law school you must become a successful learner whichever method, approach, or technique is utilised.

Understand your lecturer's personal teaching approach

Let's consider these three typical approaches and how they can be used to your advantage to help you become a deep learner.

The authoritarian expert

The authoritarian expert is a lecturer who may be eminent in their field of knowledge and who adopts an approach to teaching that may be considered by some to be paternalistic. The authoritarian expert not only knows the law well, but also has a strong desire that you know this too. This will typically be exhibited by an approach to classes that may be described as 'one-way traffic'. Here, the lecturer introduces a topic, and may ask for a few ideas from the students, but is really intent on ensuring that the most law that can be imparted in the session is so imparted.

The authoritarian expert wants to impart a lot of important material

The intention of the authoritarian expert is good. The authoritarian expert wants you to know that there is a lot of complex law in their field, and the best way to get this across is to tell you. The two problems in having the authoritarian expert as teacher are that first, they have little chance to ensure that you understand what is being spoken about (because the communication flow is one-way, you may feel too intimidated to interrupt a speech); and second, they are so intent on feeding you information that you develop a learning approach that simply soaks up the information, often uncritically, with the result that you are induced to become a surface learner, even if you would rather not be one.

The way to deal with an authoritarian expert as lecturer is to take advantage of that expertise and learn how to communicate with them.

Most lecturers are approachable and the authoritarian expert is usually no exception. Particularly prickly authoritarian experts are often less approachable than others because they do not 'suffer fools' and may resent being asked unsophisticated questions; however, if you ask a well-thought-through question you may be surprised at how responsive they can be. This is simply because you have tapped into an area of interest for them and they wish to be engaged at a higher level.

Another thing to consider is trying to understand how the authoritarian expert became such an expert. If you ask such a lecturer how they know so much, they will probably tell you that they adopted deep and lifelong learning methods; that is, they were intrinsically interested in the law, read assiduously, and asked lots of questions. Some experts develop their expertise by running cases in the area, working for law reform commissions, and writing books or articles on the area. The point is that the expert immersed themself in the material—they did not adopt a surface-learning approach—and thus developed their deep and considerable knowledge.

Understand the learning methods used by the authoritarian expert

The Socratic interrogator

The lecturer who adopts a Socratic-interrogation, or -dialogue, technique is one who harnesses the social factor of tutorials, and in some cases the element of fear, to ensure that you keep up to date with your readings and weekly work. The Socratic interrogator will use prescribed readings and questions as the basis for asking questions of individual students in tutorials. Historically, the Socratic lecturer will ask a student, selected at random, to explain a case, or judgment, or topic, or to provide an answer, by using a series of questions. The student will answer the questions until such time as they are unable to answer any further questions. At this point the lecturer then moves onto the next selected student and asks the last unanswered question of them, and the process continues in this manner for the duration of the tutorial. Today, a Socratic interrogator may be a little more flexible and may ask questions of any student at random at any time. Alternatively, some Socratic interrogators will forewarn the class about who can expect to be asked questions in a given week, or delimit the areas that questions may be

The Socratic interrogator asks lots of questions

asked about, or allow others to jump in and provide answers when another person is having difficulties.

The benefits of the Socratic-dialogue method is that in order for the class to proceed, and in order for students to contribute positively and actively, all students in attendance must normally be fully prepared to answer any question. Where this works best is when the tutorial has a participation mark associated with the unit. In order to answer questions and achieve participation marks, students must have done the readings and attempted to answer the questions or tasks.

The disadvantages of the Socratic-dialogue technique are that:

- Some students are not as good at, or comfortable with, oral communication in such settings and may feel intimidated, with the consequence that their learning suffers.
- The learning associated with the readings and answers may be more oriented towards a surface-level approach if the questions focus on regurgitation of material and process as opposed to analysis and criticism.
- The opportunities for further discussion of topics associated with the readings may be reduced if the class is completely directed by the lecturer, or if students are too intimidated to talk because they may suffer more questioning.

Lecturers who engage in the Socratic-dialogue technique can provide a springboard to deeper learning in several ways. First, the technique is designed to ensure you read all the set readings and do the tasks for the class. Thus, at the very least, you should have considered the week's materials at least once. If you genuinely think about those materials, recognise the limitations of your understanding, and consider the areas you think your lecturer might ask you about, then you are in a better position to do further readings and talk through your answers with colleagues. Second, if you have joined a study group you will find that discussing the set tasks and possible questions will cause you to go from simply remembering what a case or statute states to considering more deeply what its purpose is and how it has various limitations. Third, watching your colleagues answer questions gives you an idea about how others comprehend and interpret the unit materials. That insight into your student colleagues is valuable in providing you with comfort that others might also find certain topics difficult. Finally, if you have properly prepared, it also gives you a chance

A study group may help you practise answering questions

to reflect on what appears to be important to your lecturer and where areas of difficulty in understanding do, in fact, lie.

The student-focused facilitator

The student-focused facilitator is a lecturer who runs tutorials by asking for students to work through readings and questions or tasks largely by themselves. The facilitator acts as a learning mentor and will provide some introductory or process guidance—such as 'let's consider a certain case or problem'—but will make reliance on 'self' a student-learning priority. Facilitators will sometimes also be advocates of enquiry-based learning. This is where students solve problems largely on their own—as a result of their own enquiries—after receiving some introductory guidance as to what tools and methods might be best used to solve the problem.

The advantages of having a facilitator as lecturer is that students have a greater opportunity to control the direction of their learning—by examining the questions and issues that interest them the most, or cause them the most concern, and by providing a strong basis for a more self-directed and deeper approach to learning. If done well, the lecturer as facilitator will be working just as hard as any other type of lecturer and will force students to take responsibility for their own learning. The difficulty with the lecturer as facilitator is that when the unit is not properly designed, or the lecturer is less skilled, some students get lost in the lack of structure. Some students feel disenchanted that they are doing all the work and the lecturer is, to them, not 'giving them the law'. Other students may feel that things are formally unresolved when there is no clear statement being made by the person 'who should be in charge'.

Facilitators guide students as they learn for themselves

Having a facilitator as lecturer is, arguably, the easiest way to develop deep and lifelong learning methods. Because of the greater emphasis on student direction and participation, you have the opportunity to learn as shallowly or deeply as you desire. The way to take advantage of a facilitating lecturer is to ensure that you have prepared for a class so well that when you run into a sticking point, you can ask the lecturer, or your colleagues, for the tools or direction to resolve the issue. You may not receive a direct or complete response from the facilitator about what the final answer to a question may be, but you should have an understanding of the path you need to follow in order to obtain that answer.

Facilitators will help you understand the path you need to follow to obtain an answer

The three curricula of any course

Whether explicitly acknowledged or not, there are three different forms of curriculum within any course, and unit, of study at law school. They are:

i) the legal–academic content curriculum;
ii) the professional legal skills curriculum;
iii) the generic academic skills curriculum.

All three of these curricula are part of your law degree program and may be evident, in part, in some or all of your units of study in law school. It is necessary to understand these curricula so that you can contextualise what you are learning and how those curricula are designed to produce a law graduate with certain characteristics at the end of your studies.

The legal–academic content curriculum

The legal–academic content curriculum is the primary focus of most law school curricula. It is largely based on, or influenced by, the 'Priestley 11' content requirements discussed in Chapter 2.

The legal–academic content curriculum is the primary focus of most law school curricula

The academic curriculum for any accredited law school will usually include coverage of the content of the areas listed by the Priestley committee; however, some law schools adopt a more flexible approach to the rigid content list than others. In addition to the content suggested by the Priestley committee, your law school may add to the academic curriculum those materials that it deems to be important to satisfy its school and university philosophies. An example might be that in a unit on criminal law, your law school might teach the standard topics of determining criminal responsibility and the crimes listed by the Priestley committee, such as murder, assault, theft, etc. But in addition, your law school or lecturer might have a research slant or interest in corporate and commercial law, and so may also insist on the academic curriculum including a topic such as corporate criminal liability.

Equally, your law school or lecturer might have a philosophy that is geared towards developing in students a deeper understanding of social justice issues. Therefore your criminal law unit may have an extra topic aimed specifically at understanding drug laws, women and crime, restorative justice, or juveniles as victims or perpetrators (to name just a few options).

The academic curriculum is found in the set readings from textbooks and primary legal materials. It is typically assessed by way of essays, research papers, and final examinations.

The professional legal skills curriculum

The professional legal skills curriculum is an amalgam of activities designed to develop a deeper appreciation of the law by linking it to a practical context. This curriculum is evidenced, if not explicitly acknowledged by your lecturers, within activities that are more than just critical intellectual analyses of the law, but which have some link with professional activity. These professional legal skills have as their twin aims the development of an understanding of legal principle and an appreciation of how that understanding might be applied in practice.

The professional legal skills curriculum links theory and practice

The types of activities that are typical of those within a professional legal skills curriculum are those that require some form of communicating in a professional legal context. You will note that when you engage in these professional legal skills curriculum activities that the level and type of intellectual achievement is no different from that which we have referred to as part of the academic curriculum. The only difference is the clear link that the professional legal skills curriculum makes with legal practice, and, to a lesser extent, legal theory.

Examples of activities in which professional legal skills are developed include:

- mooting and other forms of oral advocacy;
- drafting of contracts;
- client interviewing and providing advice;
- meeting procedure;
- interlocutory applications and drafting initiating process;
- witness examination;
- dispute resolution processes;
- group presentations.

The generic academic skills curriculum

Generic academic skills are those that the university requires in all of its graduates, regardless of discipline. Generic academic skills are typically based on the development of analytical talents and proficiency in communication competencies, whether oral, written, or computer-based. Usually a law graduate will develop these generic academic skills as part of the academic content and professional skills curriculum; however, it is important to bear in mind that some generic ideas may not be fully embraced by some of your lecturers. For instance, there is a generation of lawyers who still find computers to be a daunting and foreign concept. It will come as no surprise then that some of your lecturers will use traditional communication and assessment methods, while others will embrace technology more fully. The point is that some of the generic academic competencies may not be specifically developed by all lecturers in all units. And given the need to cover the other curricula mentioned above, it is probably appropriate that your lecturers do not try to cover all generic skills in a single unit of study.

Generic academic skills may include:

- familiarity with and achievement in the scholarship of discovery, integration, and transmission of knowledge;
- an ability to integrate interdisciplinary thinking;
- effective written and oral communication skills;
- an appreciation of the ethical dimension to decision-making;
- an ability to work as part of a group;
- computer literacy.

The three curricula of any course or unit at your law school will be dependent on a range of factors including: the interests of available personnel; funding; the collective needs of academic staff; the leadership of the law school executive; university missions and goals; and professional accreditation requirements.

Later in this chapter, we note the advent of 'Threshold Learning Outcomes' as a means of identifying the necessary and desirable qualities of law school graduates. These outcomes are set to play a role in guiding the three curricula in the future.

Curricula of the future

In this section we have referred to the three curricula of the law program as being dependent on a range of factors. These factors make each law school different, in sometimes substantial ways. Over time, the changes to the academic staff at your law school, the manner in which modern technology is utilised, and your university's program for change, as well as changes to the law itself, will naturally mean that the various curricula will evolve. In addition, there are a variety of reports and interest groups that seek to improve, or change, the legal profession and the law school curriculum. Based on these we suggest that the law school curricula may develop and change to incorporate the following:

- a national legal services market;[6]
- the embedding of ethics throughout the law program;[7]
- the globalisation of legal services and the internationalisation of law programs;[8]
- the embedding of Indigenous knowledge, experiences, and perspectives into the law curriculum.[9]

Four interrelated components of any unit of study

There are four key interrelated components to any unit you study in law school. They are: the unit objectives; readings; learning activities and assessment tasks; and graduate attributes. Where a unit has been closely developed in conjunction with the law school's teaching philosophy and your university's planned outcomes, you should find that there is explicit congruity between the unit aims and objectives, the readings you do, the learning activities

Unit objectives, readings, learning activities and assessment tasks, and graduate attributes all affect what you need to learn

6 http://www.ag.gov.au/Consultations/Pages/NationalLegalProfessionalReform.aspx.

7 Michael Robertson, 'Embedding "Ethics" in Law Degrees', in Sally Kift, Michelle Sanson, Jil Cowley, & Penelope Watson (eds), 'Excellence and Innovation in Legal Education' (Chatswood: Lexis Nexis Butterworths Australia 2011), at 99–117.

8 Council of Australian Law Deans, 'Internationalising the Australian Law Curriculum for Enhanced Global Legal Practice', http://www.cald.asn.au/media/uploads/CALD5864_CouncilAusLawDeans_Final.pdf.

9 This is a project that has already been taken up by many universities around the country, e.g. Badanami Centre for Indigenous Education, University of Western Sydney, 'Embedding an Indigenous Graduate Attribute', Final Report, 2012 http://www.uws.edu.au/__data/assets/pdf_file/0007/370807/UWS_Final_Report_Embedding_an_Indigenous_Graduate_Attribute_2012.pdf. Note should also be taken of the debate relating to constitutional reform and the recognition of Indigenous Australians: http://www.humanrights.gov.au/publications/constitutional-reform-fact-sheet-recognising-aboriginal-torres-strait-islander-people and http://www.recognise.org.au.

and assessment tasks you are required to undertake, and the graduate attributes for your school and university.

How do these four components fit together?

Unit objectives

The unit objectives—as found in your unit learning guide and read in conjunction with the unit aims—explicitly list the direction your learning should take for each semester. The objectives are provided in the first week of the semester and should be a very strong guide to you about the areas in which your lecturer intends you to read, learn, and develop. In other words, you should consider these objectives as a guiding light to the tasks you are required to complete—they should be used to give you some direction as to why you are doing certain assessment tasks beyond those directions directly associated with the tasks. Unit objectives typically list the levels of understanding you should be striving to achieve in defined areas. They are expressed in aspirational form; for example, 'By the end of this unit you should be able to ...'.

Unit aims and objectives give direction to your learning

Readings

Usually the readings for your unit will be listed in the unit learning guide, which may also be known as a unit study guide, or unit outline. The readings may be listed as a precursor to weekly learning activities and are associated with particular questions, tasks, and assignments for your tutorials or seminars. Alternatively, you might be provided with a series of Acts, cases, or textbooks, and told that all and every part of those readings will be assessed in some way, so you need to start reading them all from Week One of the semester. Finally, in some units you may be asked to develop your own reading list based upon your own enquiries into a given area. The point is that the readings are the tools from which you can develop your legal, practical, and generic academic skills. They are provided for you to read, or created by you, for a reason and thus should be examined carefully. If you are familiar with the unit aims and objectives, then you are better able to understand why your lecturer deems specified readings to be important. If your unit is carefully planned, you will usually only be reading

The tools of the law are words, so you must read

those materials that specifically go towards helping you achieve the defined unit objectives, participate in learning activities, complete the assessment tasks, and fulfil the graduate attributes for your degree.

AMOUNT AND TYPE OF READING

In comparison to most other disciplines, the study of law involves a significant amount of reading. This results from the nature and complexity of the positive law,[10] as well as the quantity of material that is normally required to be covered.

What makes reading the law so difficult? It is simply because the law must be read in a certain way (see Chapters 3 and 9) and you need to be comprehensive in your approach. That is, there are rules pertaining to the legal system (such as precedent and statutory interpretation) that inform the way a piece of law should be read. Further, when reading a case or a statute, an approach that attempts to follow impermissible shortcuts to save time will frequently result in confusion. A permissible shortcut is where you can quickly determine from the table of contents, or a catchword list, that an Act or case is relevant, or irrelevant, to your enquiry. An impermissible shortcut is where, after deciding to read an Act or a case, you do not read it in full. If your lecturer has indicated that only so much of an Act or case is necessary to read, then you are entitled to only read parts of it. However, it is our view that many problems relating to a deeper understanding of the law result from skimming the primary materials, thereby occasionally missing relevant and important details that place the key provisions in their broader context.

Always read cases and Acts in full

Why is there so much material to read? First, the volume of law made by parliament has increased in modern times. This is partly due to rapid societal change and technological development, which, due to their new and unique nature, require proactive legal governance such as that provided by parliament. It is also largely due to the fact that governments and parliament can have greater control over the law and society, and hence continuing power, if they make the (statutory) law in the first place.

10 The 'positive law' is the law as 'posited' by the sovereign—effectively, the law that derives from the case reports and statutes.

Second, the internet—particularly websites such as AustLII[11]—has made access to the primary materials of the law much easier. Prior to the advent of electronic databases, law lecturers and students would have studied the statute books and cases as they found them on the law library shelves. These would be updated as fast as the library could manage, to replace the old legislation and case reports with new ones. Depending on the library budget and the time taken by the government printers to produce the statutes, or the law book publishers to produce reported case decisions, delays of several weeks or even months could arise between the time the law was made and the time when the reasonably studious law student could have access to that law.

AustLII and other electronic databases give you almost instant access to the law

Students of law, like their lecturers, can now have a recently handed-down decision of any of the superior courts in the country on their computer screen within hours of the decision. In addition, many case reports are now available for consideration—not just the reported ones. Reported cases are those that have been selected for publication in a law report series on the basis that the case has created a development in the law in a certain area and should be disseminated widely. Unreported judgments are those that do not necessarily raise significant changes to the law and are thus not 'reported'. A modern law student will be required, as a matter of course, to consider unreported judgments in any research-related assignment or task.

Third, your law lecturer may have developed and prepared a printout or list of readings specifically for your unit. These readings can sometimes be all that you have to read for your unit, but sometimes they are additional to a textbook. Some lecturers may have the benefit of different types of textbooks that complement each other, so you might find that there are three or four prescribed sets of readings, or texts, for the one unit; although many academics are conscious of the cost factor—law books are not cheap—and accordingly attempt to keep the number of prescribed books down to a minimum.

Many law lecturers develop their own learning materials packages

On this point it is important to make several notes here about reading lists for your unit. When your lecturer provides you with a reading list for your unit, whether electronically or as a handout, some of the books that are listed may be labelled as 'prescribed' (or required) texts, while others are

11 http://www.austlii.edu.au.

simply listed as 'recommended'. Those books listed as prescribed will normally be referred to significantly during the course of your unit. It may be that the prescribed texts contain the questions and activities that you will undertake in your tutorials. It may be that the prescribed texts provide an overview of fundamental principles, or alternatively they may be neat, abridged packages of primary resources. Regardless of the type of book it is, it will normally be essential for you to have access to it on a weekly basis during the course of your unit.

Textbook publishers are increasingly transferring textbooks to online formats. So another way to obtain some of the essential readings may be to download the textbook to your computer or personal digital device.

Prescribed textbooks are usually very important

Many students have jobs or supportive parents or spouses and can simply buy the books. However, many students do not. There are a number of ways around this. Short-term loans or credit cards can be helpful if you want your own copy of the books. This is often a good choice if you are in some form of employment. Less frequently, some students, who are friends or live near to each other, arrange themselves into study groups or textbook consortia. They then purchase the required readings as a group. This keeps the costs down but can be a nightmare if you do not have a clear system of time limits for use of those books and materials that everyone sticks to. You should also note that some bookstores will provide a tax exemption on those textbooks that are prescribed by your lecturer—so make sure you take evidence of your university enrolment and textbook list with you if you go shopping.

Prescribed textbooks can usually be found in your library

A financially light but more time-intensive final alternative is to use the library. Most lecturers will ensure that there are a couple of copies of the required readings in the 'special reserve', 'closed reserve', or 'short-term loan' section of your library. This will allow you to borrow the books you need for a short period of time, usually several hours to three days depending on your library rules. This is time-intensive because, unlike those who own their texts, you will need to use the books in the library or return them shortly after they have been borrowed. If you are organised, then it is quite a workable system, but you do need to plan ahead. If your lecturer has not made use of this part of your library facility and you need to use this method, then you will need to ask the lecturer to do so.

Returning to why there is so much to read, a final reason is that the law book publishers themselves are always interested in increasing their share of the market. New and different publications on all areas of law are continually being produced for consideration by lecturers and students. If a lecturer does not prescribe more than one or two texts for a particular unit, then they might refer you to others that may be of value. You may decide that you wish to do extra reading so as to increase your understanding of a topic. Browsing the law library, or your closest law bookshop, will also uncover many readings that your lecturer may not have alerted you to. You might also wish to read other texts and journals because you find the nature and style of your textbooks difficult to read or understand. Thus, you may voluntarily increase the amount of reading required to pass your units.

Engaging in extra reading can really help your understanding

Learning activities and assessment tasks

Engaging in learning activities provides an opportunity for you to test your ideas about and understanding of the law in an individual or group situation. Learning activities range from simply attending a lecture or reading a textbook through to more advanced actions, such as tutorial participation, presentations, and moot courts. Ideally, learning activities should be crafted in such a way that they complement each other within the unit and degree as a whole and allow you, the learner, to more fully engage with the process of learning about the law. Learning activities may be assessable (such as your assignments) or non-assessable (such as simply attending class). Some may be compulsory, while some may be optional.

Learning activities should be a counterpart to your readings and assessment tasks

Your assessment tasks are compulsory learning activities designed to promote learning and critical thinking about the law. In a properly constructed law degree, the assessment tasks you complete should directly link to the aims and objectives of the unit, the non-assessable learning activities, and the graduate attributes. The assessment tasks should also be achievable given your consideration of specified readings, or those you are asked to research for yourself.

Assessment tasks may be aimed at achieving one or more of a series of academic and practical proficiencies and outcomes. Table 4.2 provides an idea of what some of the typical assessment tasks you will complete are designed to accomplish.

Assessment tasks are a further means to develop your understanding of an area of law

TABLE 4.2 Assessments and accomplishments

Assessment task, outcome, or skill	Class participation	Seminar presentations	Problem-based essays	Theoretically based essays and research papers	Moots	Court reports	Viva voce	Formal exams
Case analysis	✓	✓	✓	✓	✓	✓	✓	✓
Statutory interpretation	✓	✓	✓	✓	✓	✓	✓	✓
Problem-solving	✓	✓	✓	✗	✓	✗	✓	✓
Critical thinking	✓	✓	✓	✓	✓	✓	✓	✓
Oral communication	✓	✓	✗	✗	✓	✗	✓	✗
Written communication	✗	✗	✓	✓	✓	✓	✗	✓
Computing competency	✗	✗	✓	✓	✓	✓	✗	✗
Advocacy skills	✗	✗	✗	✗	✓	✗	✓	✗
Consideration of professional ethics	✓	✓	✓	✓	✓	✓	✓	✓
Consideration of interdisciplinary and social justice issues	✓	✓	✓	✓	✓	✓	✓	✓
Teamwork	✓	✓	✗	✗	✓	✗	✗	✗
Self-directed learning	✓	✓	✓	✓	✓	✓	✓	✓

We examine assessment more fully in Chapters 11, 12, and 13; however, one extremely important final note on assessment needs to be made now. In any assessment task, you must maintain intellectual integrity. In any university environment, being honest about the foundations of your work is crucial. If you engage in plagiarism, you will forever be known as unethical. In an intellectual context this is the highest crime that one can commit. Please consider any work on assessments in the light of our comments in Chapter 12, which specifically deals with plagiarism.

NEVER engage in academic misconduct such as plagiarism

Graduate attributes

Graduate attributes are statements by your university about the common characteristics and qualities of individual graduates. These attributes are usually written in a general sense and are complemented by your law school by way of discipline-specific additions. Graduate attributes will include the particular features of your university and law school, but increasingly will be focused on the 'Threshold Learning Outcomes' adopted by the Council of Australian Law Deans.

Graduate attributes are the university-expected outcomes for your course

THE THRESHOLD LEARNING OUTCOMES (TLOs) FOR THE BACHELOR OF LAWS[12]

TLO 1: KNOWLEDGE

Graduates of the Bachelor of Laws will demonstrate an understanding of a coherent body of knowledge that includes:

(a) the fundamental areas of legal knowledge, the Australian legal system, and underlying principles and concepts, including international and comparative contexts,
(b) the broader contexts within which legal issues arise, and
(c) the principles and values of justice and of ethical practice in lawyers' roles.

---

12 Sally Kift, Mark Israel, & Rachael Field, 'Learning and Teaching, Academic Standards Project, Bachelor of Laws, Learning and Teaching Academic Standards Statement, December 2010', Australian Learning and Teaching Council, http://www.cald.asn.au/assets/lists/Education/KiftetalLTASStandardsStatement2010%20TLOs%20LLB.pdf.

TLO 2: ETHICS AND PROFESSIONAL RESPONSIBILITY

Graduates of the Bachelor of Laws will demonstrate:

(a) an understanding of approaches to ethical decision-making,
(b) an ability to recognise and reflect upon, and a developing ability to respond to, ethical issues likely to arise in professional contexts,
(c) an ability to recognise and reflect upon the professional responsibilities of lawyers in promoting justice and in service to the community, and
(d) a developing ability to exercise professional judgement.

TLO 3: THINKING SKILLS

Graduates of the Bachelor of Laws will be able to:

(a) identify and articulate legal issues,
(b) apply legal reasoning and research to generate appropriate responses to legal issues,
(c) engage in critical analysis and make a reasoned choice amongst alternatives, and
(d) think creatively in approaching legal issues and generating appropriate responses.

TLO 4: RESEARCH SKILLS

Graduates of the Bachelor of Laws will demonstrate the intellectual and practical skills needed to identify, research, evaluate and synthesise relevant factual, legal and policy issues.

TLO 5: COMMUNICATION AND COLLABORATION

Graduates of the Bachelor of Laws will be able to:

(a) communicate in ways that are effective, appropriate and persuasive for legal and non-legal audiences, and
(b) collaborate effectively.

TLO 6: SELF-MANAGEMENT

Graduates of the Bachelor of Laws will be able to:

(a) learn and work independently, and
(b) reflect on and assess their own capabilities and performance, and make use of feedback as appropriate, to support personal and professional development.

Threshold Learning Outcomes guide the development of graduate attributes

In order for your university and law school to state to the wider world that a graduate has certain specified attributes, the law school must be able to explain how those attributes are developed throughout the law school curriculum. To do this, the law school will usually state that the attributes are embedded within the learning activities, particularly the compulsory assessment tasks of the discipline. In any accredited law school, the content-based attributes of lawyers will continue to be largely drawn from the Priestley committee recommendations and research about teaching and learning in university contexts. But increasingly, the nationally developed Threshold Learning Outcomes will begin to appear in the language of graduate attributes.

How to approach your lecturers about your learning

There are many occasions when you may need to speak with your lecturers about academic or personal matters associated with your studies. We discuss non-academic matters in Chapter 14. When it comes to discussing academic matters (your learning, teaching-related issues, assignments, or the readings), it is essential that you do so in a timely and professional manner. This is because your lecturer is a very busy person and, like all important resources, should be used wisely.

So what sort of questions should you be asking your lecturer? The easiest way to answer this is by reference to what you should *not* be asking. You should not ask your lecturer the answer to a particular question or how to understand a piece of law unless you have first made a genuine attempt to understand it yourself. This comes back to the point we made earlier that university is about lifelong learning and self-activated students. If you have not attempted to resolve a problem, nor given thought to a difficult passage of prose, then requesting 'the answer' will simply reinforce a shallow approach to learning with its concomitant side effects. Most lecturers will simply refuse to answer such questions. If you were to have asked such a question in a tutorial, you might find that the lecturer asks you to provide the answer, either on the spot, by way of Socratic questioning, or for the next class. All of these options may be more uncomfortable than if you had done the reading and thinking

Questions to lecturers should focus on developing your understanding, not just on getting an answer in the first place. The types of questions you *should* ask, whether in class or outside it, are those that indicate that you have carefully considered the area of law in question and that a particular point or issue is causing you concern. A carefully considered question will alert your lecturer to a methodological or more advanced issue that can be dissected so as to increase your understanding.

We insert an important caveat here. Where you quite simply feel lost in relation to a reading or an assignment, then it is perfectly acceptable to ask for some direct assistance as to what something means, or how something should be done. Specifically, whenever you feel that you are really stuck on a point, or have not understood how to do, or why you are doing, a particular task, then you need to be courageous and approach your lecturer about it.

Why do you need to be courageous? Because some law students will feel too proud to indicate that they need help and will continue or complete an activity or assessment task without really understanding what they are doing. Unfortunately, this course of action is fraught with danger—as you could be doing the wrong thing—and does not help you in becoming a deep learner. You might feel foolish if it turns out that you have simply failed to read something in an instruction or case or statute, but you will feel even worse if you do something when confused and fail that task. The best lawyers and legal academics will ask questions of colleagues if they need help. It is not a matter of professional people swallowing their pride, but of acknowledging that to do their job properly they need to be fully apprised of certain facts, assumptions, or reasons for doing their work.

Don't try to impress your lecturer with convoluted, or clever, language when that is not required

When asking a lecturer for help in this situation, you need to be direct and honest and prepared. A lecturer is better able to help you if you ask for instructions about the point or issue that causes you concern than if you try to impress your lecturer with convoluted, or clever, language when that is not required.

You should also consider having a written a list of questions that you have identified as important for you to be able to move forward in your research or activity. Some students feel a little daunted when approaching their lecturer. Whether daunted or not, it is common to discover that you have had only part of what you needed to know answered after you leave your lecturer's office. A lecturer, whose time may be limited, is better able to advise you on all the points you need help with if you indicate that you have three or four questions than simply asking the first one and proceeding through them one by one. For example, if the lecturer only has 10 minutes to spare for you on a particular occasion, it may be that they can answer your other questions later, or via an email, or can adjust their time so that they do not spend too long on any one part of your enquiry. A final point here is that you need to genuinely understand the answers given. Again, some students may feel unnecessarily daunted by asking for clarification of a point just made by their lecturer, but if you do not understand something, then you will have wasted your lecturer's time and your own if you do not ask for a further explanation.

We are not trying to paint your lecturers as unhelpful people: indeed, the vast majority of lecturers are academics because, in part, they wish to assist their students to learn the law. The important thing for you and your lecturer is that the two of you can quickly pinpoint what it is that is causing you to be 'stuck' on a certain issue. If you have simply not done any readings, or have not read the materials designed to help you complete your assignments, then it is understandable that your lecturer will not be impressed, in addition to feeling frustrated. Ultimately, when faced with a student who has not attempted to educate themselves, a lecturer will invariably send the student away to do some work.

Approach your lecturers having done some reading or research

At the beginning of this section we mentioned the necessity to be timely and professional. What do we mean by those terms? 'Timely' means asking your questions when you are properly prepared to do so—that is, after having done some reading and thinking—and as soon after the issue arises as possible. In a tutorial situation this may mean asking the question when it arises in the classroom. Alternatively, you might need to reflect on your thoughts about a topic before asking the question. As we note in Chapter 7, it can be quite helpful to reflect with your student colleagues in a study group. Reflection allows you to make sure that your question is the one you wish to ask, and also gives you the opportunity to arrive at the answer yourself; that is, without having to be told the answer by your lecturer. If your question is about a specific word or phrase, then you should consult the place where it is first mentioned—case or statute—to determine whether there is a definition within that source. Failing that, you should consider the definitions provided by law dictionaries and textbooks prior to speaking with your lecturer. If your question is about an aspect of an assignment, then that question must be posed soon after the assignment is distributed, and preferably after you have done some preliminary research.

Ask questions in a timely and professional way

Lecturers, like everyone else, make mistakes or may express themselves imperfectly, and sometimes a problem you are having may be due to the way the assignment is described—a simple change of wording may make your task much simpler. Similarly, lecturers, however careful they may be, cannot be aware of all practical difficulties that students may face. For instance, if a key resource has been lost, stolen, defaced, or has failed to upload to a website, it may be impossible to do a task. Informing the lecturer of such a situation at the last minute may result in the lecturer simply indicating that you have had more than enough time to discover alternatives, such as a different library, and hence you must suffer any disadvantage. As discussed in Chapter 3, unless you suffer a personal misfortune or misadventure that your law school deems acceptable, it is never appropriate to speak with your lecturer about a problem you are having with an assignment on or after the due date for submission.

Asking questions in a professional manner means to adopt a more formal and precise communication style than you might if you were in a social setting. Lecturers are professional teachers and researchers, and possibly legal practitioners, and as such should be actively engaged in ensuring that graduates from their law school have communication abilities recognised by the legal profession, even if the graduate is not going to practise law. Therefore, your lecturer will be seeking to ensure that you clearly articulate the issues you wish to discuss in a grammatically correct form. Your lecturer may also assist you in the correct pronunciation of commonly used legal words or names that are not in everyday usage. Finally, do not use text message abbreviations or colloquialisms, as you might with friends.

Communicate clearly and logically with lecturers

Importantly, it is necessary to approach any lecturer—whether orally, by letter, or in email form—in a courteous manner. This is not just because we should all approach others as we ourselves would wish to be approached, but also because of the simple fact that if you need to negotiate with your lecturer—for example, you need an extension for an assignment, you want to miss a class, or you think you deserve more marks for an assignment—making the lecturer cranky or upset by your manner is not a great start. We are not suggesting that your approach needs to be grovelling, or sycophantic, just that it should simply be polite. On this point of self-advocacy we also suggest that you clearly, courteously, and confidently put your point across, or make your request known. It is important not to be unnecessarily intimidated by your lecturers simply because they have a particular manner or

Always be courteous

reputation: sometimes that manner or reputation is perception and not reality. If you do not make your point, your lecturer will never know what problems you might be encountering, or the extent of a problem that could be generic for a lot of other students.

The use of digital technology

The use of computers and other technological devices in legal practice and law studies is now commonplace. Most students today are comfortable surfing the net, or using portable digital devices such as iPads or web-enabled digital telephones, or storing data 'in the cloud'. In the same way, law schools are increasingly adopting new technologies to deliver curricula and to assist students and academics in their legal research. The following discussion highlights some of the advantages and pitfalls in the use of digital technology in law schools.

ONLINE CLASSROOMS

In addition to in-house, university-developed virtual learning environments, there are learning management systems such as Blackboard, WebCT, and WebCT Vista. These are designed to assist universities, and law schools, in communicating with their students, and they house learning materials for units and courses. They are the basis of online or blended learning classrooms, and facilitate distance education. Housed within the university's computer architecture, these computer platforms are able to be accessed and used on-campus and via the internet. They are frequently renamed by universities, and may also be referred to as: 'E-learning', 'My Uni', 'Online learning', or 'Your student portal', amid myriad other names. There are many features of these programs, but the main ones include:

Learning management systems help law schools communicate with their students

- a place to store unit learning guides, lecture notes, assessment instructions, reading resources, and audio and video files for access by students at any time;
- an independent email system for use by students and staff within units or courses;
- discussion boards to allow students and staff to discuss issues with each other, so that everyone in a unit or course can see the discussion and become involved in it;

- a place to list internet links to valuable resources;
- a way of recording, storing and distributing your marks for assessment items;
- a place in which to conduct online tests;
- a noticeboard for important announcements; and
- an area for students to develop personal learning or professional portfolios.

The increasing use of online classrooms in all university disciplines means that you need to be able to gain access to a computer on a regular basis and become proficient in using the program that your university or law school operates. Most law students have their own computer; however, if you do not you will find that universities usually have a large number of computers in specially designed learning spaces, such as computer labs or the library, where you are able to log on and use all the facilities provided by the online classroom.

Using the online classroom is a relatively simple process. Initially you will locate the specific internet address for your university's online learning site, either through your university's home page or from a lecturer's handout. You navigate to that site and log on, which usually means entering your name or student identification number, plus a password that you have been given, or chosen. Upon entering the online learning space, you will find a series of tabs, icons, or menus that your lecturer has created that allow you to access the features mentioned above.

Some of the basic skills you will need to learn in relation to online classrooms is how to: read, store or print readings, notices and lecture notes; do any online tests; use the links to access internet resources; use the classroom as a place to interact with students and lecturers; and store personal learning materials (such as your own notes).

Make it a habit to check online classrooms on a daily basis

An important point to note about online classrooms: make it a habit to check those sites on a daily basis (if you can), as your lecturer, or your student colleagues may place things there that require urgent attention.

DIGITAL PRESENTATION SOFTWARE

There are many software applications that assist students in making presentations. The most popular is PowerPoint. When using a presentation software package to assist in a presentation, whether in a seminar, workshop, or other class, the information that you wish to be viewed by an audience—such as text, graphics, photos, or video—is manipulated by the software into discrete screens of information and, typically, projected from a computer, through a data projector, and onto a large screen.

The advantages of using presentation packages such as PowerPoint are that you are able to:

- arrange your message in a visually attractive form for your audience;
- have a series of points from which to talk, organised and projected onto a screen;
- incorporate any digital data, such as video clips, into your presentation; and
- appear more professional, and entertaining, than if you were just to use paper notes or an overhead projector.

The disadvantages of PowerPoint are:

- The technology does not make up for poor preparation. A well-prepared oral presentation will always be more effective than a poor PowerPoint presentation.
- The program will not make you sound any better if you are nervous.
- The good looks of technology cannot cover poor, or missing, content.
- The overuse of PowerPoint can dull the impact of important points that you, or the many other PowerPoint users, wish to make.
- Some users of PowerPoint make the mistake of placing too much content on each screen projected, making the material hard to read.
- Reading every word that appears on a screen is boring for members of your audience who can just as easily read the material provided.
- Recent psychological research suggests that the use of audio and visual reception channels at the same time is not as effective as using *either* an audio channel *or* a visual channel.

In relation to this last point, it may prove to be more effective if, when using PowerPoint, you allow materials designed to be read or viewed to be so read or viewed, but not read aloud by you. If you wish to talk about a matter at length, it should not also appear on the screen.

PERSONAL DIGITAL DEVICES AND PODCASTING

There are many personal digital devices that can assist you in storing, recording, or creating notes and other information. These range from the ubiquitous iPhones, iPods, and iPads and their clones to USB memory sticks, Blackberry and other digital telephones, and digital voice recorders. All can store many gigabytes of information that would be very expensive to obtain in hard copy. The advantage of digital devices is that they are small and portable. The disadvantage is that unless you wish to pay for the printing, you may need to work with that digital media on your computer screen.

In addition to the storing and recording referred to above, and the non-academic storage of music and photographs, the iPod and its clones are great for receiving lectures and other useful material via podcasting. Many universities are now looking into, or already utilising, podcasting as a means of distributing lecture materials. The advantage of podcasting is that lectures may be downloaded onto the portable storage device and listened to at your leisure, time and time again. If you have the time, or if the recording is good enough to use translation software, the lecture may be turned into written form.

Lectures may be downloaded onto your iPod and listened to at your leisure

DISTANCE EDUCATION AND MOOCS

While we are very supportive of the use, and advantages, of digital technology to enhance the law school learning experience—especially where distance-mode students live a long way from campus—we are mindful of the potential disadvantage of any overreliance on technology by students. There are many reasons why law school students may wish to utilise digital technology at the expense of human interaction in classrooms. These include: work or family commitments, shyness, and distance from campus, among others. However, if digital technology means that non-distance-mode students treat classes as an optional extra, then the richness of face-to-face interactions is missed. The ability to easily test ideas and question theories and legal propositions is, subject to normal communication protocols, instantaneous in a face-to-face classroom. Many messages received from lecturers and student colleagues are conveyed in non-verbal form, such as through nods of the head and raised eyebrows. While students can test and question online, in chat rooms and discussion boards, the fact is that these are more time-consuming, less flexible, and devoid of the vividness of human interaction.

Digital technology is more time-consuming, less flexible, and devoid of the vividness of human interaction.

Having said that, we note that the advent of Massive Online Open Courses, or MOOCS, are a significant development of the distance education model. MOOCS provide opportunities for students from around the world to engage in learning from any number of universities that are making MOOCS available. The flexibility of study options, the prestige of some MOOCS institutions, the marketing power implicit in MOOCS, and the ability to cross national borders have made MOOCS a feature of higher education that will continue to develop. However, the potential problems with MOOCS—such as the debatable quality of the learning approaches, and the difficulty ascertaining who is actually completing courses—only add to the problem of a lack of jurisdictional relevance for many of the units required to be completed by Australian law students.

5

LEGAL PROBLEM-SOLVING

Judges commonly are elderly men, and are more likely to hate at sight any analysis to which they are not accustomed, and which disturbs repose of mind, than to fall in love with novelties.

Oliver Wendell Holmes[1]

1 Oliver Wendell Holmes, 'Law in Science and Science in Law' (1899) 12 *Harvard Law Review* 58, at 455.

Introduction

Despite the cynicism of former United States Supreme Court Justice Oliver Wendell Holmes, the entire system of justice is predicated on judges not only being able to accept an alternative analysis of the law based on the facts before the court, but also, on occasions, showing their enthusiasm to do so. As stated in Chapter 1, studying and practising law is about analysing the facts, then comparing those facts to the current accepted view of the law to determine whether people have acted according to the law or whether the law should be changed based on the new facts. However, if this analysis took place without any structure, the judicial system would probably break down through inefficiency. So, the process of legal analysis and the setting of precedent (a term to be explained below) take place within a set structure. Therefore, this chapter will look at a legal problem-solving model as one structure to manage the analysis and synthesis of legal problems.

The process of legal analysis and the setting of precedent take place within a set structure

Before embarking on an explanation of that model, it is important to first consider the proof-making model that is the basic model used for all litigation, because an understanding of this model will help put the legal problem-solving model into context.

As with other issues raised in this book, the legal problem-solving model set out in this chapter demonstrates the authors' views on a structured approach to legal problem-solving, but it is not the only approach you will encounter in your life at law school or in the profession. The legal problem-solving model is the first thing lawyers address their minds to when clients come to seek advice. Finding the answer, or a likely answer, to the problem guides lawyers in their advice to their clients—particularly as to issues of liability or fault. If a client wishes to litigate the dispute, then the lawyer will address her or his mind to the proof-making model in order to map out the potential litigation.

The proof-making model

Rules of court determine that certain procedural and substantive tasks have to take place if a plaintiff wishes to recover from a defendant in civil court, or if the state wishes to prosecute a person for the breach of certain laws in a criminal court. For example, in civil matters a case is brought to the attention of the court by the plaintiff filing a statement of claim setting out the facts of the matter. From there, the defendant has a short period of time (usually 28 days) in which to file a defence, setting out the facts according to the defence, after which time the matter will eventually proceed to a hearing where evidence will be introduced to support the facts that support the cause of action. The cause of action is a statement of the legal rule that has been broken that has caused the plaintiff to incur a loss (usually money), such that the plaintiff wishes to recoup that loss by suing the defendant.

The cause of action is a statement of the legal rule that has been broken

For example, let us say that you and I agree that you will sell me your car for a certain sum of money and I pay a deposit for the car and promise to pay the balance of the purchase price upon delivery of the car the following week. If you do not deliver the car as agreed, then you have breached the contract created between us. The cause of action is breach of contract. The legal rule that has been broken is your promise to perform the contract according to the terms you and I agreed upon; that is, delivering the car to a certain place on a certain day in exchange for an amount of money. The facts that support the cause of the action are the elements of what makes a contract:

Facts support elements that prove the cause of the action

i) You made me an offer to sell your car.
ii) I accepted your offer to sell the car by indicating that I would purchase it.
iii) I paid a deposit or gave something of value (consideration) for the creation of the contract, which shows I was serious about the contract and serious about binding you and me to our agreement.
iv) You had the intention to sell the car and I had the intention to purchase the car.

The evidence that will support the cause of action could be:

a) the words you used to offer the car to me;
b) the words I used to accept your offer;
c) the actual money I handed to you for the deposit and the bank statement that shows that you deposited the money in your bank account; and
d) the words we both used to agree on the delivery of the car for the balance of the purchase money.

FIGURE 5.1 The proof-making model for a contract claim

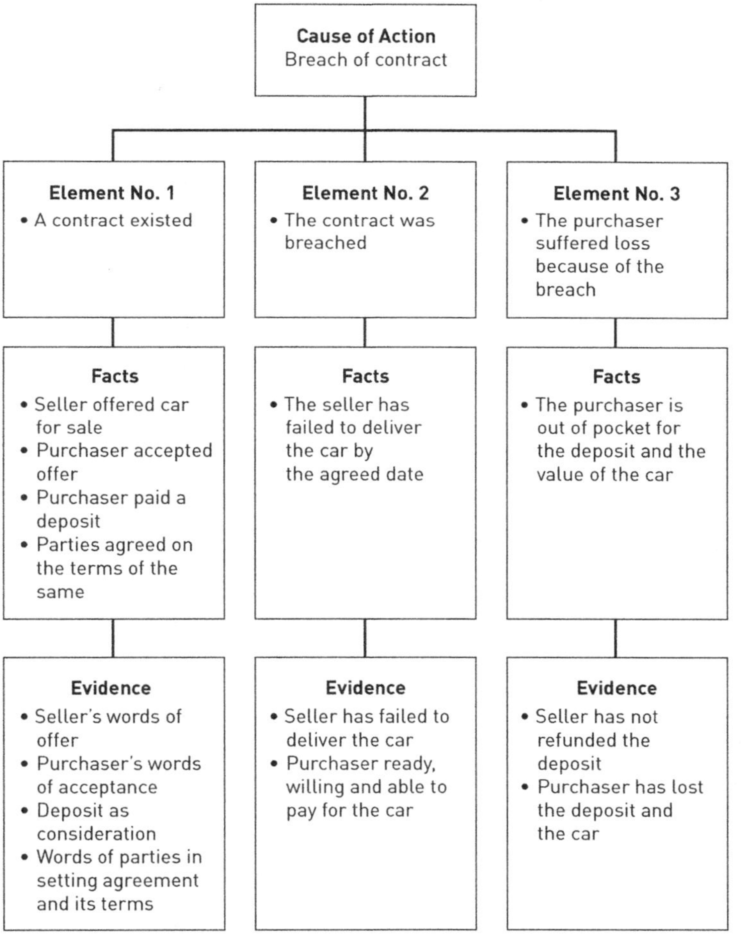

The above structure is commonly called the 'proof-making model' and is used by lawyers when constructing a case for court. It provides a road map of how the case will be presented and its basis in law. Figure 5.1 is a diagrammatic representation of the proof-making model for a standard claim in contract.

In a criminal case, exactly the same process is followed, only instead of us speaking about the 'cause of action' we generally refer to the 'elements of the crime'. In criminal matters, the elements of the crime that are made out by the facts proved by the evidence come from the actual wording of the crime in the legislation or case law that sets out the crime. A prosecutor who fails to introduce evidence that proves the facts that support the elements of the crime will not secure the conviction of the accused person. In such cases the jury will acquit (set free) the accused.

In a criminal case, we refer to the 'elements of the crime' rather than the 'cause of action'

Court judgments

In a civil or criminal case, once the case is presented using the proof-making model and the tribunal of fact (either a judge or jury) decides the outcome of the case, in the case of a judge hearing the matter alone, she or he will hand down a judgment explaining the reasons for the decision. The judgment will recount the evidence presented, and the judge will look to see if the plaintiff (civil) or the prosecutor (criminal) has presented enough persuasive evidence to support the facts contended that in turn prove each of the elements to the cause of action (civil) or the elements of the crime (criminal).

A judgment explains the reasons for the court's decision

In civil cases, if the judge is satisfied that the standard of evidence judged on the balance of probabilities proves that the elements of the cause of action have been made out, then she or he will find in favour of the plaintiff. If the judge is not satisfied that the plaintiff has proved the elements of the cause of action, then she or he will find for the defendant.

In criminal cases, the judge or jury must be satisfied beyond reasonable doubt that the elements of the crime have been proved, otherwise the accused will be acquitted of the crime. In criminal cases, where the tribunal of fact is a jury, the judge will not write a judgment as the judge is not privy to the reasoning of the jury. Therefore, the following discussion will refer only to civil cases, where judges generally set out their reasoning.

When judges write judgments, they draft them in a certain way. They usually raise most of the elements set out in the proof-making model; that is, they will generally:

Judges usually raise the elements set out in the proof-making model in their judgments

- identify the cause of action and, based on the statement of claim, identify the issue or issues before the court for judgment;

- recount the evidence presented to the court by both the plaintiff and the defendant;
- discuss whether the facts have been proved to the required standard (on the balance of probabilities in civil matters);
- state the law and see if the facts of the case before them fit neatly into the way the current law treats such facts; if the facts do not fit neatly into the parameters of the current law, then they will reason why the case before the court should be treated differently; either way, they will set out their reasons for finding the way they did;
- decide if the cause of action has been made out and conclude with orders the parties are required to follow.

It is this structure of a judgment that is of most use when developing a strategy to answer legal problems, and you will find this structure to be identical to the legal problem-solving model. It is interesting to note that some barristers tend to adopt a similar system when drafting advices on various legal issues for their instructing solicitors.

Before embarking on an explanation of the legal problem-solving model, we should address the issue of why law schools use legal problem-solving as part of their assessment regimes.

Why do law schools use legal problems for assessment?

Law schools use a variety of methods to engage students in thinking about the law. Some of these will be discussed in other chapters of this book. For now, it is important to recognise that most law schools use legal problems more frequently than any other forms of learning and assessment strategies. A legal problem is usually a question couched in the form of a fictitious fact pattern, where people have done something that raises certain legal issues. An example of a legal problem appears at the end of this chapter.

Law schools use legal problems more than any other form of assessment

The reason law schools use legal problems is essentially twofold. First, legal problems allow you to: test your ability to analyse facts and the law; apply the law to the facts; synthesise an argument; and formulate a conclusion. They allow you to discuss the relevant case law and statute, and how facts either conform to or vary from precedent. They also allow you to argue contrary to the prevailing precedent. This form of analysis and synthesis is a very important skill for student and lawyer alike. It shows the lecturer or a judge that a persuasive counter-argument exists to the prevailing precedent that should be considered. Second, legal problems help you start to think like a lawyer. The job of a lawyer is to solve legal problems. Clients consult lawyers so that they can receive advice on the solution to their particular legal problem. Therefore, the sooner you start thinking like a lawyer, the more prepared you will be to practise law. Having a framework to solve clients' legal problems is of great benefit to lawyers as well as to students.

Legal problems help you start to think like a lawyer

The legal problem-solving model

The legal problem-solving model essentially follows the method adopted by judges when they write judgments. It is a simple four-step process characterised by the acronym ILAC:

i) Issues—list the issues raised by the problem;
ii) Law—list the relevant law that will help answer the problem;
iii) Argument—using the law just stated, make an argument;
iv) Conclusion—make a firm conclusion, including why you have chosen one option over another.

Each step involves a reasoning process that we will shortly explain. Together, the steps in the legal problem-solving model build up an answer to the problem that provides legal authority and a rational and persuasive argument as to why the law should be followed or changed to accommodate the facts of the case.

Together, the steps in the legal problem-solving model build up an answer to the problem

Prior to discussing each step of the legal problem-solving model, it is worthwhile discussing how legal precedent is treated by the courts.

Precedent

Knowing the right case authority is only half of the battle in solving legal problems. Knowing how to apply the precedent that flows from the case is the other half. Precedent is a legal principle derived from a case that is followed in other cases displaying similar facts. It is important because lower courts are bound to follow precedent established by the highest court within the jurisdiction. For example, all state and territory courts are bound to follow precedent from the High Court of Australia, as the High Court is the highest court in the country. On a state and territory level, if the High Court of Australia has not established a precedent in an area of law, then state and territory courts are bound by the precedent established by their respective Supreme Court or Court of Appeal, these being the highest court in each state or territory.

Precedent is a legal principle derived from a case that is followed in other cases with similar facts

There are five basic ways in which courts deal with precedent:

i) applying precedent—where established case law is applied to a new set of facts before the court;
ii) approving precedent—where established case law is found to be good law and applicable to the case before the court;
iii) following precedent—where established case law is applied identically to the case before the court;
iv) distinguishing precedent—where established case law is not applied to the present case because there is some difference between it and the case before the court;
v) overruling precedent—where the court, considering a similar set of facts, decides that the precedent was wrong.

It is important to note that the above references to 'case law' mean not only legal rules created by courts, but also the courts' attempts to interpret statutes and the cases that have explained such attempts. Statutory interpretation will be dealt with in more detail in Chapter 9.

It is inevitable when using the legal problem-solving model that you will need to quote precedent. When quoting precedent, always ensure that first, the precedent is relevant to the fact pattern before you. That is, does the precedent help you to reach a conclusion on the legal issue raised by the fact pattern? Quoting irrelevant precedent will not assist you to answer the problem and, if it is for an assessed piece of work, it will not gain you any marks. Students sometimes think that quantity is more important than quality in

Does the precedent help you reach a conclusion on the legal issue raised by the fact pattern?

answering legal problems. Not so. Two cases that display very similar facts to the legal problem before you and are used to mount a convincing argument are more valuable than six cases that are not on point and do not help your argument.

Second, ensure that the precedent is just that. Judges make comments that may be classed as *ratio decidendi* (ratio); that is, the reason that the court decided the way it did on a case. Precedent emanates from ratio. Judges also make comments that are called *obiter dicta* (obiter); that is, a remark in passing that does not form part of the reasoning of the case. Students (and lawyers) sometimes get the two confused and quote what they think is ratio when in reality it is obiter. Just to confuse matters more, some court decisions contain multiple judgments where the judges may agree on the outcome but for different reasons. Therefore it may not be clear what the ratio of the case is. In such cases, a lower court is only required to apply the decision of the case when the facts before the court are not reasonably distinguishable from the earlier case.

Precedent emanates from the *ratio decidendi*

Now let us return to the elements of the legal problem-solving model.

Step 1—Issues

When a builder builds a house, they ensure that there are adequate foundations so that the house will not fall down. The foundations cement the house to the land. Similarly, identifying the issue or issues in a legal problem sets the right foundation for the rest of the legal problem-solving model. Without a proper identification of the issue or issues, the legal problem-solving model will fail to provide an answer to the problem.

Identifying the issue sets the right foundation for the rest of the legal problem-solving model

The issue in a case is the question of law to be decided by the court. For example, is there a valid contract between the parties? There are two important things to note from this example. First, the issue has been phrased as a question. Phrasing issues as questions is a very useful skill. Posing a question that discloses the issue encourages you to find an answer; it is human nature to answer a question posed. It also encourages you to answer the question based only on the particular legal problem and, therefore, helps ensure that you do not become

The issue in a case is the question of law to be decided by the court diverted from the issue itself. One of the big mistakes students make in answering legal problems is that they digress from the issue and discuss irrelevant issues. Posing the legal issue as a question helps focus your mind on the answer to the specific issue.

Second, once you have studied contract law, you will recognise that this example ('is there a valid contract between the parties?') is very broad in terms of the area of law it has sought to identify. The issue as stated is too broad to be of much use. While it is acceptable to commence identifying the issue or issues in a legal problem by using a broad approach, you need to do more than just identify the broad area of law. The reason for this is that identifying the broad area of law leaves you open to discuss issues irrelevant to the main issue that is raised by the facts of the legal problem. It is important to narrow the issues to pinpoint more directly the area of law you will need to argue in order to successfully reach a conclusion. Using the same example, we can narrow that broad issue down to four possible issues that disclose the precise area of law raised by the legal problem. Again, once you have studied contract law, you will appreciate that the four basic elements of a valid contract are:

Broad issues must be narrowed down to more specific issues

- an offer by the offeror (the person making the offer of a contract);
- acceptance by the offeree (the person receiving the offer of a contract);
- consideration or something of value moving from the offeree; and
- intention to create a legally binding contract.

You should try and narrow the issues further so that the area of law to be addressed in the answer is pinpointed even more accurately. To give you an example, let us say that a pharmaceutical company has advertised in the newspaper a drug that is 'the cure for the common cold'. They promise that if you use the drug for two weeks at the beginning of winter according to the instructions on the packet, you will not catch a cold. To show how confident they are about the product, the company states that if anybody uses the product according to its instructions and then catches a cold, they will pay a reward of $1,000 to any such person. They have deposited $100,000 in an account at their bank as proof that the product will not fail. Let us say that Mr X uses the product according to its instructions and then catches a cold. Mr X claims the $1,000 from the pharmaceutical company but they refuse to pay. Mr X seeks your legal advice. What are the issues? Given the above facts, the issues could be stated as being:

i) Has there been an offer to enter a contract?
ii) Has there been an acceptance of the offer to enter the contract?
iii) Has good consideration moved from the offeree (Mr X)?
iv) Have the parties indicated an intention to enter into a legal relationship (contract)?

The issues have now been more accurately stated and direct us to the exact area of the law of contract that we wish to discuss. Once again, the issues have been posed as questions that require answering by the legal problem-solving model. As well as this, they identify precisely the area of law that will allow you to focus on the relevant case authorities (and legislation, if applicable) and start arguing the solution to the legal problem.

Pose the issues as questions that require answering by the legal problem-solving model

Step 2—Law

Like the previous step, step 2 is also a foundational step that enables you to answer the problem persuasively. Without quoting the correct law, the argument in step 3 and the conclusion in step 4 will be deficient or just plain wrong!

Legal authority tends to be divided into two categories—primary and secondary sources. Primary sources are, for example, case law and legislation that provide precedent and authority for legal propositions. Secondary sources are, for example, commentary by academics and practising lawyers in textbooks and journal articles. Your lecture notes that you take from lectures are classed as secondary sources. When looking for legal authority to help you solve a legal problem, primary sources are the best. If there is no primary source of material relevant to the problem—which admittedly rarely occurs—then it may be permissible to use secondary sources, but at the end of the day, they do not carry the same weight of authority as primary sources. In court, secondary sources do not carry any weight with the judge, but may be persuasive in their thinking about an issue if new law needs to be made.

Primary sources provide precedent and authority for legal propositions

When quoting cases you should note the following matters for consideration and mention where relevant.

THE JURISDICTION AND HIERARCHY OF THE COURT

It may be important to note whether a decision you are quoting emanated from a state or territory court, or a federal court. Remember that lower courts are bound by the decisions of higher courts. Figure 5.2 sets out a basic flowchart as a guide to the hierarchy of courts in Australia.

It is important to note that there are other specialist courts and tribunals that operate at state and territory level that are omitted from Figure 5.2. For example, in New South Wales there exists the Land and Environment Court, which sits at the equivalent level of the New South Wales Supreme Court, and in Victoria there exists a specialist Drug Court, which operates at the Magistrates' Court level.

Precedent flows from the top of the chart to the bottom. For example, a precedent established in the High Court of Australia is binding on all lower courts (all courts underneath the High Court in the flowchart). Similarly, a precedent established in a state or territory Court of Appeal is binding on all lower courts within that state or territory. Where the High Court or Federal Court of Australia has not pronounced on an issue, then the state or territory Supreme Court's authority is precedent. State or territory courts do not bind other state or

Precedent flows from the top of the hierarchy to the bottom

FIGURE 5.2 The hierarchy of courts in Australia

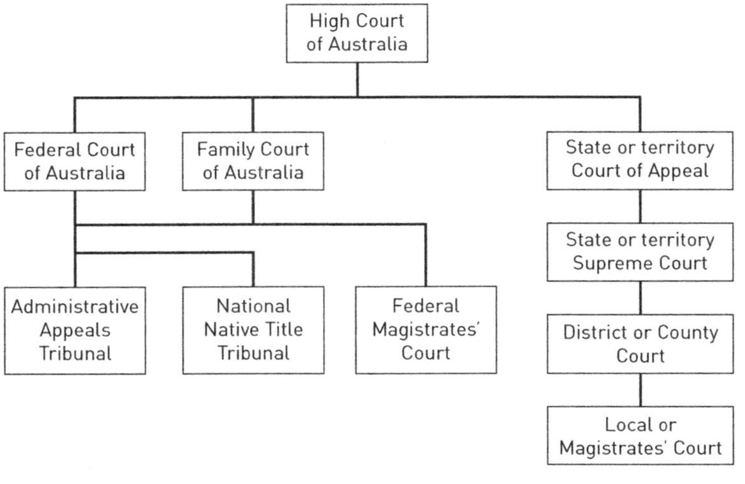

territory courts, but may be influential in the minds of judges. Similarly, overseas courts are not binding on state or territory or federal courts, but again, may be influential. Another important element to note about quoting judgments and the use of precedent generally is that more recent decisions overrule previous decisions where the decisions conflict.

WHETHER THE JUDGMENT IS RATIO OR OBITER

Obiter may help you mount an alternative argument to distinguish or overrule precedent

As stated above, judges generally make two kinds of comments: *ratio decidendi* and *obiter dicta*. When quoting from judgments, make sure that you distinguish between the two. Ratio will support you when you wish to apply, approve, or follow precedent. Obiter may help you mount an alternative argument to distinguish or overrule precedent.

THE COMPOSITION OF THE COURT

A full bench decision is more persuasive than that of a single judge; a unanimous decision is more persuasive than a bare majority

If appropriate, when quoting cases, you may mention the fact that the decision was from a single judge of the court. The reason this may be worthy of mention is that such a judgment does not generally carry the same weight as the full bench of the same court (this only applies in a state or territory Supreme Court or Court of Appeal, or the Federal, Family or High Court of Australia). Where there is more than one judge hearing a case, a bare majority is also less persuasive than a unanimous decision. Logically, if one or more judges have doubts about the majority decision, then the next court to hear the matter, either at the same level of court or higher, may similarly have doubts and overrule the precedent established by the bare majority. Courts are not bound by their own previous decisions, meaning that a court can reverse its own decision at any time, providing it is consistent with the decisions of a higher court.

Only discuss relevant facts to show why the case is pertinent to answering the problem

Step 2 requires you to outline briefly the facts of any cases you believe to be relevant. You are not expected to provide a lengthy and detailed case note of each case. Just discuss the relevant facts to prove that you know why the case is pertinent to answering the problem. The most important concept here is providing the relevant facts: those facts that are similar or dissimilar to the facts before you in the problem. Facts that are dissimilar to the facts before you may be important if you wish to distinguish or overrule precedent in your answer. Similarly, with legislation, state only those Acts of Parliament and their concomitant sections that are relevant to answering the problem. Some sections in legislation are very long, therefore feel free to discuss only those parts of a section that are relevant to your answer.

Step 3—Argument

Steps 1 and 2 are intended to lay the foundations to answer a legal problem. They define the issue or issues to be addressed and provide the building blocks to the answer; that is, the relevant law that will provide you with the information to argue your answer persuasively. While steps 1 and 2 are very important, however, they may have little or no impact if step 3 is not properly executed. Step 3 is the most important step in the model. It is the place where you analyse the relevant law and show how it applies to the issues and the facts before you, after which you then argue both sides of the answer prior to reaching a conclusion in step 4.

Step 3 is the most important step in the model

It should be stated that step 3 is the most intellectually challenging of all the steps and it is the step that many students fail to grasp properly. In our experience, students in the early semesters of their degree almost universally fail to properly deal with the 'argument' or 'application' component of legal problem-solving, especially in the time-pressured context of final examinations. It is the step that takes practice to accomplish satisfactorily.

The process in achieving a satisfactory step 3 is fourfold:

i) start with the general proposition or propositions;
ii) link the law with the facts before you;
iii) make an argument; and
iv) use the proof-making model.

START WITH THE GENERAL PROPOSITION OR PROPOSITIONS

After reading the prescribed textbook or attending the relevant lectures and tutorials in the area of law you are studying, you will note that there are certain general propositions attached to each area of the law. These general propositions arise from the case law and legislation that has developed over the years. As a starting point, state these general propositions as a simple statement of the current status of the law, and then base the remainder of your argument on either applying these general propositions or distinguishing them based on the set of facts before you. Stating the general propositions provides a good introduction to the step 3 analysis and keeps you focused on what you need to argue to be successful. For example, in contract law the general proposition that covers a situation where a person has paid back a lesser amount of money as full discharge of a debt could be encapsulated in the following general proposition that states: 'Part payment of a debt does not discharge the debt (*Pinnel's Case (Penny v Cole)* (1602) 77 ER 237).' In answering a legal problem question about this issue, therefore, it is good practice to start with this general proposition from the leading case that concisely states the law. You can then go on to list any exceptions to the general rule. In this example, a notable exception is the proposition: 'If you accept something to which there was no existing entitlement, then that "something" may be good consideration to discharge the debt (*Williams v Roffey Bros and Nicholls (Contractors) Ltd* [1991] 1 QB 1).' You have thus set out the law and an important exception to the law that together act as a good starting point to discuss the legal problem.

The general propositions arise from the case law and legislation that has developed over the years

Often there are qualifications to the general propositions and these should be stated as well as part of the starting point to your argument. For example, a general proposition about the performance of a contract is: 'A contract will be discharged by performance when exact performance has been tendered (*Cutter v Powell* (1795) 101 ER 176).' However, because of the unfairness of this rule the courts developed several qualifications of the rule, such as: 'Where a contract has been substantially performed but not exactly performed, the court may deem the contract as having been discharged (*Hoenig v Isaacs* [1952] 2 All ER 176).' As above, we have begun step 3 of the legal problem-solving model by concisely stating the law and a notable exception to it, which will be of relevance to the legal problem we are seeking to answer.

Include exceptions and qualifications to the general proposition

This discipline of stating the general proposition and any exceptions or qualifications to it is a good way to focus the student's and the examiner's minds on where the answer is starting and where it is likely to take us.

LINK THE LAW WITH THE FACTS BEFORE YOU

In step 2, you have quoted certain cases and legislation as relevant law for a reason. The chances are that there is something in the facts of the problem before you that has rung a bell in your mind compared to some cases and or legislation you have read. Good! Identify what facts in the cases or legislation rang that bell and link them with the facts before you. The factual link is what will dictate your ability to apply or distinguish precedent properly. You have already stated the facts of the cases in step 2, so you do not need to repeat that task. What you need to do is provide the link between the facts before you and the cases quoted in step 2. In other words, ask yourself: why did I quote the case or legislation in the first place? Express the link between the facts before you and the relevant law clearly and persuasively. Most importantly, the linking of the facts requires you to articulate clearly how the legal principle you are citing directly connects to the facts of your problem. Remember, it is not just the similar facts that will help you state a persuasive argument, it is the legal principle that arose from the particular fact pattern that you need to apply to, or distinguish from, the facts before you.

What cases/legislation rang a bell when you first read the problem?

MAKE AN ARGUMENT

Argue why the precedent—that is, the legal principle or proposition—should be applied to the facts before you, or why the legislation should apply. In the case of precedent, obviously it is because the facts are so similar between the facts before you and the case precedent that will allow you to argue that the principle of law established by the precedent should be followed. Conversely, where the facts are different but the legal issue is the same, the facts can be distinguished between the two fact patterns that will allow you to argue that the principle of law established by the precedent should be distinguished. In the case of legislation, argue why the legislation should apply to the fact pattern before you. Argue why the cases that explain the parameters of the legislation should be applied in the facts before you, or why the parameters of the legislation itself are relevant to the facts. Step 3 requires you to justify your argument using the relevant law. In other words, back up your argument using the relevant law.

Back up your argument using the relevant law

Once you have presented the argument that supports your answer (and ultimately your conclusion), make sure you argue any likely counter-argument. Remember, when lawyers go to court, they already know the law—otherwise they should not be acting as lawyers! What lawyers try to do in court is to exploit the grey areas in the facts. They seek to persuade the court that the facts before the court are in some way different from the case precedent or fall outside of the legislation, thereby allowing the court to not have to follow the precedent or apply the legislation; or they seek to persuade the court that there is a valid defence to the cause of action.

In court, lawyers seek to exploit the grey areas in the facts

But for every plaintiff there is a defendant. Defendants do not bother defending a case if there is not an equally persuasive argument to that of the plaintiff's (or at least the perception of an equally persuasive argument in the mind of the defendant's lawyer). A good discipline for students when using the legal problem-solving model is to try and briefly discuss any counter-argument that may exist—in other words, take up the defendant's position in the legal problem. Again, the persuasiveness in your argument will be dependent on how you apply the relevant law. Always make sure that you link your argument to the relevant law.

Briefly discuss any counter-argument that may exist

USE THE PROOF-MAKING MODEL

Remember the proof-making model discussed earlier in this chapter? The most persuasive arguments are based on law. The proof-making model states that evidence proves facts that prove the elements of the cause of action. So to be successful in court, and in solving a legal problem at law school, you will need to rely on reiterating the relevant facts as if they were evidence in the fact pattern before you that will be linked to the relevant law that together will prove the cause of action.

The proof-making model states that evidence proves facts that prove the elements of the cause of action

One last point! Every law student should go to their state or territory Supreme Court and watch the parade of trolleys being wheeled into the court by the numerous paralegals working for the large commercial firms. In these trolleys are the evidence to be presented and every last agonising fact that may or may not be relevant to the case (lawyers hate getting caught without an appropriate piece of evidence in court). The point is this: in most matters that come before a court there are a vast number of facts supported by much evidence. The legal problem before you is probably either half an A4 page in length or at the worst a couple of A4 pages in length. In the fact pattern before you there will be missing facts (if this were not the case then you would have to read reams of paper just to be able to understand one legal problem—this is hard to do in a standard three-hour exam!). Therefore, at times during the four-step process, and particularly in step 3, you will have to make logical conclusions about the facts. When this need arises, make sure you 'ad lib' in a sensible way that does not overly favour your preferred answer to the problem. In other words, ad lib some of the facts in a realistic and sensible way and do not assume facts simply to get you past a difficult area of the law.

At times during the four-step process, you will have to make logical conclusions about the facts

Step 4—Conclusion

One of the great challenges in the law is that there is sometimes no correct single answer to a legal problem. So do not be concerned if, after completing step 3, you have two equally persuasive arguments (remember, lawyers exploit the grey areas of already established law, so apparently there are nearly always potentially two answers!). However, in step 4, you need to select one answer as being your favoured approach to the problem. It is important to note that most law academics will not fail you if you select one of two well-argued persuasive answers that they do not agree with. Generally, you will only fail an assessed legal problem if you select the answer the marker disagrees with and it was poorly argued. Students will score poor marks even if they select the answer the marker agrees with, but it is poorly argued and without proper relevant legal authority.

Select one answer as being your favoured approach to the problem

So where the law is perhaps inconclusive, you must put your ambivalence aside and argue strongly for your interpretation. Like a conclusion to an essay, your conclusion in a legal problem is your last chance to argue as persuasively as you can for your interpretation of the law based on the facts before you. It is permissible to state that there are two approaches that could both be successful if argued in court, but at the end of the day your lecturer will want you to argue for one solution over another. As a lawyer you will be required to do the same for a client, so this is good practice.

Where the law is inconclusive, put your ambivalence aside and argue strongly for your interpretation

An example

Here is a worked example of the legal problem-solving model using the same fact pattern as presented above. For convenience, the facts are repeated below. Do not be concerned that you may not have yet studied contract law. At this point in time, just try and understand the structure of the legal problem-solving model. This fact pattern is based on the landmark contract law case *Carlill v Carbolic Smoke Ball Company* [1893] 1 QB 256, which is still good law today.

Facts

A pharmaceutical company has advertised in the newspaper a drug that is 'the cure for the common cold'. They promise that if you use the drug for two weeks at the beginning of winter according to the instructions on the packet, you will not catch a cold. To show how confident they are about the product, the company states that if anybody uses the product according to its instructions and then catches a cold, they will pay a reward of $1,000 to any such person. They have deposited $100,000 in a bank account as proof that the product will not fail. Let us say that Ms Smith uses the product according to its instructions and then catches a cold and the pharmaceutical company refuses to pay Ms Smith the $1,000. Advise Ms Smith as to whether she can claim the $1,000. (Answer this problem using only the common law and not statute.)

STEP 1—ISSUES

For Ms Smith to be able to claim the $1000, she would have to be able to prove that a valid and enforceable contract existed between her and the pharmaceutical company. In this respect the problem raises the issues of whether the four essential elements of contract were present between the parties, those of: offer, acceptance, consideration, and intention. Translated into questions to be answered, the four issues could be expressed as follows:

i) Is the advertisement an offer or an invitation to treat (an invitation to submit an offer)?
ii) Does Ms Smith have to communicate acceptance of the offer (the general rule is that the offeror must 'receive' the acceptance before it is deemed effective)?

iii) Is the detriment (loss) suffered by Ms Smith sufficient consideration (consideration must something of value)?

iv) Is the pharmaceutical company's offer of a reward evidence of its requisite intention?

STEP 2—LAW

Dealing with each issue separately, the following case law will be of some help in seeking a solution to the legal problem faced by Ms Smith. It is important to note that wording of the question prevents the use of consumer legislation that would assist in solving the legal problem in the answer—the person that set the question clearly wants students to display the requisite skills of case analysis in a legal problem.

Issue (i)—Is the advertisement an offer or an invitation to treat?

In *Partridge v Crittenden* [1968] 2 All ER 421 an advertisement offering wild birds for sale allegedly breached the *Protection of Birds Act 1954* (UK). The court found the seller not guilty under the Act because the advertisement was not an offer but an invitation to treat; therefore the charge of 'offering for sale' had not been made out.

In *Carlill v Carbolic Smoke Ball Company* [1893] 1 QB 256 the facts were very similar to the current facts. In that case an advertisement appeared in a London metropolitan newspaper advertising the use of the Carbolic Smoke Ball, stating that it would prevent influenza if used according to its instructions. The Carbolic Smoke Ball Company advertised that they had deposited £1,000 with a London bank in order to pay £100 to anyone who contracted influenza after using the smoke ball. Mrs Carlill used the smoke ball according to its instructions and shortly thereafter contracted influenza. She claimed the £100 and the Carbolic Smoke Ball Company refused to pay. The House of Lords found that the advertisement was a genuine offer to the world and not an invitation to treat because of the £1,000 on deposit in a bank to show the offeror's sincerity. In other words, the Carbolic Smoke Ball Company intended their advertisement to be an offer.

Issue (ii)—Does Ms Smith have to communicate acceptance of the offer?

In *Carlill v Carbolic Smoke Ball Company* [1893] 1 QB 256 the court found that the offer by the Carbolic Smoke Ball Company was a binding promise that could be accepted by performance by anyone that purchased the smoke ball and used it according to its instructions. The court found that the performance of Mrs Carlill, in purchasing the smoke ball and using it according to its instructions, dispensed with the communication requirement of acceptance of an offer.

In *Brogden v Metropolitan Railway Co* (1877) 2 App Cas 666 a contract was signed by Brogden, the supplier of coal, and sent to the purchaser, the Metropolitan Railway Company, who left it in a desk drawer without signing it. The purchaser purchased coal and the supplier supplied coal according to the terms of the contract. A dispute arose between the parties and the supplier claimed there was no contract between the parties because the purchaser had not formally accepted the supplier's offer by signing the contract and sending a copy back to the purchaser. The court found that because the purchaser and the supplier had commenced performing the contract according to its terms, they had conducted themselves as if there was a binding contract between them. Therefore, the court found that there was in fact a binding contract between the parties.

Issue (iii)—Is the detriment suffered by Ms Smith sufficient consideration?

In *Hamer v Sidway* 124 NY 538, 27 NE 256 (1891) William Story promised to pay his nephew, Hamer, US$5,000 if he would stop drinking, smoking, swearing, and gambling until he attained the age of 21 years. Hamer did so, but when his uncle died, his executor (the administrator of Story's will) refused to pay the $5,000 to Hamer. The court found for Hamer on the basis that a contract had been established between him and his uncle, the consideration for which was the detriment Hamer suffered as a result of his promise. The court found that this detriment—that is, the forbearance (refraining) from drinking, smoking, swearing, and gambling—was sufficient enough in terms of value for it to be classed as good consideration for the contract.

In *Carlill v Carbolic Smoke Ball Company* [1893] 1 QB 256 the court found that the detriment in performing the contract by using the smoke ball according to its terms constituted good consideration.

Issue (iv)—Is the pharmaceutical company's offer of a reward evidence of its requisite intention?

In *Nyulasy v Rowan* (1891) 17 VLR 663 Rowan offered to buy 400 shares from Nyulasy for £8 per share, the offer to remain open for three months. After a period of time Nyulasy accepted Rowan's offer, but Rowan reneged on the offer stating that it was just a joke. The court found in favour of Nyulasy on the basis that if an offer appears serious on its face, then if the offeree accepts within the stipulated time, there is a binding agreement between the parties. The court found that there was nothing in Rowan's offer that indicated that it was not to be taken seriously.

In *Carlill v Carbolic Smoke Ball Company* [1893] 1 QB 256 the court was satisfied that the action by the Carbolic Smoke Ball Company in offering £100 as payment to anybody that used the smoke ball and contracted influenza, coupled with the advertised deposit of £1,000 for payment to anybody contracting influenza, was sufficient evidence of their intention to enter into a binding contract with any person who accepted the offer by their performance of the terms of the contract (that is, buying the smoke ball and using it).

STEP 3—ARGUMENT

Issue (i)—Is the advertisement an offer or an invitation to treat?

As a general proposition, an offer may be described as an indication by one person to another person that they wish to enter a contract with the other person on certain terms. Advertisements are often classified as invitations to treat, or mere puffery designed to entice customers into a store so that a contract can be formed in the store. In other words, store owners invite customers, through the advertisement, to come into the store and create a contract. The advertisement is no more than an invitation to a customer to come into the store and make an offer to purchase goods on certain terms. The law states that no offer can be classed as such unless the person making the offer (the offeror) intended it to be an offer. The logic of this situation is best explained by the scenario of a customer coming into the store and finding that the item advertised was out of stock. If the store owner had intended to be bound at the advertisement stage, then the customer would be able to sue the store owner. This would clearly be unfair as the store owner cannot predict how many people will respond to the advertisement and how many contracts would be created so that enough stock could be ordered. Therefore, the law says that it is only upon the customer attending the store and offering to buy the in-stock item that an intention to contract is created, unless the store owner *intended* an advertisement to be an offer.

The pharmaceutical company in the case under discussion has made a similar type of invitation to that in *Partridge*; that is, an invitation to purchase an item. Therefore, at first instance we may conclude that, like the court's finding in *Partridge*, the advertisement is no more than an invitation to treat and the references to it curing the common cold are mere puffery or advertising language designed to entice customers to offer to purchase the product. However, a distinguishing feature between these two cases is the fact that the pharmaceutical company has offered a reward for anybody who tries the drug and still catches a cold. This fact alone distinguishes it from the facts in *Partridge*.

Applying *Carlill*, the offer by the pharmaceutical company would appear to be an offer as opposed to an invitation to treat or mere puffery given the intention with which the advertisement was placed. In particular, the $100,000 on bank deposit and the offer to pay $1,000 to anyone who contracts a cold after using the product would indicate that the pharmaceutical company was sincere about the offer and intended that it be an offer capable of acceptance. Why would they deposit such a sum of money if they did not intend to pay a reward to anyone who contracted a cold after using the product? Because of this, and the fact that the terms of the offer were very specific, the offer seems to carry the intention that people will purchase the product and use it according to its instructions, thereby creating a contract between the parties as opposed to an invitation to treat, or a mere puff, which carries no intention to be bound.

The counter-argument to the above is a strict reading of the facts in line with *Partridge*, thereby classifying the advertisement as purely an invitation to treat published to entice prospective customers to approach the pharmaceutical company with a view of negotiating terms in order to enter a legally binding contract.

Issue (ii)—Does Ms Smith have to communicate acceptance of the offer?

As a general proposition, an offer can only be accepted by people to whom the offer was made. A qualification of this proposition is the fact that an acceptance must be communicated to the offeror. In this case the advertisement is classed as an offer to the 'world at large'. This means that the offer does not specify who can accept it; rather, it means that the pharmaceutical company contracted only with those people that accepted the offer by purchasing the drug and using it according to its instructions. In these sorts of contracts, where there is no specified form of acceptance, acceptance is indicated by conduct or performance.

In the case under discussion, we have an offer to the world at large, acceptance of which is by conduct. While *Brogden* was not the same sort of offer as we have in our case, the similarity in the cases is the fact that acceptance was by performance of the contract according to its terms. *Carlill's* case is of course more similar to our fact pattern, in that the offer was of the same type as the offer our case. Applying both *Brogden* and *Carlill*, it can be said that there has been a valid acceptance of the offer by the pharmaceutical company based on Ms Smith's (the offeree's) performance of the contract according to its terms. In an offer to the world at large, the pharmaceutical company must expect acceptance by performance rather than acceptance by direct communication between the pharmaceutical company and all of its potential offerees (customers).

The counter-argument to the above proposition is that because of the nature of the promise—that is, to 'cure the common cold'—acceptance should be communicated to the offeror so as to put the offeror on notice that the offer has been accepted and that the drug is going to be used by a bona fide consumer according to the terms of the contract as set out in the advertisement. It could be argued that because of the breadth of the promise and its seriousness, the offeree should communicate acceptance to the offeror and that the advertisement was written with that requirement in mind.

Issue (iii)—Is the detriment suffered by Ms Smith sufficient consideration?

As a general proposition, consideration is something of value that passes from the offeree but not necessarily to the offeror. Consideration must be bargained for. The idea behind consideration is that it is the price of the promise made by the offeror. This in turn proves the genuineness of the offeree to enter the contract with the offeror. Consideration may be either a benefit (most commonly—but not always—money) to the offeror or a detriment to the offeree.

Applying *Hamer*'s case—and noting that the facts are different to our case—the fact that Hamer suffered some sort of detriment as a result of the contract was seen to be sufficient consideration. Such detriment moved from (was provided by) Hamer, and while there could not be said to be any benefit for the uncle, such benefit need not exist for sufficient consideration to be made out.

Once again, *Carlill*'s case is of more benefit given the similarity of the facts. Like our case, in *Carlill*'s case the detriment was the fact that Mrs Carlill went to the trouble of purchasing the smoke ball then used it for a period of time to no avail. In our case the consideration is the detriment suffered by Ms Smith in purchasing and using the drug according to its instructions, then contracting a cold.

The counter-argument to the above is one raised in *Carlill*'s case; that is, in terms of our fact pattern, that the price of the drug was merely consideration for the contract to purchase the product, and not consideration for the promise of the reward should the drug not work. Accepting that proposition, the only other argument could be to state that Ms Smith had not suffered detriment by using the drug. Therefore, it could be concluded that if there was no detriment, then there was a total failure of consideration. Perhaps it could be argued that taking one tablet does not constitute detriment to the point of it being sufficient consideration. Consideration needs to be sufficient, but need not be adequate; therefore it can be said that consideration need not be of equal value to the promise, but must be something of value. Perhaps Ms Smith did not suffer enough detriment to constitute sufficient consideration.

Issue (iv)—Is the pharmaceutical company's offer of a reward evidence of its requisite intention?

As a general proposition, to create a contract the parties must expressly or impliedly display a common intention to create legal relations (create legal obligations). As a qualification of the general proposition, it is said that there is a rebuttable presumption in business and commercial agreements that parties intend to create legal relations. This presumption may be rebutted by express words that the parties did not intend to create legal relations.

In our case we have an agreement between a company and a customer. Therefore the presumption that the parties intended to create legal relations applies and there is no evidence that the offeror rebutted such a presumption by express words.

Applying *Nyulasy* and *Carlill*, we can state that the advertisement run by the pharmaceutical company was serious in its intent. In particular, the depositing of the $100,000 in a bank showed the seriousness with which the pharmaceutical company treated the agreement it had with Ms Smith, or indeed any offeree who chose to accept the offer. The offer could not be classed as being one so outrageous that no one would believe it to be a serious offer.

The counter-argument to the above analysis is that it may be possible to argue that, given that the chances of a pharmaceutical company coming up with a cure to the common cold are so remote, the advertisement should be treated as lacking the requisite intention. In other words, the advertised claims are so outrageous that nobody could possibly treat them as being serious. The advertisement is therefore lacking the requisite intention to be binding upon anybody that takes up the offer. The advertisement should be more properly categorised as being mere 'puffery', or advertising jargon not to be taken seriously.

STEP 4—CONCLUSION

Issue (i)—Is the advertisement an offer or an invitation to treat?

The advertisement is not an invitation to treat because it is classed as an offer to the world at large and there is an expectation that offerees will treat such advertisements as being genuine offers capable of acceptance by performance. In such cases it is foreseeable that Ms Smith would treat the advertisement as an offer and accept the offer by way of performance.

Issue (ii)—Does Ms Smith have to communicate acceptance of the offer?

Ms Smith does not have to communicate her acceptance to the pharmaceutical company. In contracts that commence by being offers to the world at large, the law states that acceptance can be by performance of the offer according to the terms of the contract.

Issue (iii)—Is the detriment suffered by Ms Smith sufficient consideration?

The detriment suffered by Ms Smith in purchasing the drug and using it according to its instructions is sufficient consideration for the contract to be binding.

Issue (iv)—Is the pharmaceutical company's offer of a reward evidence of its requisite intention?

Commercial or business contracts made between parties at arm's length (on equal footing) are presumed to carry the requisite intention. This contract is such a commercial contract and, given that the pharmaceutical company has not expressly rebutted the presumption, and the fact that they have worded the advertisement seriously and provided a reward for parties accepting the offer, this means that the requisite intention is present in the pharmaceutical company's offer to contract.

6

CLASS TYPES

'The building is named for the late Christopher Columbus Langdell, who was the Dean of Harvard Law School in the late nineteenth century. Dean Langdell is best known as the inventor of the Socratic method.'

David lowered his hand and looked sincerely at the building.

'May he rot in hell,' David said.

Scott Turow[1]

1 Scott Turow, 'One L' (London: Harmondsworth, 1978).

Introduction

Universities are places of adult education and, like other places of education, they strive to teach in an innovative way that engages students and motivates learning. Universities recognise that students are not a homogeneous group that learns efficiently via a single teaching method. If this were the case, then teaching would be a simple, cost-efficient task. On the contrary, university lecturers seek to employ a variety of teaching methods that will enable all students to achieve their learning objectives for any given course—Chapter 4 discussed some of the various teaching and learning styles of lecturers and students.

Students are not a homogeneous group that learns efficiently via a single teaching method

For example, some students prefer a mass-lecture approach, where the skeleton of the topic is set out and then the students go away and fill in the gaps through their own research. Other students prefer the small-group approach to teaching, whereby they have the opportunity to engage with the lecturer and other students in an effort to reach a joint understanding of the material.

Because different students prefer different learning styles, many lecturers teach by employing a variety of teaching methods. The important thing for you to understand is that within a single subject, you will not necessarily find each teaching method maximises your ability to learn efficiently and with a deep understanding of the material. While this is unfortunate, it is a necessary element of tertiary education. But rest assured, even if you encounter a teaching method that is not your preferred one, first: it will only be one part of the overall teaching strategy employed and you will therefore be past it sooner than you think; and second: you will be surprised how effective all teaching methodology can be to your learning strategy. Finally, and this is cold comfort for you, even though you may not prefer a certain teaching method, other students may prefer it, so on the law of averages, you are at least receiving your preferred teaching method for some part of each subject.

You will be surprised how effective all teaching methodology can be to your learning strategy

The purpose of this chapter is to examine some of the popular methods of teaching employed by lecturers. Through this insight you should be able to ascertain the correct use of any teaching strategy and thereby be able to use it more efficiently in your overall learning strategy. Some hints will be discussed to enable you to maximise the benefit of each teaching methodology to your overall learning strategy. What is most important about this chapter is for you to realise that adult education means taking responsibility—or at least sharing responsibility—for your own learning. This is a very important concept for you to understand for two reasons. First, and this is particularly relevant in the study of law, studying the law is about analysis and synthesis. As discussed in Chapter 5, analysis is an intellectual process where you consider the various elements to a fact pattern and the relevant law. Then, using reasoning and the process of reconstructing the elements through the skill of synthesis, you determine an outcome to the legal problem. This process is one that only you can initiate. Lecturers cannot think for you. Further, they will not sit in the law office you eventually work in and conduct the processes of analysis and synthesis for you every time a client comes to see you with a legal problem. So taking responsibility for your own learning will pay dividends upon you entering the legal profession as it will ensure you can think like a lawyer.

Adult education means taking responsibility for your own learning

Second, while universities try not to employ poor teachers and communicators, it is inevitable that you will encounter some lecturers who struggle to communicate the essence of the area of law you are studying. In such cases, it is not acceptable to throw your hands up in the air and blame the lecturer (as tempting as that is). If you do not understand a concept you are studying, then make it your business to find out how to understand it and, more importantly, why you did not understand the concept in the first place. Perhaps you missed a key case or piece of legislation. Perhaps you did not understand the lecturer's explanation of the concept or the example given by analogy. Perhaps you failed to read the right materials before the class. Whatever the reason, ensure that it does not happen again. Alternatively, have a strategy in place to ensure that you will not fail to understand an important concept again. Ensuring you do not fail to understand important legal concepts is a hallmark of a student taking responsibility for their own learning and is the essence of what adult education is all about.

If you do not understand a concept, make it your business to find out how to understand it

Lectures

The view taken by many lecturers, particularly last century, is that lectures deliver the content of a subject to students and through this task they set the parameters of each subject. For this reason, lectures could be characterised as providing little interaction between lecturers and students. Other lecturers take the view that lectures should be interactive and, for example, pose questions to students and expect a response from them, or are happy to take questions as they arise throughout the lecture.

Many law schools still use large-scale lectures where up to 500 students (sometimes more) gather to hear their subject coordinator deliver content based on general principles and the case law that supports those principles. The lecturers often mention different reasoning given by different judges in landmark cases, and have you begin to think about the different reasoning and how the law may be better articulated. Other lecturers simply outline the key cases and refer you to other cases that need to be read in order to understand the general principles and the exceptions to the general principles.

Lectures can set the parameters of each subject

Some law schools have moved to 'small-group' teaching and learning, where small classes of 20–50 students gather to discuss cases and legislation in a more collaborative, problem-solving way. Others use small groups as an opportunity to combine a mini-lecture with a tutorial-style problem-solving class.

The use of the lecture is being questioned by many educationalists today for two basic reasons. First, higher education research and theory has recognised the importance of active learning methods that allow students to take responsibility for and engage in their own learning, as opposed to the more traditional didactic methods of teaching and learning where students were seen as passive receivers of information who merely regurgitated information in an assessed task.

The use of the lecture is being questioned by many educationalists today

Active learning acknowledges that the best kind of learning allows students to: read, write, discuss, collaborate, and engage in solving problems. Most importantly, students must engage in tasks that promote higher-order thinking such as analysis, synthesis, and evaluation—the very things already discussed as being the essential skills of a lawyer.

Second, the technological revolution has delivered content to every student in a variety of ways. Accessed through personal computers or mobile devices comes a world of information about every imaginable subject. Any area of the law can be searched, and information from the most basic to the highly complex can be at your fingertips in a matter of seconds. For example, judgments from most superior courts in Australia are available within hours of them being handed down. In the High Court of Australia even the parties' submissions in certain cases are available for downloading. Therefore, there is no longer a need for university lecturers to gather a large or small group of students together simply to deliver content or information. Students have no incentive to catch a bus or drive their car to a university campus and listen to lecturers delivering information that they can get through a hundred different websites, as well as their electronic textbook. The sun has set on lectures that merely provide students with information. Unless active learning techniques are being utilised in lectures, they have little use in the modern university. To this end 'blended learning' is becoming an increasing feature of student life. Here, lecturers may use podcasts, audio-visual, and other forms of technology to enhance or replace lectures. If done well, these blended-learning sessions can be an exciting form of active learning. We talk more about audio-visual and blended-learning technology later in this chapter.

There is no longer a need for lecturers to gather students together simply to deliver content

Tutorials

Tutorials are a time to expand on the content contained in the prescribed readings set by the lecturer and your own research on the subject area. Most importantly, they enable active learning to take place, with opportunities for collaborative learning and problem-solving using techniques such as enquiry-based learning (discussed in Chapter 4). Depending on the university, tutorials are generally classes of only about 30 students, although at some universities tutorials can be as large as 60 students. This is not desirable as tutorials should not be intimidating for students, given the necessity for interaction between students and tutors.

Tutorials enable active learning to take place

Tutorials are usually directed at answering specific theoretical questions or legal problem-solving, and they are predicated on students preparing for the tutorial class in order to make sense of material covered in the tutorial class. The concept of 'class-flipping' is gathering momentum, particularly in the United States, where content is delivered—usually via electronic means—to students at a time that suits them; and then some time later learning occurs using active learning

'Class flipping' is based on using technology to leverage learning in the classroom

techniques. Class flipping, or 'flip teaching', is based on using technology to leverage learning in the classroom, so that lecturers can spend their time interacting with students thereby value-adding to the student experience. Wasted time in lectures that merely deliver content is avoided and lecturers can spend that time in more meaningful learning activities with students.

Tutorials are a good opportunity to interact with your tutor. They allow you not only to test your knowledge and interpretation of the materials, but also to seek answers to questions in your mind that you have not managed to resolve through your research prior to the tutorial.

Hopefully, if the class is no more than 30 students you will feel comfortable asking the tutor, or your fellow students, about grey areas in your understanding of the topic under discussion. A capable tutor will not make you feel stupid by asking a question; rather they will use your question as a valuable tool to direct discussion. Remember, the chances are that if the question is in your mind, it is similarly in the mind of more than half the class. So you are in effect asking a question that is on the mind of many others—this alone makes it a very important question.

A capable tutor will use your question as a valuable tool to direct discussion

If your tutor is a good communicator and understands the process of legal analysis and synthesis, then she or he will ensure that both sides of any legal problem are canvassed. For example, in most legal problem-style questions, you are asked to advise a client. Usually, such advice will need to be expressed from a plaintiff perspective; that is, from the perspective of the person aggrieved who is wishing to initiate court proceedings (in criminal matters, your advice will generally be from the defendant's point of view to enable an analysis of the defences available in criminal law). During step 3 of the legal problem-solving model discussed in Chapter 5, where you are expected to analyse the facts and the law, you should be prepared to discuss any likely defence available based on the fact pattern.

Tutorials give you the opportunity, among other things, to explore the case for the plaintiff (civil)/prosecution (criminal) and the defendant (civil and criminal), and through this process allow you to explore the facts and test various hypotheses based on the permutations and combinations of answers thrown up by the fact pattern. It is in this forum of discussion that effective analysis can take place. It is the opportunity to interact with the tutor and other

The opportunity to interact with the tutor and other students is invaluable

students that is invaluable and you should always ensure you leave a tutorial with all of your questions fully answered.

Tutors have differing approaches to tutorials. Some use a Socratic method of teaching (discussed in Chapter 4), named after the philosopher Socrates who used questions to develop ideas in the minds of his pupils or, in the political sense, to elicit admissions from his opponents. In education, this system is used to quiz students about certain issues with the hope of developing the idea towards a conclusion. Some tutors will ask you to answer questions throughout tutorials. This sort of tutorial requires preparation so that you are able to answer the questions put before you. Usually if a tutor runs this sort of tutorial, it is linked to a class participation mark. Here, the questioning lasts until the student is 'intellectually exhausted'; that is, until they cannot answer any more and the tutor moves on to the next student. This type of 'exhaustive' learning is useful to a tutor, who can easily ascertain your level of understanding of the law, and useful to you as you need to anticipate possible permutations of evidence that could produce different results in the fictitious client's problem that you are trying to solve.

Some tutors will ask you to answer questions throughout tutorials

Some tutors may split you up into groups and allocate a certain question or issue to the group, who will then report back to the rest of the class on a likely answer. Other tutors simply ask for volunteers to answer certain questions and lead the discussion themselves.

It does not matter what style of tutorial your tutor runs; the maximum benefit can only be obtained by you preparing for the class. Even if you have had a busy week and can only manage to read a couple of cases and a few pages of commentary from that week's readings, it is still worth the effort as the more familiar you are with the concepts being discussed, the quicker you will reach the required level of understanding. For deeper learning you can go back and review the readings and your notes from the tutorial.

The maximum benefit can only be obtained by you preparing for the class

Workshops

Workshops are designed to be even more interactive than tutorials. They are usually designed to have specific entry points for student participation. For example, tasks such as the analysis of a landmark case or a piece of legislation or the drafting of a document will be scheduled for a critical moment in the workshop, usually after the opportunity to understand a threshold of theoretical information has been achieved. After completing certain tasks, students may then be asked to report back to the class as a whole in order to share their analysis with the class, and a discussion may ensue based on the findings of individual students or teams of students.

Workshops usually have specific entry points for student participation

Workshops work best when theory is linked with some practical or hypothetical task, such as the drafting of a document or the answering of a legal problem or theoretical question. Workshops also lend themselves well to group work, which will be discussed below. Overall, workshops are most effective when there is a high level of student involvement that forms part of the learning strategy. In such cases, the lecturer has determined that more involvement by students is an integral part of the learning strategy. This is mostly the case where there is the potential for deeper learning through a practical application of the law being taught.

Workshops are most effective when there is a high level of student involvement

You will get more benefit out of a workshop if you have prepared by ensuring that you have completed all of the suggested readings and any other preparatory tasks. However, workshops will often have a surprise element to them. That is, often they will require participation in tasks that you have not been warned about. This is usually a deliberate element of the learning strategy devised by the lecturer. To achieve the maximum effectiveness from such sessions, you should try and participate to the best of your ability in the workshop tasks. Often the tasks may involve several elements, both assessable and non-assessable. For example, the task of being involved in a team negotiation may test your ability not only to understand the dynamics of negotiation based upon the prescribed readings, but also to work in a team. This is an important skill given the frequency of team work in, for example, large-scale litigation or in the operations of a community legal centre.

Workshops will often have a surprise element to them

The worst thing you can do is to treat the task as being trite, or below you, and approach the task with a negative attitude. You are attending law school not only to gain a degree, but also to learn as much as you can about the law and the skills of being a lawyer. It should not matter that a task is assessed or not; but where workshop tasks

Workshops only work if everybody participates

are assessed, it is important to ensure that you get involved in a way that benefits you and the class as a whole. After all, workshops generally only work if everybody participates.

Seminars

Seminars usually involve students presenting answers to specified problems or questions to a small-group class. Because of this, seminars tend not to be very wide in their subject matter and focus on specific issues. Usually, you are given a specific question to answer during the semester. Some lecturers allocate such questions at the beginning of the semester, while others hand out the questions with a set period of notice, say two weeks before the due date, so that all students have the same preparation time. Either way, do not leave preparation for the presentation to the last minute. It always takes time to prepare answers to be presented in class, and a common complaint is that students never give the preparation of the answer the time it deserves. Note that some seminars may involve students handing in a written paper as well as presenting an answer to the class.

Do not leave preparation for the presentation to the last minute

Be conscious of word limits of the paper to be handed in and the time limit on the paper to be presented to the class. Do not go over the word limit or the time allocated for your presentation, as you may have marks deducted. In the case of presentations, such behaviour penalises other speakers who may come after you.

Do not go over the time allocated for your presentation

Moots

Moots may or may not be categorised as a class type. Some law schools classify them as a type of assessment or skills-based activity. However, other schools run domestic or international intervarsity moot competitions as subjects in themselves. In such cases, moots can be classed as a class type.

Moots are best described as a legal debate. That is, teams debate each other on a topic drafted as a legal problem and adopt a courtroom-style approach to the presentation of the debate. The legal problem is set in a certain jurisdiction and the rules of that jurisdiction will apply to the moot teams. For example, most constitutional law moots are set in the High Court of Australia, the court of original jurisdiction in constitutional matters. Therefore, the rules and court procedure of the High Court would be adopted and the moot teams would have to comply with those rules. Moots, as an assessed task, will be discussed in Chapter 11. For the moment, it is worthwhile mentioning how typical moot classes are run and how to get the most out of such classes.

Moots are best described as a legal debate

Whether the class is preparing to represent the law school in an intervarsity moot or whether it is purely an internal mooting class will determine the way the class is run. In cases where the class is preparing for an intervarsity moot, a less-adversarial atmosphere will pervade the class at the start so that students can concentrate on learning mooting and advocacy fundamentals, and link these with trial questions and research tasks that will prepare the team for the real questions to be used in the competition. Once the teams have prepared the written and oral submissions, the adversarial nature of the class will return when students practise their advocacy skills and test their arguments on each other. Guest judges often brought in to provide an objective view of their performance in readiness for the real competition.

In internal moots, teams will be preparing their cases often as part of an assessed task. Therefore, students will need to learn how to operate as a team and how to achieve the outcomes of preparing the case both in written and oral forms. This often means keeping their preparation secret from other teams and utilising their tutor as a facilitator/resource. Teams may have to meet outside of class and may relocate during scheduled classes to prepare in private for the moot that is usually held during class time over several weeks towards the end of semester. Whatever the style of moot preparation adopted by the class, mooting requires not only individual work, but also a strong sense of team work. This is probably the most important factor to think about if you are involved in mooting at any level. You are expected to work by yourself in researching the law and preparation of the argument. However, you are also expected to work as a team in developing the argument and the tactics to be adopted in the moot itself. This means that you need to be prepared to share information and listen to other people's views on the issues raised by the moot questions. Most importantly, you need to accept that there may be people who have the same sort of ability as you thought you had when it comes to research, writing

Mooting requires not only individual work, but also a strong sense of team work

submissions, and presenting submissions verbally in the moot court. Sometimes the humbling process of acknowledging other people's abilities is the most valuable lesson to learn from mooting.

There are a number of tasks in any given moot. Some students shy away from mooting because they think it will involve them standing up in front of a group of people and speaking in public. This is not always the case. The research and drafting of submissions are the foundations to a successful moot team. Without a competent team to complete those tasks, a moot team will nearly always fail. Brilliance as an advocate will not make up for poor preparation and poorly drafted written submissions. It is a shame that many talented students do not get involved in moots because of the above incorrect perception.

Brilliance as an advocate will not make up for poor preparation and poorly drafted written submissions

For those who are interested in pursuing a career as an advocate, moots are the activity for you. They will give you great experience in arguing the law on your feet in a mock-court situation. Some moot competitions are even conducted in real courtrooms with the generous approval of the respective state or territory attorney-general and chief justice. This in itself is a wonderful experience for students.

Moots give you great experience in arguing the law on your feet in a mock-court situation

Role-plays

Like some forms of moots, role-plays are more a class task rather than a class type. They generally require students breaking up into groups and assuming the roles of certain characters defined by fact patterns devised by the lecturer. Role-plays are a chance to apply theory to practice in a controlled set of circumstances. Most importantly, they generally require you to play a character as opposed to yourself, and the role-play may define certain character traits that will be important to the outcome of the role-play. You should always endeavour to abide by the instructions in a role-play, as such instructions have been specially devised by the lecturer for a purpose—a purpose that generally becomes apparent during the role-play, or in a debrief of the role-play.

Role-plays are a chance to apply theory to practice in a controlled set of circumstances

Some role-plays may ask you to just be yourself in terms of how you apply theory to practice. In such cases, do not replace your own character with some perceived character based on the facts. In these sorts of role-plays the lecturer is probably looking to you to bring your own experiences to bear on the role-play.

Most role-plays conclude with a debrief that will give you the opportunity—either with your opposite number in the role-play, or in a class situation—to discuss how the role-play unfolded and to do some self-assessment of what you would have done better if you could do the role-play again. A well-conducted debrief will also allow the dissipation of any aggression that surfaced during the role-play. It is most important to remember that if you are role-playing in a class, you should seek to maintain good relations with your fellow students. Do not let a role-play divide the class or students within the class.

A debrief will give you the opportunity to review your performance

Small-group work

Small-group work is a teaching strategy favoured by many lecturers as it tends to allow for more student involvement in small group-based discussions. As a student participating in small-group work, you should be conscious of either dominating the group dynamic or failing to contribute adequately to the group work. Either end of that spectrum means that the chances are, you are probably not contributing in a way that will assist the group in achieving its objectives. Those that dominate small groups do not allow a cross-section of ideas to come forward for consideration. Those that contribute few ideas limit the options for the group to achieve its objectives. The right sort of balance is to consider ideas based on your educated view, which has been derived from your research or your experience, or both, and to apply efficient time management to the task at hand.

Be conscious of either dominating the group dynamic, or failing to contribute adequately

Some small-group work carries a self- and peer-assessment task. In such cases you will be asked to assess your own contribution to the team and that of other members. This form of assessment can be very effective in small-group work, but it can also be abused. Interestingly, most lecturers report that students in this sort of assessment tend to be tougher on themselves than their peers. Usually

You may be asked to assess your own contribution to the team and that of other members this sort of assessment carries a veto from the lecturer. In other words, the lecturer can change a mark if they choose. If you are faced with such a task at the conclusion of a small-group work exercise, you should try to mark as fairly as you can using the objective criteria set down by the lecturer.

Informal learning

It is a mistake for lecturers to think that you will only learn through formal lectures or tutorials or other university-organised classes. Research on the effectiveness of 'informal learning' shows it not only often produces better learning outcomes, but can also enhance a student's engagement with their studies and the university environment. The literature recognises two types of informal learning, both explained below by learned practitioners in the field.

> In recent years there has been increasing acknowledgement of the importance of socially based, informal modes of learning that occur outside of the classroom. These types of 'out-of-class' interactions in Higher Education settings are commonly referred to as students' *informal learning* experiences and are characterised by their unplanned nature, happening anywhere, at any time and without the presence of a teacher. While informal learning can also refer to self-directed study, in the context of this paper informal learning is predicated on informal social interactions between students. These informal 'out-of-class' learning experiences and interactions with peers are reported to have a positive impact on student satisfaction and learning and are also known to build students' sense of self-worth and confidence. (references omitted)[2]

This first definition of informal learning reflects what many universities are now realising is an effective form of learning; that is, to build informal learning spaces for students who will naturally form into groups or learn individually in university-based environments that are friendly and encourage such forms of learning. Informal learning spaces are being built by universities that: are warm

Universities are increasingly building spaces to encourage informal learning

2 Kate Goodwin, Gregor Kennedy, & Frank Vetere, 'Getting Together Out-of-class: Using Technologies for Informal Interaction and Learning' (paper presented at the 2010 Ascilite Conference, Sydney, 2010), at 387 of the Proceedings to the Conference.

in winter and cool in summer; have clean toilet facilities; have power points for charging mobile devices; are wireless-enabled; have kitchen facilities; have free lockers; are secure during different times of the day; and are inviting. If your law school has these sorts of facilities, or there are similar facilities close to your home or your friends' homes, you should avail yourself of the opportunity to learn from each other informally by discussing the concepts and questions facing you in class.

The second type of informal learning can be explained as follows:

> We must move away from a view of education as a rite of passage involving the acquisition of enough knowledge and qualifications to acquire an adult station in life. The point of education should not be to inculcate a body of knowledge, but to develop capabilities: the basic ones of literacy and numeracy as well as the capability to act responsibly towards others, to take initiative and to work creatively and collaboratively ... Schools and universities should become more like hubs of learning, within the community, capable of extending into the community ... More learning needs to be done at home, in offices and kitchens, in the contexts where knowledge is deployed to solve problems and add value to people's lives.[3]

This second definition raises the issue of workplace learning. You should not think that this just means testing the knowledge and skills you acquired at law school in a law office. While many students do find work in a law firm while studying law, a law firm is not the only place to learn the skills of problem-solving or to develop your interpersonal skills. Almost any workplace can provide you with the opportunity to develop basic capabilities that will be of use in the practice of law. As already discussed in Chapter 2, most practical legal training courses include a certain minimum number of hours in the workplace. They do this deliberately to ensure that the doctrinal rules of law and graduate capabilities learnt at law school are given the opportunity to be tested in the workplace, and that you will begin to understand the culture of work through direct experience.

A law firm is not the only place to learn the skills of problem-solving

3 Charles Leadbeater, 'Living on Thin Air: The New Economy' (London: Penguin, 2000), at 111–12.

If you have the opportunity to work part time while studying (or full time, if you are a part-time student), and this does not have a detrimental effect on your study, then you should try to do so as it will benefit you in the long run for two reasons. First, you will enjoy another opportunity to learn; and second, once you have graduated, future employers will often look kindly on someone who has been able to work, participate in extracurricular activities, and at the same time maintain good grades.

Student participation

Figure 6.1 sets out the levels of student control over their participation, and the lecturers' expectations of your participation level in each type of class. It can be seen that your control over your level of participation in each type of class is inversely proportional to the lecturer's expectation

Your control over your level of participation is inversely proportional to your lecturer's expectation

FIGURE 6.1 Student participation and lecturer expectations in different class types

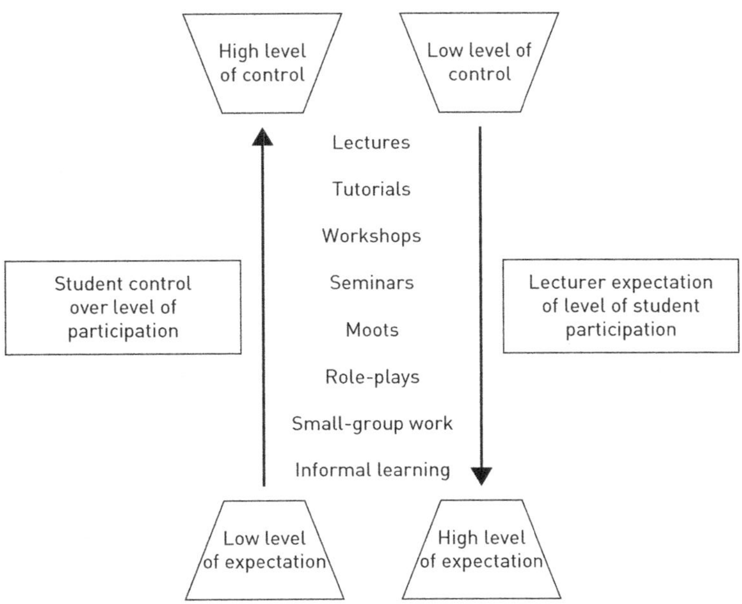

of your level of participation. For example, in a lecture, you have a greater amount of control over your participation because lecturer expectation of your participation is lower than, say, for a seminar or small-group work, where lecturer expectation of your participation is higher.

Figure 6.1 may be of use to students who wish to consider lecturer expectation of their participation when selecting which law school to attend or which elective units to enrol in. This sort of decision is important when you consider what kind of learning style suits you the most. If you prefer a learning style that allows you to have a high level of involvement, then a law school or subjects that give you that option will be more attractive to you than one where lecturer expectation of your involvement in classes will be minimal. Sometimes, finding out academic expectations are a matter of asking the lecturer (or subject convenor) responsible for deciding the teaching method of the subject you are interested in studying.

You may consider lecturer expectations when deciding which elective units to enrol in

Taking notes

Depending on how certain subjects are taught, you may have to take notes in class or while you are reading, watching, or listening to materials prescribed for the subject, or those that you have sourced through your own research. Even if you have the benefit of technology such as voice-recognition software, you will need to order your thoughts in a way that is clear and assists you in your studies. You need to work out a system of recording your learning that will act as an effective aide memoire of all the material you encountered and the legal problems you have solved through your study of each subject.

You need to order your thoughts in a way that is clear and assists you in your studies

When taking or generating notes, use headings and subheadings to break down the material and distinguish the arguments of the plaintiff/prosecution and the defendant, or philosophical and theoretical points. Make sure you understand the case precedents and are clear on the ratios in each case, or at least where to find them. If you are answering a theoretical question, separate out the various philosophical and theoretical arguments and clearly state any crossover points where theorists have criticised or addressed other

It is vital to redraft your notes into an easily understandable summary of how to solve legal problems

theories. It is vital to redraft your lecture, tutorial and reading notes into an easily understandable summary of how to solve the legal problems you will encounter in your law studies. This serves two purposes. First, it will make revision easier than having to try to reconstruct the information from memory. Second, it will be a great aid to your exam preparation. Examination questions will normally be drafted as legal problems, so great experience can be gained by sitting yourself in a quiet room and answering your tutorial questions or sample legal problems from books and previous exam papers under mock exam conditions. Then, with a detailed answer, you are in a position to check your understanding of the material and your ability to answer the questions.

The rise of educational technologies

Many years ago, the only tool university lecturers had to communicate their message was their voice and a piece of chalk and a blackboard. Stories abound at some of the old 'sandstone' universities—such as the universities of Sydney and Melbourne—of lecturers filling up several rotating blackboards with scientific formulas. As each blackboard was rotated, a senior student was on the other side of the blackboard rubbing it clean so the lecturer could continue writing. These sorts of lectures were characterised by lecturers delivering lectures to the blackboard with, in more recent times, a microphone hung around their neck so that the students could at least hear what was being said, even if they did not actually see the face of the lecturer.

At one sandstone law school in Australia, many hundreds of students probably have fond memories of a certain high-profile judge delivering lectures to a painting on the side of the lecture hall wall while jiggling change in his pocket, seemingly oblivious to the fact that there were any students in the lecture hall at all. This same judge rarely used lecture notes because he was either acting as senior counsel or judge on most of the leading cases in that particular area of law. While this practice was prima facie arguably not the most effective form of communication, students were undoubtedly privileged to have the benefit of such a great thinker on what at times were difficult concepts to grasp. However, this sort of lecturing is now rare in universities where active learning is demanded of lecturers. In fact, the days of lectures that merely deliver content or information are numbered.

The days of lectures that merely deliver content or information are numbered

Audio-visual aids

These days, a vast number of audio and visual aids are employed by lecturers. Usually these aids are employed to assist in the learning process. In fact, this is the only reason that such aids should be used in the first place. However, some lecturers like the 'gimmickry' of using such aids and you, the unfortunate student, will have to be patient while the lecturer indulges in the desire to show off the latest gadget. At the end of the day, teaching is about communication, and gadgets do not necessarily ensure effective communication that leads to good teaching. The proper approach to the use of educational technologies is to use them only if they assist the learning process. Such technologies should not be used simply for the sake of using them.

Audio-visual aids should not be used simply for the sake of using them

Lecturers once used the humble overhead projector, projecting clear acetate transparencies with handwritten or photocopied information to their class. Today, the overhead projector has been replaced by the data projector connected to a computer with Microsoft PowerPoint or Apple's Keynote running a slide presentation. Slides often include animation and hyperlinks to video clips from providers such as YouTube or the Khan Academy or dozens of other providers of such media. These slides usually find themselves on to the university's learning management system, where students can download them prior to or shortly after a class.

The overhead projector has been replaced by the data projector connected to a computer

While there are rules to the use of these sorts of visual aids (such as do not cram too much information onto each slide, and ensure that the typeface is at a minimum of 28 points in size so that it can be read), lecturers new to teaching may breach the protocols that make these aids a useful tool for teacher and student. Having such aids available before the class they are being used in means you do not have to madly write the content of the slide down; however, some lecturers do not publish slides until after the class they were used in. In such cases you will need to try and capture the essence of the slide if you think the information is not readily available through an alternative source.

Try and capture the essence of the slide

The internet

The growth area in educational technologies is the internet. Many units are now either partially or wholly internet-based. The internet allows lecturers to communicate large amounts of information that saves time in lectures and saves the university the cost of printing such material. The internet can deliver small- or large-class teaching via podcasts, contemporaneous tutorials, and even automated assessment such as multiple-choice quizzes that give you instantaneous feedback on your performance. Some lecturers have become very creative when it comes to using the internet and have it as part of their assessment program.

Many units are now either partially or wholly internet-based

In addition to the posting of materials, lecture notes, and tutorial questions and answers on the internet, one of the more successful uses of the internet in higher education is the use of chat rooms. Chat rooms are similar to an electronic tutorial, where either a student or a member of the teaching staff can raise an issue and allow the entire student cohort and teaching staff to discuss the issue, with everybody being able to read the views of every other person in the chat room. It is most important to be patient and polite when using such learning opportunities, and to treat all those participating in chat rooms with respect.

Chat rooms are similar to an electronic tutorial

Textbook publishers are now providing universities with integrated learning packages that include electronic materials, such as podcasts from experts in the academic and legal professional worlds, and feature interactive elements that help you to test your understanding of concepts. Online tutors can be packaged up with these resources, as well as access to myriad resources from around the world to assist in the learning process. Because of the rapid rise of the development and use of educational technologies, universities today are embracing flexible learning as a method of engaging with students who do not live close to the university, or students who have work at times where they cannot attend face-to-face classes. Blended models of delivery are also popular. These combine face-to-face and online delivery to provide students with a choice as to the most convenient mode of university education for them.

Universities today are embracing flexible learning

The rise of Massive Open Online Courses (MOOCS), discussed in Chapter 4, is another area of innovation resulting from the development of educational technologies. MOOCS allow students from anywhere in the world—providing they have internet access—to study at some of the most prestigious universities, such as Harvard, MIT, and Yale. MOOCS are characterised by being a free course of study available via the internet on a diverse range of subjects that may

Open educational resources are changing the face of higher education or may not lead to the granting of a degree. You can take single subjects or study for a whole degree—the choice is yours. Usually, to pass the assessment you will need to pay a fee, which is how the universities fund the development of the MOOC. Most importantly, the content of the course is available to anyone that wishes to study it, whether they sit the assessment or not. These open educational resources are changing the face of higher education, as reliable and authoritative content is now readily available to you, so you do not need to rely on your own university to supply it.

The technological revolution has only just begun and where it will end is anybody's guess. However, it is likely that mobile access to learning through tablets and wearable technology will dominate the educational landscape in years to come. Having mobile access to learning is desirable given the demands and costs of higher education. Many students need to work or have carer responsibilities that prevent them from attending face-to-face classes some or all of the time. Further, learning should be undertaken at a time when you are receptive to learning and when that learning can be most beneficial to you—not at a time when the university says you should learn. Mobile educational technologies allow you to learn at a time that suits you, not an inflexible university timetable.

Mobile educational technologies allow you to learn at a time that suits you

The use of the three-dimensional virtual world Second Life is another interesting development in higher education, with some universities already experimenting with the use of avatars as teaching staff that are available any time of the day or night. Whether avatars could ultimately replace teaching staff in a direct contact sense (academics will still need to program the avatars and generate the knowledge to be taught and learnt) is a matter of conjecture, but the rationale for all higher education to be face to face is dwindling.

Some universities are experimenting with the use of avatars as teaching staff

The rise of 'learning analytics'—where universities and lecturers can find out how you best learn and then tailor-make a learning plan for you—is gaining momentum. Again, technology allows data to be gathered very easily, such as how many times and to what extent you are accessing your subject's learning management system, what information you are seeking, and what areas of assessment you are weak on. All of this type of information can be used to point you in the right direction and assist you to develop your strengths and weaknesses in your law degree.

Through 'learning analytics', lecturers find out how you best learn and then tailor-make a learning plan

While the rise of educational technologies signals new delivery methods of higher education and in particular new ways to learn, most importantly—as with many elements of human progress—it provides you with more and better choices as to how you will study. You are now, or in the near future, going to be in a position to decide how university study will fit around your life, not how your life will fit around university study.

The rise of educational technologies provides more choices as to how you will study

Student and lecturer interaction

The level of interaction between student and lecturer is the sort of issue that can elicit a different response from any number of lecturers. There probably is no right answer outside of the various policy positions set out in each university's rules and regulations. As stated above and in Chapter 4, adult education is about being responsible for, and therefore taking control of, your own learning. In this respect the job of the lecturer is not simply to give you everything you need—in terms of concepts to be understood, and analysis and synthesis to be undertaken—after which you simply regurgitate it all in an exam.

The job of the lecturer is not simply to give you everything you need and for you to regurgitate it in an exam

Your lecturers are there to facilitate the achievement of your learning goals, which are found in the description of your law degree and set out in each subject learning guide. Lecturers assist you by setting out the parameters of each unit, and then help you achieve an understanding of the legal concepts involved in each topic within a unit. Most importantly, lecturers help you to learn the skills of analysis and synthesis (discussed above and in Chapter 5). To reiterate: the former means breaking the issue or issues up into their requisite parts so that you can understand them better. The latter means reconstructing the elements so that they make sense, allowing you to reach a logical and well-reasoned conclusion. Lecturers should encourage you to argue in a reasoned fashion based upon your research. Further, the analysis and synthesis processes should include consideration of both sides of the argument; that is, the plaintiff's and the defendant's cases. For theoretical questions this means analysing the various theories and commentaries in the

Lecturers set the parameters of the subject and help you achieve understanding of the legal concepts

same way that legal problems are analysed, so that a reasoned opinion can be put forward.

While lecturers are not there to be your personal tutor or best friend, they are there to encourage you and hopefully inspire your desire to learn. Lecturers should be enthusiastic in helping you achieve your learning goals, and should employ teaching techniques that appeal to a variety of student learning preferences. While they are unlikely to be the fountains of all knowledge, even in individual subjects, they should always be able to help you find the answer to any questions you may have. This does not generally involve just telling you the answer; rather, it means assisting you to find the answer yourself, as this promotes deeper learning.

Lecturers should encourage you and inspire your desire to learn

Finally, student and lecturer interaction is a partnership of sorts. Your role is to initiate the process by seeking out information and taking responsibility for your own learning. This means completing the set readings and, where possible, casting the research net a little wider than the listed readings each week. It means breaking down the elements of each topic, and analysing how the elements work and interrelate with each other, and how they provide answers to certain issues in society. It means designing and managing a study regime that will allow you to successfully complete all of the assessed tasks in the subject and achieve some sort of deep or lasting knowledge of the legal concepts addressed in the unit.

Student and lecturer interaction is a partnership of sorts

In summary, the lecturer's role is to guide you in achieving your learning objectives. This means setting out the unit in a logical and easy-to-understand manner. It means setting clear parameters of each topic. It means helping you learn how to analyse and synthesise legal issues and be able to articulate those issues in a competent and coherent fashion. It means being available when you need assistance in the process of understanding legal concepts. Finally it means providing direction to your learning strategies when needed.

Lecturers provide direction to your learning strategies when needed

Missing classes

Missing face-to-face or electronic classes can be a concern to both you and the lecturer responsible for the subject you are studying. It should be of concern to you because you are missing important learning opportunities that are the key to understanding concepts and achieving deeper learning of those concepts. This could put in jeopardy passing the subject and ultimately graduating. From the lecturer's point of view, missing classes may be detrimental to the class dynamic, for example where there is small-group work to be completed. In this respect, your absence may also inconvenience other students in the class.

Missing classes may be detrimental to the class dynamic

The following comments are the authors' views of how to deal with students missing classes. Always check with your lecturers as to their own attitude towards missed classes.

Most universities do not have a compulsory attendance requirement. The theory is that universities are places of adult education; therefore you, the adult learner, are best placed to determine the value of formal classes to your learning objectives. Where universities—or more particularly lecturers convening subjects—do have a compulsory attendance requirement, it is usually because there is a class-participation component to the subject's assessment. It makes sense if a subject requires you to participate in the class discussions or other tasks that you be compelled to attend a majority of the classes, otherwise lecturers have to weigh up quality-versus-quantity issues that may produce inconsistent results. Where there is a compulsory attendance requirement, expect it to be around 80 per cent.

Some classes may have a compulsory attendance requirement

You should note that most universities do not consider work commitments an excuse for missing classes (or handing in assignments, as discussed in Chapter 3). Universities take the view that if you have to work full time, then you should enrol in a part-time program of study (that most universities offer), or select a law degree that is delivered flexibly or blended using online technology. This will enable you to balance your need to work with your desire to earn a degree.

Most universities do not consider work commitments an excuse for missing classes

Ultimately, most lecturers realise it is inevitable that students will miss classes. The reasons may be: sickness, family problems, work pressures, or misadventure. If your problems are very serious in nature, you should consider speaking to one of the university counsellors. This is a free service at most universities. University counsellors can help formulate a plan to get you over the problem, or

University counsellors can help formulate a plan to get you over your problems point you in the direction of a simple solution, so that you can achieve your learning objectives in any given unit. This point will be revisited in Chapter 14.

Most importantly, if you have problems you should speak to your lecturer as soon as possible. If you feel uncomfortable speaking to your lecturer for whatever reason, then speak to a counsellor who can help smooth the approach to the lecturer. The earlier you speak to your lecturer, the more chance they have to help you get past the problem and successfully complete the subjects you are currently studying. The later you leave it, the less chance you have of your lecturer being able to resolve any study issues with you. Ultimately, you should ensure you make a concerted effort to catch up and to satisfy the assessment tasks set down in the units you are studying. Speak to your lecturer about how to satisfy those tasks. If your lecturer sees that you are making an extra effort to get back on track in the subject, then they will be more inclined to help you.

Make an extra effort to get back on track, and your lecturer will be more inclined to help you

7

MANAGING YOUR TIME WELL

Six hours in sleep,
in law's grave study six,
Four spend in prayer,
The rest on nature fix.

Justinian (trs. Edward Coke)[1]

1 Translation by Edward Coke (1552–1634) of a quote from Justinian, 'The Pandects', Book 2, Chapter 4, 'De in Jus Vocando'.

Introduction

Successful law students are those that organise their time early and commit themselves to a realistic study plan. Spending a few moments at the beginning of each semester working out how the next several months will develop is essential to having a less stressful time studying law. Managing your time well calls for you not only to consider what your lecturers want you to do in the form of assignments, and noting when your exams are, but also to think carefully about the work that it will be necessary to do in order to complete those tasks, and determine how other demands on your time will make an impact on those studies. As we indicated in Chapter 4, you are the person who is primarily responsible for your learning, and that includes submitting your assignments on time and attending compulsory classes and exams.

Take time at the beginning of each semester to work out how the next months will develop

Orient yourself to your units

Most lecturers will spend the first few moments in any first class discussing the objectives of the unit and what is required of you in terms of contribution to classes, submission of assignments, and passing exams. It is important that you note these important activities and dates in your diary, or time management system (for more on this, see the next section), and consider how much work is involved in doing those tasks.

Diarise all important activities and dates, including assignments and exams

Equally important is for you to comb through the unit learning guide, which you will normally receive from your lecturer in the first class or online via the university's virtual classroom platform. The learning guide is similar to a contract between you and the law school. It explains your responsibilities and duties—such as turning up to class, and completing set readings and assignments—in addition to those of your law school and lecturer—such as providing appropriate learning materials, facilities, and guidance. Careful consideration of that learning guide is vital. What you hear discussed in class might be slightly different from the way it is expressed in the learning guide, and if there is a significant difference between what you heard and what you read, you need to ensure that you are doing the required activities properly. So if there is a difference between what your learning guide states and what your lecturer tells you in class, you must ask for clarification. Normally your lecturer will print and publish any corrections or changes to learning guides; however, if this does not appear to be happening, then send your lecturer an email and seek a written reply. This is important as it may be used as evidence in any dispute you may have with your lecturer; and it is also an important legal skill in verifying the terms of any brief you are given and ensuring there is a paper trail evidencing your instructions.

Your unit learning guide is like a contract between you and the law school

Where you are dealing with a casual teaching staff member, it is more important to ensure that you check any ambiguous instructions you may have been given. This is not a reflection on the quality or professionalism of casual lecturers, but is due to the fact that casual staff at universities are less frequently available for consultation, and hence an assignment may fall due while you are trying to track down a potentially inaccessible casual staff member. In addition, casual staff members may need to follow a 'chain of command' and, upon receiving your request, may have to consult with a coordinating lecturer or other full-time colleague for advice.

Casual staff members may have to consult with a full-time colleague for advice

Time management: Hints, warnings, and techniques

Proper time management is a critical component in your development as a law student. In our experience, the key difference between those students who succeed in their law studies and those who struggle is the inability of the poorer students to develop and maintain a program of study that allows them to balance the demands of study with other aspects of their life. We recognise that there will always be a variation in abilities between students; some students will 'naturally' be better at grasping certain concepts than others. Even where most of those in law programs are considered to be the 'elite' students and could all be labelled the 'best and brightest', there will be some who are clearly better university students than others. However, accepting those differences in abilities, even the more gifted students will find law studies difficult unless they are able to plan their time properly. We also recognise that there will be some students who struggle because they cannot engage with, or become interested in, the readings and tasks. Those students may have chosen to study law when they have talents and abilities in other areas. Alternatively, those students may have chosen to study law at a time in their lives when they might have been better off travelling, studying, running a business or family, or engaging in any number of competing interests. The point we wish to impress upon you here is that, despite the fact that you might be one of the brightest students, or perhaps one who is still trying to work out if law is the right academic discipline for you, studies in law can be made so much simpler if you are able to arrange your time properly.

Successful time management is a key to successful law studies

Submitting assignments on time

Submit all your assignments on time. Typically, late submissions will be penalised by a deduction of marks per day late or even by a complete fail for that assignment. Thus, it is much more difficult to achieve a good result for any assignment if you submit it late. Where you have a good and acceptable reason for your late submission you should always inform your lecturer about it (and/or follow any instructions that have been brought to your attention for late assignments). We recommend that you examine any university or school policy regarding the submission of late assignments and ensure that you meet the grounds, or criteria, required to submit a task late. If you are aware of something that might affect your studies during the semester, it is much better to seek advance approval for an extension of time when you know of a forthcoming time-management conflict than to leave it until the last minute, or, worse still, hope that your lecturer will take pity on you when you simply hand it in late without notice. A typical example of conflicts that may allow the granting of an extension would be where you have a formal family occasion, such as a wedding, to attend, or you have been selected to represent your university in a sporting or scholastic event.

Ensure that you meet the grounds, or criteria, required to submit a task late

Procrastination

Procrastination is a way of thinking that causes a person to put off engaging in a task in situations where the task should have been started, continued, or completed. Procrastination in its severest forms is a form of irrational justification that can cause the person to delay doing a task to a point where the task may be submitted late, submitted in an impoverished or incomplete form, or simply not submitted. In the context of law school, procrastination can cause you to fall behind in your studies, with the result that you will be struggling to get up to date with all your work. In a degree program, where time management is so important, falling behind is an unattractive option.

Procrastination is a form of irrational self-justification

The causes of procrastination vary from individual to individual, but may be due to:

- fear of failure, especially in new tasks such as learning the law;
- being a perfectionist and thus delaying doing something because you are concerned that it may not be good enough;
- seeing a task as too large to complete, as opposed to examining how a large task may be broken down into smaller, manageable parts;
- not understanding the process to be followed, thereby being confused about what you need to do; or
- underestimating the amount of time required to complete a task—this is especially obvious when you leave an assignment to the last few days and realise that you needed to spend more time on it.

If you recognise that you procrastinate, then you need to be active in working through the problem so that it does not hamper your studies. Ways of dealing with procrastination include the following:

Be active in working through the problem so that it does not hamper your studies

- Consciously recognise that you are procrastinating (for example, you may always be tidying your room, home, or office instead of working) and make a conscious decision not to act that way; for example, by living in a messy room while typing up that essay.
- Ask lecturers and colleagues for help, or advice, if you find something confusing or daunting. There are many times when a small tip from a lecturer or friend will allow you to see how a task can or should be completed, where before you thought it was simply too difficult.
- Develop a clear picture of how long a task will really take to complete and stick to a plan to complete it.
- Acknowledge that any piece of writing and any presentation can be improved, and that part of the process of learning is gaining constructive feedback about how to improve your performance.

- Understand that successful studies require you to complete the tasks assigned, by the due date. While we acknowledge that the process is more than simply osmotic, it is the case that simply engaging in the process of doing your assignments will allow knowledge and understanding to be developed. Completing tasks on time provides a psychological sense of satisfaction and a developing professional approach to learning the law.
- Appreciate that some parts of a task are more enjoyable than others, but decide to spend time on the not-so-enjoyable parts anyway.

What time management techniques should I adopt?

There are many techniques and modes of 'managing' time. Some students are used to using diaries or filofax-type folders. This may be because they work in an environment in which diaries are commonplace or paper-based systems of information management are used. Most universities provide students with student union diaries at the beginning of semester. Increasingly, some students are more comfortable using portable digital devices such as smartphones and tablet computers, or a laptop or desktop computer. These digital technologies incorporate software programs and apps that:

- remind the user of important dates and activities;
- record the location and duration of lectures, social activities, work, and other commitments;
- allow the user to link multiple devices, including those of a spouse, employer, or friend;
- assist in managing the timeline for a task or project;
- provide feedback and incentives as you complete parts of a task;
- may be shared with those who may encourage you, such as: mentors, family, and fellow students.

In many firms of legal practitioners, the firm will use an in-house intranet system that allows all appointments, matters, and hearings to be recorded on a central database. This system allows staff to be aware of exactly what they need to undertake and complete in a given period, and also allows partners and supervisors to monitor the productivity and availability of staff. What is important is that you develop and use a method that works for you. Below, we suggest some ways in which

Develop and use a time-management system that works for you

you can arrange your time; however, we are not being prescriptive: if you have a method that works better for you, then use it. The vital thing is to become organised.

During the first few days of any semester at any university you will generally receive a learning guide that gives you details about: when and where classes are to be conducted; what you need to read and do in order to be prepared for those classes; and a clear indication of when your assignments are due. All of these details need to be considered, and, where necessary, diarised. As you are taking a degree that has a link to professional legal practice, it is important to ensure that your assignments are properly completed and submitted on time. In the same way that a judge or magistrate will be reluctant to assist you should you be unprepared or fail to attend court, so too will your lecturers be unimpressed if you miss due dates. Where you are engaged in full-time studies, you may find that there are assignments or tasks that all need to be done in the same week, or even on the same day. At least with good preparation and time management, you will be better able to deal with such pressures.

Use your diary to manage study and other commitments that may occur in quick succession

We recommend that you develop a weekly plan and a semester plan and the following tables provide some guidance as to how you might do this. Clearly, you will be using your own diary or digital device, but the suggestions can be transferred easily to whichever system you are using. We recommend that you carry your time-management system with you and look at it regularly. If it is a diary, then have it open on your desk. If it is a smartphone or tablet computer, then make sure that you have the sound and message settings turned on to keep you on track.

Develop a weekly plan and a semester plan

Table 7.1 gives a simple overview of what a standard week might look like for a student who is undertaking studies, and has some casual work, a social life, and other interests. For the purpose of this hypothetical student, we have assumed that they do not have children or other significant care responsibilities. We have made a few other assumptions:

- The law school units comprise three hours of face-to-face or online time per week.
- Our student puts in four hours of preparation for each unit of study, plus one hour of reviewing notes before classes.
- Our student understands the importance of exercise and relaxation—meditation is used as means of maintaining focus.

- Our student wishes to be part of a study group.
- 'Travelling home' includes visiting friends and family, and other venues.
- When engaged in serious periods of study, our student will have a break for 10 minutes every hour to move around, eat and hydrate, and reflect on what they are doing
- For our student, the day begins early and ends relatively early (however, your own body clock and personal 'best time for study' may be different).
- Unmarked periods of free time may be utilised for social activities, relaxation, or assignment preparation.
- The weekend has been quarantined for sport, relaxation, and social/cultural time.

This table is an attempt to show our hypothetical student's regular weekly time commitments. The message we hope to share here is that your activities and time can be managed so as to complement your studies, or it can be mismanaged and harmful to your studies and general well-being. Hopefully, you will note that when you factor in a responsible amount of preparation time for each class, the weekly timetable is quite full. If one views studying at law school as a full-time job, then what you see in Table 7.1 is quite a reasonable workload.

View studying at law school as a full-time job

TABLE 7.1 Overview of a hypothetical week during semester

Time	Mon	Tues	Wed	Thurs	Fri
0600	Meditation	Meditation	Meditation	Meditation	Meditation
0700	*Review: Criminal Law notes*	Walk/run	*Review: Legal Ethics notes*	Gym	Walk/run
0800	Travel to law school		Travel to law school		
0900	**Seminar: Criminal Law**	*Preparation: Legal Ethics*	**Lecture: Legal Ethics**	Travel to law school	*Preparation: Criminal Law*
1000	**Seminar: Criminal Law**	*Preparation: Legal Ethics*	**Tutorial: Legal Ethics**	*Review: Constitutional Law notes*	*Preparation: Criminal Law*
1100	**Seminar: Criminal Law**	*Preparation: Legal Ethics*	**Tutorial: Legal Ethics**	Lunch	*Preparation: Criminal Law*
1200	Lunch	*Preparation: Legal Ethics*	Lunch	**Seminar: Constitutional Law**	*Preparation: Criminal Law*

Time	Mon	Tues	Wed	Thurs	Fri
1300	*Preparation: Contract Law*	Lunch		**Seminar: Constitutional Law**	Lunch
1400	*Preparation: Contract Law*	Travel to local community legal centre (CLC)	*Review: Contract Law notes*	**Seminar: Constitutional Law**	Travel to study group
1500	**Lecture: Contract Law**	Volunteer work at CLC	**Tutorial: Contract Law**		*Study group*
1600	Travel home	Volunteer work at CLC	*Preparation: Constitutional Law*	Travel to work	*Study group*
1700	*Preparation: Contract Law*	Volunteer work at CLC	*Preparation: Constitutional Law*	Casual work	Travel home
1800	*Preparation: Contract Law*	Travel home	Travel home	Casual work	
1900	**Online discussion group: Contract Law**	*Preparation: Constitutional Law*	Sport training	Casual work	
2000		*Preparation: Constitutional Law*	Sport training	Casual work	
2100				Travel home	

Bold type: Face-to-face/online classes
Italics: Preparation/review
Underlining: Work/volunteer work
Normal type: Other

Table 7.2 is an overview of our hypothetical student's semester. This table records our student's time commitments, whether study-oriented, work-related, social, or family-based. It shows you exactly how much free time you might have and how that free time may best be used. For instance, if, like our hypothetical student, you know that you have an essay due in Week 10 of your semester, then you need to plan for it by blocking time in advance of the due date so that you are able to do your research and drafting. You might wish to use different-coloured pens, or digital highlights, in order to show different activities and deadlines. We suggest that you use a significant bold colour to indicate the due dates for assignments. Note that while each university generally follows standard semester dates, there are some significant differences between universities in regards to mid-semester breaks, exam periods, and (for parents and carers) school

TABLE 7.2 Overview of a hypothetical semester

Week of semester	Mon	Tues	Wed	Thurs	Fri	Sat	Sun
1	Purchase textbooks					Sport Music concert	
2	Preparation for Contract Law submission				Attend court for Criminal Law field trip	Sport	
3	**Contract Law discussion board submission due**				Write up Criminal Law field trip	Sport Night out	
4	**Criminal Law field trip report due**					Sport	Family birthday party
5				Staff training at work		Sport Music concert	
6	**Criminal Law bail application**				Begin preparation for Legal Ethics viva voce	Sport Friend's wedding	
7		CLC conference			Continue preparation for Legal Ethics viva voce	Sport	Begin writing Contract Law memorandum of advice
8	Intra-session break					Weekend away	

9	Public holiday		**Legal Ethics viva voce exam**		Research Constitutional Law paper	Sport Music concert	Finalise Contract Law advice
10			**Contract Law memorandum of advice due**		Begin writing Constitutional Law paper	Sport Friend's birthday party	
11	Online/blended learning week—no classes on campus					Sport	Finalise Constitutional Law research paper
12				**Constitutional Law research paper due**		Sport Friend staying over for weekend	Friend staying over for weekend
13						Sport Music concert	Organise notes for each unit
14						Sport End-of-semester dinner with study group	Prepare summaries of unit notes
15	Stuvac					Sport	Legal Ethics final review
16	Legal Ethics exam	Contract law final review	Contract Law exam			Sport	Criminal Law final review
17	Criminal Law exam			Constitutional Law final review	Constitutional Law exam	Sport Music concert	

holidays. We suggest that you forward plan your semester by recording your study vacation—or 'stuvac' as it is known—as well as any standard, or ad hoc, breaks—such as class-free weeks—you may have in each unit. This information is generally available from your unit outlines or your university's website.

Again, we hope you note that when you consider that the weekly timetable must be superimposed onto the semester-length timetable, our hypothetical student is very busy. Following such timetables rigidly may not be possible because of illness and other misadventures that occur in life. But a genuine attempt to plan your weekly and semester activities and to follow such timetables will avoid or relieve a significant amount of tension that would otherwise build up.

Study groups

Study groups are a fantastic way to meet people who you will be learning with for the next three to five years. We say learning 'with' because, as we noted in Chapter 4, law schools are increasingly developing a learner focus. In our experience, studying law can be positively enhanced by joining intellectual forces with people who are your friends, or who live or work near your home or work. In addition to making friends and future professional contacts, creating a study group is a great way to reduce your individual study workload while developing your analytical skills. A further advantage is that a study group that works well can be a valuable support base for you when things go wrong. For instance, you may have to miss some classes due to work, health, or family pressures—having a supportive study group can go a long way to staying up to date with your lecture notes and reducing associated stresses.

Study groups can be a valuable support base when you need help

Initial perceptions of other students

The problem that many students in law schools have in creating a study group—particularly if they do not have any school friends or other contacts within the law school—is overcoming their initial reactions to the traditionally competitive people and environment they encounter. It is a normal reaction to consider your student colleagues as rival high achievers and part of the elite within the university environment. This stems from the point we made in Chapter 3 that law studies generally require a high university entrance

Self-concept can change when former high achievers suddenly find they are no longer the 'star' mark. It is also true that many students in law programs have a very high self-concept as a result of being a high achiever throughout their schooling and other studies. Research shows that one's self-concept can change when former high achievers suddenly find themselves in a position where they are no longer the 'star', or may be struggling in their law studies.

In our experience there is a lot of unwarranted nervousness associated with being in a law school environment. This reaction may be exacerbated by a general trepidation about university studies, particularly if you are the first to attend a university from your family, and may be increased when you discover the huge reading lists associated with your units. Some of this nervousness can be translated into social behaviour that may be considered aggressive or even rude. A large part of this is due to students who have always been the best in their high schools not wishing to acknowledge that law studies can be difficult: this bravado, or overconfidence, is very much centred upon the psychological concept of 'face'. The result is that it is sometimes difficult to work out exactly who a person really is, and thus whether you could study with them, until you have been able to get to know them better.

If you know people from your high school, workplace, or local area then it is pretty easy to join in a study group with them. If you are not so well connected, then we suggest two main ways of working out who might be appropriate persons to begin to study with. The first is by determining who lives or works near a location that is convenient to you. Study groups tend to flourish when the members of the group can conveniently get to meetings at agreed times. Some law schools use name tags at orientation to allow people to learn each other's names and so easily ask where they live, thereby facilitating the development of such study groups. A second way of developing a study group is to sit in on a few classes and develop a feeling for those students who appear to be constructive participants in class and are obviously doing their readings, or who are espousing a similar view to their studies to your own. There is nothing worse than entering into a relationship, no matter how short or long term it may be, and finding that the members of the group have a completely different view to you about the procedure to be adopted when you meet. Here we are not referring to intellectual differences, as these can be very healthy in developing critical thinking skills, but situations where the study group is really a social group that will be looking to you to provide most of the effort.

Study groups flourish when the members can conveniently get to meetings at agreed times

This leads us to mention the type of study group we do not recommend. This is the group that you might like to join on the basis that its members have similar social, cultural, or political interests, or where members of that group are in some other way attractive to you. If such a group has as its main—or sole—purpose the getting together for fun, or a non-law study task, then you are not in a study group. We recommend joining such groups for the purpose of non-law development and getting to know people, but not for the purpose of study. Study groups need to be focused on certain delimited tasks and rarely work when simply an adjunct to other activities.

Study groups need to be focused and rarely work when simply an adjunct to other activities

Regardless of the problems that are sometimes encountered when first getting to know new colleagues, creating a study group can be a worthwhile exercise. Besides the advantages we note below, study groups may give you the opportunity to develop lifelong professional and personal friendships.

Review of class notes

Notes compiled before and during lectures, tutorials, and seminars are often a valuable guide to the designated readings that, typically, are the subject of assignments and exams. Even where you have pre-read for a class, your class notes, without further reflection and consideration, are rarely a completely accurate and useful set of materials upon which you can rely for other assessment tasks. This is because, unless you know shorthand or have tape-recorded proceedings, it is generally impossible to fully transcribe all the interactions in a class, in addition to words you might have spoken yourself. Further, even a complete recording of class discussions is not going to provide you with an integrated understanding of how a topic, discussed in one class, fits into the 'whole' of your unit of study. That is, even where you understand what was discussed in a class, such understanding does not automatically mean that you have a flawless comprehension of how that topic fits into the broader aims of the unit of study.

You need an integrated understanding of how one topic fits into the unit of study

Re-examining what was discussed in class and reviewing your notes in the light of the readings is an important component in your development as a serious student of law. It is one thing to be given information in a class that exposes a misunderstanding you had about a principle in a case, or how a particular statute should be read, but it is another to synthesise this new information properly with your previous understanding of the material. It is important to reconfigure your notes for completeness and accuracy.

Re-examine what was discussed in class and review your notes in the light of the readings

The advantage of doing this task as part of a study group is that the study group may play a number of roles in your review process. The study group may reduce the workload by individual members agreeing to undertake particular parts of a syllabus—for example, specified weeks of the semester—thus allowing you to spend more time on those parts of the syllabus that you have volunteered to take primary responsibility for. In no way does this approach allow you to not consider the relevant readings in other areas—as you will also have to attend class and engage in the learning activities—however, it does mean that your fellow study group members can give you the benefit of their in-depth study into each particular area.

Individual members may agree to undertake particular parts of a syllabus Another advantage of reviewing class notes in a study group is that you are forced to consider and explain your conclusions about cases and topics before others. This has several benefits: you develop oral and written communication skills akin to those used in the law school program; you have a forum in which to bounce ideas and ask further questions; and you are in a 'safe' and supportive environment.

You are forced to consider and explain your conclusions about cases and topics before others

Précis of class questions

As study groups develop, they can begin to engage in forward planning. Rather than reacting to what has happened in class, a proactive study group will work through future class exercises, and pre-read and discuss cases together so as to make formal class time all the more valuable. A typical unit in law school will have weekly readings, exercises, or questions. A proactive study group will, subject to university rules and instructions regarding plagiarism, begin to pull apart those readings and exercises together in addition to answering the class questions. This form of group study can be a confidence-builder for those members of the study group who may be finding the unit difficult. Such students can go into their formal classes with a fuller idea of the direction of the class, as well as a series of questions for the lecturer that will assist them in developing their understanding of a particular topic. It also gives a forum for the more advanced members of the study group to test their views and develop mentoring skills. On this point, it is well worth mentioning the oft-cited saying that 'one of the best ways to learn something is to teach it'.

Be proactive in your studies, not reactive

Case notes

In most units of study in law school there will be a reading schedule that frequently contains a lengthy list of cases. These cases are usually appeal cases, as opposed to those decided at first instance, or trial. This list of cases needs to be read, understood, and considered in the context of the wider topic and unit aims. In Chapter 9 we provide guidance on how to read and understand case law. Here, we provide a method by which you and your study group can get the most out of your notes on particular cases. There are a number of different ways in which you can set out your case notes. The one we provide is a balance between completeness and efficiency.

A case note should provide you, and your study group, with a snapshot of a case. It needs to be written in such a way that you can quickly gather all the important information you need when you are writing an essay or exam. Typically, a case note will provide the following information.

A case note is a valuable tool that should provide you with a snapshot of a case

Name of the parties

The party names may frequently be abbreviated, provided that the meaning is clear. For instance, in criminal matters the prosecution is often not spelled out or even mentioned in a case note (for example, *Director of Public Prosecutions v Brown* could be cited as *DPP v Brown* or simply *Brown*). Where there are several parties, the case will often be referred to by the first-named party (for example, *Brown, Smith, and Jones v Nguyen* may be referred to as *Brown & ors v Nguyen*; here, the 'ors' refers to 'others'). In some circumstances, the case will be so well known that you simply need to refer to the common reference (for example *Commonwealth v Tasmania*, a famous constitutional law case from 1983, is commonly referred to as the *Franklin Dam* case because the Franklin Dam was the location over which the constitutional question arose).

Case citation details

This is where you need to provide the full details about where to find the case. This will usually be a reference to a report series (for example, (1972) 128 CLR 509) or, increasingly, to the specific details of an unreported judgment (for example, *R v Favero* CCA (NSW), 19 October 1999, Sully J, unreported.). For more on this point, see Chapter 10 in which we discuss report abbreviations.

The court that decided the matter, or considered the issue(s)

This is important from the perspective of the doctrine of precedent (for more on precedent, see Chapter 8).

The judge(s)

Over time, you will notice that in different units there are some appeal court judges (within the Supreme Court of your jurisdiction, or the Federal Court or the High Court) who appear to be referred to quite frequently by your lecturer or in your readings. This is because those judges have developed a reputation as being leading law-makers in a particular area (as compared to the other judges on that court, who may have other areas of expertise), whose judgments have been ground-breaking, or have been cited regularly. Where relevant, it is also necessary to know what the composition of the majority and minority in a particular case is. This is because you may need to be aware of the way in which an individual judge or court has changed attitudes over time: knowing which judges decided a certain way at certain times can be of great assistance.

Some judges have developed a reputation as being leading law-makers

Relevant (or material) facts

The key word here is 'relevant'. Knowing the facts is important because the facts allow you to place the legal principle being studied into context. The facts also provide you with a great memory link to assist you in remembering what the case was about in a legal sense. What is critical here is that you do not make your case note too long by loading up the facts section. One way of cutting down on the length of the facts section is to include only those facts that are relevant.

So what are relevant facts? Relevant facts are those that have a bearing on the decision in some way. For instance, in a criminal law case, a note to indicate that the accused person was a certain height may be highly relevant if the case is about the correct identification of an assailant (you would definitely indicate something about height in your facts section); however, the height of the accused (if reported) would be irrelevant in a note for a case where the accused has admitted doing certain acts (so the accused has been properly identified) and the issue before the court is whether the accused had the relevant *mens rea* (or guilty mind) associated with the crime. Importantly, the relevant facts may often include a brief history of the matter. This is necessary so that you understand why the case you are reading about is before the court.

Relevant facts are those that have a bearing on the decision in some way

Issue(s)

In any case there must be one, and sometimes more, issues necessary for decision by the court. Your identification of the issues needs to be precise enough so that you know exactly why the court is required to decide the issues. Often the judge will state the issues very clearly and simply—sometimes as part of a heading and sometimes as an opening statement—and you simply need to restate them. In other cases you might need to read the judgment more carefully to discern exactly what the case is about.

Your identification of the issues needs to be precise

Some of these issues may be about the procedure adopted by the lower court. Where you are mainly studying substantive law as opposed to procedural law (which is typical in first year), the procedural issues may not be as important as the substantive law issues and you may be able to dispense with them as part of your case note (see Chapter 8). But please check this with your lecturer, because sometimes the procedural law is woven into the fabric of the substantive law.

Decision/holding

The decision (or, where there are multiple issues, the decisions) is what the court finally held (decided) about the issues. The holding may be simply that an accused remains convicted of a crime, or that a particular party was successful in its civil action. It is important to know these holdings in order to understand how the particular parties in a case had their issues resolved. However, they are best understood in relation to the reasoning used by the court in coming to its decision.

Reason for the decision

The reasoning behind the decision, or the *ratio decidendi* (ratio), is the key part of the case note (see Chapter 5). In order to determine the ratio, you will need to read the case carefully. After understanding what each judge has decided, you need to note what each judge says about why they came to the decision they did. Producing these notes is not always easy; some judges make their reasoning very clear and explicit, while others—particularly in older decisions—have a writing style that is less easy to decipher. The process for determining the ratio for your case can become even more complicated when the judges come to the same decision, but use different means to do so—there are thus multiple ratios to consider. The ratio is also difficult to determine when the judges agree with other judges about some parts of their decisions, but disagree on other aspects.

The key to a comprehensive case note is to ensure that you have noted the reasons for each and every issue by each judge. This can be achieved by referring to the specific words used by each judge. An abbreviated form of the case note could include a basic understanding of each judge's reasoning by way of paraphrasing the ratio.

Ensure that you have noted the reasons for each and every issue by each judge

Relevant *obiter dicta* points

Sometimes, what the judges say about issues not directly requiring a decision are very important to note too. As discussed in Chapter 5, *obiter dicta* (obiter) is not the law that will be applied by other courts according to the rules of precedent. But it remains important in giving readers an idea about how judges think and thus their views on how the law might be decided if cases on such points were specifically brought before them. *Obiter dicta* may be important to note in cases where your lecturer is especially keen on you developing an understanding about how the law has changed or may be changed.

Page references to related cases and topics in the prescribed readings

This section of your case note gives you the chance to explicitly link other cases and readings to your case note. It is a great way to express interconnections between topics and ideas and, as discussed in Chapter 4, is essential to your overall understanding and developing expertise in law.

Table 7.3 is an example of a case note.

TABLE 7.3 Example of a criminal law case note

Parties	*The Queen v Crabbe*
Citation	(1985) 156 CLR 464
Court	High Court of Australia
Judge(s)	Gibbs CJ, Wilson, Brennan, Deane, and Dawson JJ (joint judgment)
Facts	Crabbe drove his road train through the wall of a motel and bar near Ayers Rock (NT). Five people died. Crabbe was found guilty after a trial in the Supreme Court (NT). The trial judge directed the jury about recklessness as a form of *mens rea* for murder. As part of those directions the trial judge stated (quoted in the High Court joint judgment at 466): 'A man commits murder if he kills somebody, having at the time that he did the action which caused the death ... (a) state of mind ... such that he knows that what he's about to do is likely to kill someone, but nevertheless goes ahead and does that act with reckless indifference to the consequences ... or ... he foresees the possibility that what he does might cause death, or really serious bodily injury, nevertheless takes no reasonable available step to ascertain whether or not it will.' And later the trial judge stated (at 467): 'He's further guilty of murder if you're satisfied beyond reasonable doubt that he foresaw the possibility that there might be some people in the bar, but didn't take any step that might have been available to him to find out whether there were any people there or not, before he went ahead and drove the vehicle in.' On appeal, the Full Court of the Supreme Court (NT) held that the trial judge had misdirected the jury on the definition of recklessness and ordered a new trial. The Crown appealed the decision and reasoning of the Full Court.
Issue(s)	At common law, does recklessness as a form of *mens rea* for murder mean that the accused must know, or foresee, the 'possibility' or 'probability' of death resulting from the act(s) of the accused?
Decision/holding	Appeal dismissed. New trial to take place. The High Court stated (at 469): 'It should now be regarded as settled law in Australia, if no statutory provision affects the position, that a person who, without lawful justification or excuse, does an act knowing that it is probable that death or grievous bodily harm will result, is guilty of murder if death in fact results. It is not enough that he does the act knowing that it is possible but not likely that death or grievous bodily harm might result.' The High Court also held that 'probable' means 'likely to happen'.

Reason for the decision	The High Court reasoned as follows (at 469): 'The conclusion that a person is guilty of murder if he commits a fatal act knowing that it will probably cause death or grievous bodily harm (but absent an intention to kill or do grievous bodily harm) is not guilty of murder if he knew that his act might possibly cause death or grievous bodily harm is not only supported by a preponderance of authority but is sound in principle. The conduct of a person who does an act, knowing that death or grievous bodily harm is a probable consequence, can naturally be regarded for the purposes of the criminal law as just as blameworthy as the conduct of one who does an act intending to kill or do grievous bodily harm. Indeed, on one view, a person who does an act knowing its probable consequences may be regarded as having intended those consequences to occur.'
Obiter dicta	'... not every fatal act done with the knowledge that death or grievous bodily harm will probably result is murder. A surgeon who competently performs a hazardous but necessary operation is not criminally liable if the patient dies, even if the surgeon foresaw that his death was probable. Academic writers have pointed out that in deciding whether an act is justifiable its social purpose or social utility is important' (at 470).
Related cases and topics	*Pemble v The Queen* (1971) 124 CLR 107 (Barwick CJ stated that recklessness was a test of possibility at 118–21; McTiernan J at 127 and Menzies J at 135 stated that the test was one of probability). *La Fontaine v The Queen* (1976) 136 CLR 62 (Barwick CJ questioned the possibility test at 69; Stephen J stated that the test was one of possibility at 85–86; Gibbs J at 75–77 and Jacobs J at 94–100 held that the test was one of probability; Mason J left the question open at 91). *Crimes Act 1900* (NSW), s 18 (requires 'reckless indifference to human life', not 'recklessness to death or grievous bodily harm' as stated in *Crabbe*.) *Royall v The Queen* (1990) 172 CLR 378 (*Crabbe*'s case applies to s 18 of the *Crimes Act 1900* (NSW), but only as to the accused foreseeing the probability of death: per Mason CJ at 395; Deane & Dawson JJ at 416; McHugh J at 456; Brennan J at 400; and Toohey & Gaudron JJ at 431.)

Working while studying

Working while studying can be both problematic and advantageous. The problem of working while studying is, quite simply, that you have less time to devote to your studies. Given that the expected workloads can be quite steep, our view is that an ideal combination of work and study mean that you attempt to find a balance between financial security and successful study. We recognise that a significant majority of students now need to work in order to fund the growing expenses associated with law studies. However, we note that once you have embarked on your course, the law school will generally consider that you have contracted to do the work and readings associated with your studies. That being the case, it is usually quite difficult to ask the university to be lenient as regards assignments and exams just because you have work constraints on your time.

Working while studying requires careful balancing of the two

Apart from the financial benefits, the advantage of working while studying is that you will get to see the law you are learning being applied. For a keen observer, any occupation provides an opportunity to see the interaction of the law with the broader community. Whether you work in fast food, social welfare, retail, or telemarketing, the ideas that you are exposed to in your law studies will be evident when you reflect upon your work practices. If you happen to work as a legal clerk within the legal profession, or in the courts or a government department, you will have the benefit of seeing the law—and significant legal actors—in action. A further benefit of a law-related job is that you will have the chance to speak with legal professionals about their ideas on topics that you are studying. It is these insights that can really cause you to reconsider your first thoughts about your readings and personal prejudices.

Any occupation provides an opportunity to see the interaction of the law with the broader community A final benefit of working in a law-related position is that you will be in a position to start networking. A network of friends and professional colleagues can be of great assistance during your studies when you need some advice about certain ideas you are considering. A network also gives you an opportunity to develop an insight into the realities of work in the legal profession. Should this insight be appealing, then your network may provide you with a chance to obtain a job as a legal professional upon graduation.

A network can help you develop an insight into the realities of work in the legal profession

Studying law is an important activity and, when coupled with the financial costs associated with course fees, should not be undertaken lightly. Like most things in life, having a balanced approach to your law studies is essential. Simply reading the law and not developing other aspects of yourself—such as sporting, artistic, cultural, or social pursuits—may result in your becoming insular in your approach to the law. Many learned and respected lawyers have often stated that maintaining good physical health and nurturing personal development outside the law are very important in the maturation process of those involved in the law. We recommend that you spend the first few weeks of law studies keeping a brief diary or journal about all your experiences. In it you should note:

- how long it takes you to undertake your studies;
- what location seems to be the most conducive to your studies (your room, library, a friend's place);
- when you are most effective at study (are you an early-morning person, good during the day, or a night owl?);
- how much sleep you are getting or not getting;
- whether your diet has changed (for better or worse);
- how often you are engaged in non-law activities (such as physical exercise) that you typically enjoy (and whether you need to increase them—this is especially important when you consider how much reading, and thus sitting, you will be doing); and
- what impact certain social and family activities have on your studies (these can often be very positive when occurring at certain times of a week or month).

After three or four weeks of your first semester, you should consider your personal notes and evaluate what you need to do to stay healthy, happy, and balanced while continuing to be successful in your studies.

Our aim in this chapter has been to give you an idea about the practical realities of law studies, as well as ways in which you might be able to better complete them. Hopefully some of the things you have read in this chapter will be worth considering and implementing.

8

CORE CONCEPTS: THE LEGAL SYSTEM AND LEGAL ETHICS

There is a vague popular belief that lawyers are necessarily dishonest. I say vague, because when we consider to what extent confidence and honors [sic] are reposed in and conferred upon lawyers by the people, it appears improbable that their impression of dishonesty is very distinct and vivid. Yet the impression is common, almost universal. Let no young man [sic] choosing the law for a calling for a moment yield to the popular belief. Resolve to be honest at all events; and if in your own judgment you cannot be an honest lawyer, resolve to be honest without being a lawyer. Choose some other occupation, rather than one in the choosing of which you do, in advance, consent to be a knave.

Abraham Lincoln[1]

1 Memorandum for law lecture, 1850.

Introduction

Studying law, like any new discipline, requires an understanding of its history, basic concepts, and jargon. During the course of your introductory law units you will be exposed to a range of new ideas and terms. In some of those units you will be guided to develop a greater understanding of some of these basic points. The level of guidance you receive may be quite explicit—you might be asked to read certain books or articles that focus on the idea or task in question—or sometimes implicit—your reading of certain cases or researching certain materials from the library may be designed to cause you to develop certain views on, and knowledge about, the way to complete a particular task. In other units you may find that your understanding of certain terms or concepts will be assumed knowledge, and therefore you may need to read more widely, or be proactive in class, in order to ensure you understand those terms and concepts.

Studying law requires an understanding of its history, basic concepts, and jargon

This chapter is written to provide you with a basic understanding of some of the core ideas and basic terms that are typically encountered during studies in law school—and no more. This chapter is not designed to replace designated unit readings, nor to stop you from consulting one of the many law dictionaries that cater to law students. What it does is provide you with a concise starting point from which you can form and develop your understanding of these fundamental components of the law.

The history of Australian law

Many of your law school units will examine the history of Australian law or, at least, parts of it directly relevant to the unit of study. The following provides an overview of selected events, facts, and constitutional turning points. You should ensure that you read more fully about matters of history so that you develop an appreciation of why the law and legal system that we have is the way it is.

Aboriginal and Torres Strait Islander peoples

The legal system in Australia is almost solely based upon a British inheritance. However, archaeological evidence suggests that Aboriginal and Torres Strait Islander peoples have occupied the Australian continent for over 40,000 years.

In addition to the statements by Aboriginal and Torres Strait Islander peoples themselves, anthropological research suggests clearly that there existed, and exists, a complex system of laws and customs governing the behaviour of our Indigenous peoples. These laws and customs were passed from generation to generation via the words and behaviour of the Aboriginal and Torres Strait Islander peoples. In large part, a system of recording and writing these laws and customs was unnecessary as the laws and customs were incorporated into the very fabric of Indigenous daily life.

There existed a complex system of laws and customs governing the behaviour of our Indigenous peoples

This lack of a written record of laws and customs went partway to allowing the English colonisers of Australia[2] to justify the concept of the reception of English law. Put simply, 'reception' is a legal concept that provides that, in the absence of a pre-existing system of law in a particular place, a colonising government has the ability to transplant its law onto the colonised territory. This is so because where a colonised territory is considered *terra nullius*—a land with no law—the law of the colonisers is to be imposed and used automatically. In the case of the colonisation of Australia, the lack of written Indigenous laws and the utilisation of the reception of English law meant that the rights and obligations normally accorded to a conquered people were not respected. The effect of this on the development of Australian law was that the Indigenous legal system was not recognised, Indigenous laws were not incorporated into the transplanted English law, and it was not deemed necessary to make a treaty with Aboriginal and Torres Strait Islander peoples. The practical consequences of reception can be seen through the lens of multiple historical perspectives. Suffice to say, the lack of formal recognition of Aboriginal and Torres Strait Islander peoples, until more recent times, has resulted in significant cultural, social, and economic disadvantage, in addition to displacement and death.

Indigenous laws and customs pre-date the reception of English law into Australia.

A practical problem for Aboriginal and Torres Strait Islander peoples today, which results from the reception of English law into Australia, is how to negotiate the clash of legal systems. Put simply, Aboriginal and Torres Strait Islander peoples continue to be governed by the law and customs of their culture, while also being forced to accept and respond to the English law that

---

2 For simplicity of expression, we refer here to 'Australia', 'Australian', and 'Australian law'. In fact, the reception of English law was into the colony of New South Wales.

has been imposed upon them via colonisation. In some cases, the negotiating to be done is easy and seamless, while in many others, compliance with the inherited Indigenous laws results in clear clashes with the dominant Australian laws. An excellent example of this is the customarily sanctioned responses of Aboriginal and Torres Strait Islander peoples to serious personal harm. For Aboriginal and Torres Strait Islander peoples, one response to such harm might be the legitimate use of spearing a perpetrator as a traditional punishment. While spearing may result in serious injury or death, it is an outcome that Indigenous customary law accepts. In English and in modern Australian law, the serious injury or death of an offender at the hands of another would invoke criminal laws, involving wounding, murder, and/or provocation. In the customary legal system, the spearing is culturally condoned as between the participants; in the English/Australian system, the spearing becomes a matter for control by an independent government.

Compliance with inherited Indigenous laws may result in clashes with dominant Australian laws

The English inheritance

Modern Australian law derives from an English inheritance called the 'common law' system. The following provides an overview of some of the more notable features of the English inheritance.

Modern Australian law derives from an English inheritance: the 'common law'. The development of the law in common law jurisdictions, such as Australia, is a journey through British history. While there was law and custom regulating the behaviour of people in the British Isles for millennia, we will begin in the eleventh century, after the Norman Conquest of England in 1066. The Normans did not attempt to transplant French law into England, nor did they develop a new set of laws for their new kingdom. Instead, the sovereign dispensed justice as he saw fit when disputes arose between members of society. As the Norman-governed society grew, dispensing justice became the responsibility of others. The sovereign delegated this authority to knowledgeable members of his court who could act according to the sovereign's wishes. These trusted members of the sovereign's court became known as 'judges'.

One of the primary matters heard by the judges of the early courts related to the sovereign's revenue. The Normans saw the preservation of royal revenues as primary among their objectives because money was used to raise armies and fight wars. Judges were sent on tours of the various regions throughout England to check on local matters and to ensure revenues were being collected. Therefore, it is not surprising that the first permanent royal court was the Court of the Exchequer, which sat at Westminster to exclusively hear disputes about revenues. Under King Henry II (1154–89) the judges went on circuit to the various regions of England, where their tasks became wholly judicial and the complex organisation of common law rules and custom began to develop. The Court of Common Pleas was established to deal with matters outside of revenue issues, and it was this development that is generally acknowledged as the formalisation of the common law—a complex system of judge-made rules that judges applied so that they could decide the cases before them.

A complex organisation of common law rules and custom began to develop in the twelfth century. The judges heard the parties who came before the court to argue their case, after which the judge would dispense justice, adjudicating as to which party was successful. As the judges' pay then depended on court fees, the width of the judges' work expanded to envelop the court in an ever-more complex set of rules that could be applied to disputes with similar facts. As the rules became more complex, people were employed to advocate a case for parties and this, eventually, saved the court time and ensured that those before the court had their matter dealt with according to the rules. Over time, these advocates became variously known as pleaders, apprentices, serjeants, and finally barristers. In addition to the advocates, some legal work was done by people who became known as attorneys or solicitors. These non-court non-advocates solicited work from potential disputants who were not familiar with the complex rules of court.

A complex set of rules developed that could be applied to disputes with similar facts

EQUITY

One important development in the common law system was the development of equity. As mentioned, the complex set of rules created by the judges came to be known as the common law. However, the common law's rigid approach to adjudicated solutions became problematic, and the rules of equity were developed to remedy unfair common law decisions.

The rules of equity were developed to remedy unfair common law decisions

The development of the rules of equity are generally attributed to the Lord Chancellor and the Court of Chancery. In the middle ages, disputants were entitled to petition the sovereign who relied on the advice of the Chancellor—said to be the 'keeper of the sovereign's conscience'. By the end of the fifteenth century, petitions were referred directly to the Chancellor, who, in attempting to maintain a sense of parity between petitioners, was referring to earlier decisions to provide a consistently 'fairer' result to a dispute, rather than applying the rigid principles of the common law. In the seventeenth century, conflict arose between the common law judges and the Chancellor as to whether the common law or the rules of equity took precedence. James I resolved the conflict in favour of the Chancellor and the rules of equity. By the early nineteenth century, the Court of Chancery had developed a body of precedent with clear principles. The courts of common law and equity were separately administered, and litigants had to be very careful to ensure that they commenced proceedings in the right court, depending on the remedy they sought. In England, equity was administered by the three common law courts (Court of Exchequer, Court of Common Pleas, and Court of King's/Queen's Bench) until they were all fused by the *Judicature Acts 1873–75*. Together, the decisions of courts of common law and equity are known by the term 'general law'.

The Court of Chancery developed a body of precedent with clear principles

Since the establishment of the rules of common law and equity, the parliaments of England (and subsequently Australia) have sought to codify a number of those rules. Codification generally occurs when the development of the common law has produced some clear injustice, or where there is community sentiment that the general law should be changed. In Australia, parliament is vested with the power—under the respective constitutions of the states and the Commonwealth of Australia—to pass laws dealing with certain subject matter. States may pass laws for the 'peace, order and good government' of that state. This is a wide power. However, it is still possible for a state to pass legislation and for that legislation to be struck down by the courts for failing to promote the 'peace, order, and good government' of the state.

The powers conferred on the Parliament of the Commonwealth of Australia to pass legislation are largely to be found in s 51 of the *Commonwealth of Australia Constitution Act 1900* (Imp). These enumerated powers are the basis for most laws passed by the Commonwealth of Australia.

Table 8.1 provides a brief timeline of some of the key events in the constitutional development of the nation. It is not a complete list, but it provides you with some ideas about key changes to the legal system from which you can base your understanding of current legal system processes.

TABLE 8.1 Australia's constitutional development—a timeline

Year	Event, fact, or issue	Ramification or discussion
Pre-1788	Indigenous customary law	Diverse (not common) spiritually based laws existed in Australia's Indigenous communities, received by oral, intergenerational storytelling
1787–8	Letters Patent; Reception of English law into colony of New South Wales	The Imperial *Letters Patent* (2 April 1787)[3], established the first criminal and civil courts in the colony of New South Wales upon settlement in 1788. Indigenous laws were not recognised—doctrine of *terra nullius* used as basis for rejecting pre-existing law; applicable British laws govern the colony
1823	*New South Wales Act* (Imp)	Establishment of Supreme Court in the colony of New South Wales
1828	*Australian Courts Act* (Imp)	Limited self-government for the colony of New South Wales
1855	*New South Wales Government Act* (Imp)	Creation of parliament for the colony of New South Wales
1865	*Colonial Laws Validity Act* (Imp)	Colonial parliament able to make own laws, but cannot override imperial law that applies with 'paramount force'
1891 & 1897	National Australasian Convention and National Convention	Debates over Federation and the development of a draft Bill for a federal constitution
1900	*Commonwealth of Australia Constitution Act* (Imp)	Establishes federal constitution and nation of Australia; colonies become states of new nation; creates federal parliament
1902	*Constitution Act* (NSW)	Creation of New South Wales Constitution
1931	*Statute of Westminster*	No imperial legislation to be made for the dominions (in the Australian context this meant the federated country of Australia, but not the former colonies)
1975	*Privy Council (Appeals from the High Court)* (Cth)	No right of appeal from High Court to Privy Council; possibility of appeal from state Supreme Court to Privy Council remains
1986	*Australia Act* (Cth)	Complete legislative and judicial power vested in Australian institutions; Head of State (executive) still Queen of England
1992	*Mabo* case	Recognition by High Court that Australia was never *terra nullius* in fact

3 http://foundingdocs.gov.au/item-sdid-70.html

Jurisprudence

For many new students, law school learning is perceived to be all about remembering the facts of cases and finding out what the law is (as that law is applied in practice). Fortunately—though for some unexpectedly—the study of law is more than a one-dimensional professional discipline. Studying law requires an understanding about how the law fits into its societies; how it is, or is not, equivalent to notions of justice; and importantly, what the law should be. These ideas are explicitly dealt with during consideration of the interaction of the law with other academic disciplines (such as: sociology, economics, and history) and the study of jurisprudence.

Jurisprudence is the philosophical study of law and may be studied as a discrete unit within your law program or as part of other core units.

Jurisprudence is the philosophical study of law

According to Cornell University,[4] jurisprudence has the following major strands:

- The first and the most prevalent form of jurisprudence seeks to analyze, explain, classify, and criticize entire bodies of law. Law school textbooks and legal encyclopaedias represent this type of scholarship.
- The second type of jurisprudence compares and contrasts law with other fields of knowledge such as literature, economics, religion, and the social sciences.
- The third type of jurisprudence seeks to reveal the historical, moral, and cultural basis of a particular legal concept.
- The fourth body of jurisprudence focuses on finding the answer to such abstract questions as What is law? How do judges (properly) decide cases?

There are two main jurisprudential schools that have clear links to liberalism, which is defined by Honderich as follows:[5]

4 http://www.law.cornell.edu/wex/jurisprudence (accessed 22 August 2013).

5 Ted Honderlich (ed.), 'The Oxford Companion to Philosophy' (London: Oxford University Press, 1995), at 483.

> Liberalism is a major political idealog[y] of the modern world. [It] is distinguished by the importance it attaches to the civil and political rights of individuals. Liberals demand a substantial realm of personal freedom—including freedom of conscience, speech, association, occupation, and more recently, sexuality—which the state should not intrude upon, except to protect others from harm.

These two jurisprudential schools are the 'natural law' school and the 'legal positivist' school.

Natural law

Natural law attempts to reconcile what exists in the world with what could or should be

Natural law is a view of the world that attempts to reconcile what exists with what could or should be. Natural law developed from ancient Greek and Roman times, when philosophers and statesmen such as Plato, Aristotle, Cicero, and Seneca attempted to develop an objective conception of law by the use of reason. Cicero famously stated:[6]

> True law is right reason in agreement with nature; it is of universal application, unchanging and everlasting; it summons to duty by its commands, and averts from wrongdoing by its prohibitions ... It is a sin to try to alter this law ... We cannot be freed from its obligations by senate or people, and we need not look outside ourselves for an expounder or interpreter of it.

The early ideas of the ancient Greek and Roman philosophers were developed in the thirteenth century by St Thomas Aquinas, who wrote:[7]

> in human affairs a thing is said to be just from being right according to the rule of reason. But the first rule of reason is the law of nature ... every human law has just so much of the nature of law as it is derived from the law of nature. But if in any point it defects from the law of nature, it is no longer a law but a perversion of the law.

Aquinas's thoughts were later developed by Thomas Hobbes, John Locke, and, in more recent times, John Finnis. Many of these developments retained a

6 Cicero, 'De Re Publica' (London: Heinemann, 1928), Chapter 22.

7 Thomas Aquinas, 'Summa Theologiae', in 'Thomas Aquinas, Selected Writings' (London: Penguin, 1998).

link between law and morality. One critic of natural law explains it, in part, as 'the theory that there are certain principles of human conduct, awaiting discovery by human reason, with which man-made law must conform if it is to be valid'.[8]

Legal positivism

Legal positivism is a philosophical view of law that rejects the natural law stance. Positivists view the law as broadly being that which is identifiable and posited by a sovereign, and reject the link between law and morals. That is, positivists argue that the natural lawyer's reasoning about what the law 'ought' to be cannot logically interact with conceptions of what the law actually 'is'. Positivists thus see the study of law to be just that: the study of the law, and not a moral analysis of the law. Positivists do not preclude a relationship between law and morals, in the sense that they may question the way in which a society uses law; however, positivists believe that the analysis of law can be undertaken in a scientific way, without recourse to values.

Positivists examine the law as 'is'

The eighteenth century saw the development of the modern positivist attack on the natural law position. Beginning with David Hume and Jeremy Bentham, the positivists argued that the gap between what 'is' and what 'should be' could not be logically overcome, and thus the approach to the law should be based upon what one can observe as being recognised as law, not morals, in a given society. Hume and Bentham were followed in the nineteenth century by John Austin, who introduced the 'command theory' of law, and in the twentieth century, the positivist flag has been flown by H.L.A. Hart and Hans Kelsen. Modern critics of positivism included Lon Fuller and Ronald Dworkin. You will note that many of the twentieth-century writers attempted to reconcile the natural law view with positivism.

Positivists argue that the gap between what 'is' and what 'should be' cannot be logically overcome

There are several offshoots of these main schools of jurisprudence, being socialist, feminist, realist, and postmodernist schools of thought.

Central principles and concepts

In order to provide an exhaustive and comprehensive guide to the central principles and concepts of the legal system in Australia, this book would need

8 H.L.A. Hart, 'The Concept of Law' (Oxford: Clarendon Press, 2nd edn, 1997), at 182.

to be significantly longer. Our aim here is simply to provide you with initial impressions about some of the key principles and concepts that you will come across during your law studies.

Adversary system

The adversary system is the court process in which the parties to a dispute are adverse, or opposed to each other. The common law system is well known to be adversarial, because parties use their lawyers to submit arguments on their behalf. These arguments are designed to buttress their case and attack the case of their opponent. A neutral judge or jury then decides which of the arguments is believed to the requisite standard of proof (see 'Proof', later in this chapter). What you should be aware of is the fact that most legal systems are in fact adversarial in nature. The civil law system—also known as an inquisitorial system because the judges have a more active role as inquisitors—has parties adverse to each other as well.

The common law adversary system is used in Australia

The key differences between the common law adversary system and the civil law inquisitorial system is that:

- In the common law adversary system, the judges must decide cases on the basis of what is presented to them in court. Common law judges have the arguments and submissions placed before them by the lawyers for the parties and they have little opportunity to ask for extra information. In the civil law inquisitorial system, the judges have a much greater role in determining what it is that they wish to hear or examine.
- In the case of criminal law, the pre-trial period after a person is accused of a crime is generally quite short in the common law adversary system, whereas the trial may be quite lengthy as certain evidentiary issues are examined in depth before the judge. In the inquisitorial system, the investigation stage is very long owing to the civil law approach to the determination of evidentiary issues pre-trial, and, as a result, the trial is quite short.

Doctrine of precedent

The doctrine of precedent is one of the hallmarks of the common law system. The doctrine is in essence a series of rules that restrict the way in which precedents—previously decided cases on similar facts or law—can be used.

It thus controls and limits how judges can use and develop the law within the court system. The rules give a coherence and predictability to the development of the law by systematising the layers of courts and by not giving unlimited power to judges to decide cases in any way that they see fit.

The rules give a coherence and predictability to the development of the law

Several of the fundamental precepts and rules within the doctrine are set out below, and these will provide you with an idea of how the system works in Australia.

- The part of a judgment that is binding as a precedent is the *ratio decidendi* (defined later in this chapter).
- *Obiter dicta* (defined later in this chapter) do not have effect as precedents.
- Courts lower in the hierarchy of courts must follow a binding precedent from the courts higher in the hierarchy.
- Decisions of courts lower in the hierarchy of courts are not binding on the courts higher in the hierarchy.
- The High Court is the top of the Australian court hierarchy.
- Decisions of the High Court are binding on all other courts in the country.
- Decisions of superior courts in one jurisdiction are not binding on the courts of another, but may be highly persuasive.
- In the interests of consistency in the legal system, a court will follow precedent of the same court within the judicial hierarchy even where that precedent may be criticised. However, where the interests of justice require change, a court may establish a new precedent.

In *State Government Insurance Commission v Trigwell* (1979) 142 CLR 617 Mason J explained his view of the role of the courts in the Australian common law system, in particular, the limitations to judge-made law:

> If it should emerge that a specific common law rule was based on the existence of particular conditions or circumstances, whether social or economic, and that they have undergone a radical change, then in a simple or clear case the court may be justified in moulding the rule to meet the new conditions and circumstances. But there are very powerful reasons why the court should be reluctant to engage in such an exercise. The court is neither a legislature nor a law reform agency. Its responsibility is to decide cases by applying the law to the

> facts as found. ... [T]he court cannot, and does not, engage in the wide-ranging inquiries and assessments which are made by governments and law reform agencies as a desirable, if not essential, preliminary to the enactment of legislation by an elected legislature ...These considerations must deter a court from departing too readily from a settled rule of the common law and from replacing it with a new rule.[9]

Interestingly the decision of the High Court in the *Mabo* case (*Mabo & ors v The State of Queensland* (1992) 175 CLR 1) created some controversy because of the law-making that it contained. As Deane and Gaudron JJ stated at para 56:

> If this were any ordinary case, the Court would not be justified in reopening the validity of fundamental propositions which have been endorsed by long-established authority and which have been accepted as a basis of the real property law of the country for more than one hundred and fifty years. ... Far from being ordinary, however, the circumstances of the present case make it unique. ... [T]he two propositions in question provided the legal basis for the dispossession of the Aboriginal peoples of most of their traditional lands. The acts and events by which that dispossession in legal theory was carried into practical effect constitute the darkest aspect of the history of this nation. The nation as a whole must remain diminished unless and until there is an acknowledgment of, and retreat from, those past injustices. In these circumstances, the Court is under a clear duty to re-examine the two propositions. For the reasons which we have explained, that re-examination compels their rejection. The lands of this continent were not terra nullius or 'practically unoccupied' in 1788.

You should consider the material on sources of law in Chapter 9.

The court system in Australia

Table 8.2 gives a simplified version of the court system in Australia. It does not provide details about specialist courts or tribunals.

9 His Honour has also written a useful and informative article about precedent that is worth examining: Sir Anthony Mason, 'The Use and Abuse of Precedent' (1988) 4 *Australian Bar Review* 93.

TABLE 8.2 The court system

Decisions of the High Court are binding on all lower courts	High Court								
	Federal	**NSW**	**Vic**	**Qld**	**SA**	**WA**	**Tas**	**ACT**	**NT**
Courts at this level are bound by the High Court, but bind all courts below them in that part of the judicial hierarchy	Full Court	Appeal courts	Appeal courts	Appeal courts	Appeal courts	Appeal courts	Appeal courts	Appeal courts	Appeal courts
Courts at this level are bound by any courts above them in the judicial hierarchy, but bind all courts below them	Federal Courts (eg Family Court)	Supreme Court & specialist courts (eg Land and Environment Court)	Supreme Court & specialist courts (eg Children's Court)	Supreme Court & specialist courts (eg Mental Health Court)	Supreme Court & specialist courts (eg Industrial Relations Court)	Supreme Court & specialist courts (eg Family Violence Court)	Supreme Court	Supreme Court	Supreme Court
		District Courts	County Courts	District Courts	District Courts	District Courts			
	Federal Circuit Court of Australia	Local Courts	Magistrates' Courts	Magistrates' Courts	Magistrates' Courts	Magistrates' Courts	Magistrates' Courts	Magistrates' Courts	Magistrates' Courts

The rule of law

The rule of law is an English legal doctrine that essentially means all people are equal before the law. It does not matter if a person is a government official, a police officer, a judge, or a bricklayer—all people will be treated the same before the law. A notable exception is the sovereign.

All people are equal before the law

The rule of law has three important components:

- the absolute predominance of regular law, so that the government has no arbitrary power over the citizen;
- the equal subjection of all to the ordinary law administered by ordinary courts; and
- the citizen's personal freedoms are protected by the ordinary law, rather than by any special constitutional guarantees that favour certain sectors of the community.

The reason that this concept of the rule of law is important is because our courts are the guardians of the rule of law and the law itself serves to perpetuate the rule of law, thereby protecting all citizens equally. The preservation of the rule of law is, some would say, the most important answer to the question: 'What is law all about?'

The law serves to perpetuate the rule of law, thereby protecting all citizens equally

You should recognise that while the rule of law is an important common law doctrine, there will be times when you may consider that the rule of law may be used by those in power unfairly. For example, the Coalition and Labor Federal Government's push to pass legislation to enable the Northern Territory Emergency Response (the 'Intervention') in 2007 and the Stronger Futures Policy in 2011 (respectively) may be seen as a welcome means to achieve protection for children who were said to be exposed to sexual abuse.[10] However, an alternative perspective is that the laws enacted in 2007 and 2011, which addressed few of the recommendations in the *Little Children are Sacred* report, were only brought about because of the archaic retention of the 'race' power in s 51(26) of the Constitution. That is, the race power enabled the suspension of the *Racial Discrimination Act 1975* (Cth) and deprived Aboriginal Australian communities of certain human rights, such as control over their money, food choices and social activities.

---

10 http://www.inquirysaac.nt.gov.au/pdf/bipacsa_final_report.pdf and *Ampe Akelyernemane Meke Mekarle "Little Children are Sacred"* Report

Separation of powers

The law is a powerful device. If it is used unfairly or unwisely it may cause incredible damage to citizens in any legal system. To avoid the arbitrary—or unfair—use of law by the government of the day, the philosophical notion of the 'separation of powers' has been adopted in Australia. The Commonwealth Constitution provides for the formal separation of powers in ss 51, 61, and 71. You should examine these sections by visiting AustLII.[11]

The separation of powers effectively means that each of the three arms of government—the parliament/legislature, the judiciary, and the executive—is limited to performing functions that are typical of each. For instance, the executive should not perform judicial functions, such as sentencing convicted offenders. Nor should the judiciary attempt to make new law when that role should be left to parliament; the judiciary traditionally has the role of applying the law. Of course there is sometimes overlap between the three sets of functions allocated to the respective arms of government, and many of the more famous and controversial legal and constitutional events and issues occur as a result of that overlap. The *Mabo* case is viewed by some commentators as an instance of the court making new law as opposed to applying the law as it existed.

International law

International law developed out of the diplomatic relationships between states (as countries are known in the international sphere) over the centuries. International law has two main sources:

- Treaties, or written agreements between states to comply with an agreed set of statements—treaties may be bilateral (between two states) or multilateral (between many states). Treaties may also be described (a little inaccurately) as conventions, covenants, and protocols.
- Customary international law—this is the common law in the international sphere. Customary international law arises from the longstanding customs and practices of the states concerned.

International law is the law that applies between states; it works through the agreements between states

In addition to treaties and customary international law, the international community also places reliance upon the resolutions of international bodies

11 http://www.austlii.edu.au/au/legis/cth/consol_act/coaca430 (accessed 22 August 2013).

(such as the United Nations) and the works of internationally respected jurists when determining the legal status of international matters.

There are three main difficulties for international law. First, international law gains its power by the agreement of states to abide by the agreements and relationships they enter, with due recognition for historical practices. International law only works when the states, the subject of international law, cooperate or conform. If a state decides that it does not wish to comply with international law, it can refuse to comply. This leads us to the next major difficulty. Because international law depends for its success on state parties voluntarily observing it, a state that decides not to observe the law cannot be punished, or brought into line, like private citizens can in the domestic setting. If a private citizen breaches the law, then that person may be brought before a court and sued (civil) or prosecuted (criminal). In the international sphere, however, there is no international court or enforcement body that can force compliance. States may agree to decisions being made against them in the international courts, but the states have consented to that scenario by virtue of the 'opt-in' devices that underpin these courts.

In the international sphere there is no enforcement body that can force compliance

Finally, international law does not operate in a vacuum. It requires state parties to come together and work through issues in situations where those state parties may have extremely large differences in regard to: domestic politics and agendas; cultural, political, or religious leanings; economic or military power; and physical or human resources.

International law may be contrasted with domestic law in that international law derives its power from the agreement between states to adhere to the commitments they make, whereas domestic law derives its power from an all-powerful sovereign (the three arms of government), which can force its citizens to adhere to that domestic law.

Common terms

In addition to being exposed to the central concepts and themes running through the law, you will find in your years at law school that there is a never-ending range of new terms to understand. What we provide below is, again, a brief taste of what some of the more prevalent terms you will encounter mean.

Common law

The 'common law' is a term that has acquired several meanings over the centuries. Your lecturers may use this term frequently, and may also use it in the variety of ways open to them without explanation as to its different senses. It is therefore essential that you can understand the essence of this term in the different contexts in which it may be used:

- Common law is the term most commonly used to refer to judge-made law, also known as the law made in and by the courts, or even the general law. Common law in this sense may be contrasted directly with the statute law as made by parliament (see 'Statutes and parliament', below).
- Common law is also the term used to describe the law that originated from the courts of common law. These common law courts created the criminal law, contract law, and the law of torts. Common law in this sense may be contrasted with the law that derived from specialty courts, such as the courts of equity and admiralty. For example, the common law provides that in the event that someone breaches a contract, or other civil obligation, the result will normally be that the person breaching will pay the party harmed an amount of money (known as 'damages') to compensate the harmed person for their loss. However, the law developed via equity may allow a person who has been wronged by a breach of contract to apply for an injunction (stopping the breaching party from doing something) or cause them to specifically perform something they had contracted to do.
- Common law is a term that may also be used to describe the system of law that is used in 'common law countries'. Common law countries include: England, Australia, New Zealand, India, and Fiji. Common law as a system of law may be contrasted with the legal systems based upon Roman and Napoleonic statute (the civil law (or inquisitorial system), or those that are based upon political (socialist) or religious power (Sharia law)).

Statutes and parliament

Statute = Act = legislation

'Statute law' is a term that is also known by various synonyms including simply 'statute', 'Acts', 'legislation', and 'parliamentary law'. Statute law is the law made by parliament and therefore is easily contrasted with the common law, as the processes for the generation of the two types of law are completely different. There are two legislative bodies that affect any one Australian citizen at any one time. They are the federal parliament, or Commonwealth parliament, and the state or territory parliament from the place where the citizen normally resides. In addition to the two parliaments that normally affect a person living in one jurisdiction, there are bodies to which parliament delegates power to make law. Examples of bodies that make delegated legislation are local councils and government departments. Delegated legislation is known by a variety of names including: by-laws, regulations, ordinances, and rules.

Substantive v procedural/adjectival law

'Substantive law' is the law related to specific rights, duties, and obligations that exist and are recognised in our legal system. Examples of substantive law include the criminal law and contract law. 'Procedural' or 'adjectival law' is the law that has as its main purpose the establishment of a system for the use of substantive law. For example, in the courts we use court rules and rules of evidence to allow us to deal with a case in an ordered and just way. Without those rules the substantive interests of the parties may not surface or be established.

The role of 'procedural law' is to establish a system for the use of substantive law

Ratio decidendi and *obiter dicta*

Ratio decidendi (ratio) is literally 'the reason for the decision'. The ratio is the part of a case that is of precedent value. It is the part of a case that binds future judges where the rules of precedent apply. *Obiter dicta* (obiter) are the 'by the way' comments used by judges when they state a personal preference or make a decision on a matter that is not an issue in the case.

The ratio is the part of a case that binds future judges

Proof

'Proof' is a term that denotes a number of things. In addition to the mode by which a party attempts to prove something in court, or the elements of an offence or action, proof is normally used in relation to the question of who has the burden of proof, and what is the standard of evidence that must be satisfied in a court. 'Burden of proof' refers to the obligation, or onus, on a party to make its case. In criminal matters, the prosecution (normally) always has the burden of proving the case against the defendant, or accused. Except in limited circumstances a defendant in a criminal matter has no corresponding evidential burden. In civil matters, the plaintiff has the burden of establishing a case and the defendant has an equivalent burden to show that the plaintiff is unsuccessful.

In criminal matters, the 'standard of proof' that the prosecution must reach in order to be successful in a prosecution is 'beyond reasonable doubt'. In civil matters, the standard that must be reached by either party to be successful is 'on the balance of probabilities'.

Burden of proof refers to responsibility; standard of proof refers to quality

Legal ethics

We have referred to legal ethics and professional conduct a number of times throughout this book. The reason for the multiple references to legal ethics is that it is central to the work of those who practise law. If your desire is to become a legal practitioner, you must be intimately aware of legal ethics. Below, we provide a brief explanation of the regulation of legal practitioners and indicate some of the core ideas that may be derived from the legal ethics literature.

Regulation of the legal profession

The legal profession is regulated by professional bodies and legal services commissioners in each state and territory. The authority to regulate is granted by each state and territory parliament. Each jurisdiction has its own legislation, such as the *Legal Profession Act 2004* (NSW), and common law and tribunal findings. While each jurisdiction operates largely autonomously, there is significant similarity between regulatory laws and ethical rules due to various attempts at developing a unified national system for the legal profession. For instance, all jurisdictions now recognise the admission of legal practitioners in other Australian jurisdictions, thus providing for easier movement between states and territories for legal practitioners (discussed in Chapter 2).

The professional bodies in each state and territory have different names and memberships but are usually known as the local 'Law Society',

'Law Institute', or 'Bar Association'. These bodies have been created by solicitors and barristers, and work for the benefit of members. An important function that many of these professional bodies have is to monitor and discipline the behaviour of members. If a solicitor or barrister engages in misconduct, the professional bodies are often the place where investigations and disciplining begin or occur.

'LAWYER' OR 'LEGAL PRACTITIONER'

A quick point about terminology. Throughout this book we have primarily used the term 'lawyer' to refer to law school graduates and/or those practising law. The existing legal profession legislation makes the following distinctions between lawyers and legal practitioners:

- An Australian lawyer is someone admitted to the legal profession.
- An Australian legal practitioner is an Australian lawyer who holds a current practising certificate.

What this means is as follows:

- Once you graduate from your law degree you are considered to be a 'law school graduate'.
- If you undertake a course in practical legal training—such as a Reading or Readers' Course with a Bar Association, or a Graduate Diploma in Legal Practice—you may then be eligible for admission to the legal profession. If you apply for admission to the legal profession, and are admitted, you will be entitled to call yourself a 'lawyer'.
- If you are admitted to the legal profession, are eligible to obtain a practising certificate, apply for a practising certificate, and are granted such a certificate, then you may call yourself a 'legal practitioner'.
- By virtue of their practical legal training, and local rules, a legal practitioner may be called a 'solicitor', 'barrister', or 'solicitor and barrister'.

In each state and territory there is legislation prohibiting the use of the title of (or falsely representing that one is a) legal practitioner.

THE FUTURE FOR A NATIONAL PROFESSION

In 2009, the Commonwealth Attorney-General's Department initiated and has since overseen a National Legal Profession Reform project. This project has seen the development of model legal profession national legislation, and, with the Law Council of Australia and the Australian Bar Association, model rules of professional conduct. The model rules of professional conduct have been accepted by some professional bodies, and are thus in force, in several jurisdictions. The model legal profession national legislation has not been accepted by the professional bodies of all jurisdictions and, in those jurisdictions where professional bodies have accepted the draft national legislation, the parliaments of those jurisdictions have not yet passed that law.

What is legal ethics?

It would be necessary to have a significantly longer book in order to discuss fully all the ethical tenets of the legal profession. Indeed, you will be studying a whole unit in professional responsibility and legal ethics as part of your law course. Here, we wish to impart, in general terms, some of the key principles and perspectives that underpin professional practice.

LEGAL ETHICS MAY NOT STRICTLY COINCIDE WITH EVERYDAY ETHICS

There are a number of schools of thought regarding how legal ethics should be taught and what legal ethics is designed to do. Some take the view that legal ethics should be considered a profession-specific example of a broader body of general ethical thinking. Others view legal ethics as a set of broad principles that guide a legal practitioner's behaviour in practice. And still others see legal ethics as a discrete set of rules of practice that simply need to be complied with, as one would comply with any rules. The problem is that none of these views, in isolation, is completely satisfactory. For instance, if one's perspective is that legal ethics is simply an extension of general ethics, then arguably some of the rules of legal ethics may need to be changed because they are inconsistent with general ethics. If one's view is that legal ethics is simply a body of 'positive law' rules, then a legal practitioner would be perfectly entitled to circumvent the purpose of those rules if a sound legal argument could be found to justify the circumvention. Accordingly, we suggest that legal ethics needs to be seen as a delicate, and nuanced, set of interlinked principles, guides and rules, which requires consistent and sustained consideration throughout one's professional life. However, at the risk of not heeding our own advice, we now list some of the better known central ideas.

LEGAL ETHICS ENTAILS DUTIES AND RESPONSIBILITIES

There are three broad areas in which legal practitioners owe duties. They are duty to the client, duty to the court, and duty to the law.

Duty to the client

The creation of a professional relationship between legal practitioner and client means, in simple terms, that in exchange for the fee paid by the client a practitioner owes the following duties to the client:

- Duty of confidentiality—a practitioner must not disclose material provided to the practitioner by the client in confidence, except where compelled by law or with the client's consent. The duty of confidentiality lasts for life and, accordingly, if a practitioner is retained by a new client against a former client, the practitioner may be required not to represent the new client if there is a real possibility that the former client's confidentiality may be breached.
- Duty of loyalty—subject to limited exceptions, a practitioner owes complete fidelity to their client and must not prefer the practitioner's own interest, or those of another person, over the interests of their client in relation to the client's legal matter.
- Duty of competence—upon entering into a retainer (contract) to represent a client, a practitioner is required to act professionally and to the standard expected of a reasonably competent legal practitioner. Failure to act competently may result in the practitioner being sued by the client.
- Duty to protect the client's money—not all practitioners hold money on behalf of a client, but for those who do, the money is considered to be 'trust money' and the practitioner must comply with trust money provisions in their jurisdiction. This means that if a client gives the practitioner money,

then the practitioner must not use that money in any way except by clear direction from the client, or as directed by a court. Put simply, a practitioner is not entitled to take the money from the trust account to pay for the practitioner's fees, or give to someone else, unless the client has given clear authority for the practitioner to do so.

Duty to the court

The fact that law and justice are so publicly dispensed in the courts has resulted in strict obligations upon practitioners to uphold the dignity of the courts and assist the courts to make decisions based on the best evidence and arguments available:

- Duty not to mislead as to the facts—a legal practitioner must not state to the court something the practitioner knows is, or believes may be, untrue. Where a practitioner becomes aware that the court has been accidentally misled, the practitioner must inform the court of the error.
- Duty not to mislead as to the law—a legal practitioner has an obligation to ensure that the most current law is being used by the court. In circumstances where a practitioner is aware that the court is proceeding on the basis of incorrect or outdated law, the practitioner must bring the relevant law to the courts attention, even if it is against their client's interest.
- Duty not to misuse their position—a legal practitioner's status means they have certain rights in court that no-one else has. A practitioner must not abuse those rights. For example, a practitioner must not use the privilege against defamation—the right to say things in court without being sued for possibly defamatory comments—as an opportunity to launch an unfounded attack upon an opposing client, practitioner, or third party.

Duty to the law

Lawyers, upon admission to the legal profession, become officers of their Supreme Court. Accordingly, and especially while performing legal work, legal practitioners are required to uphold the law and comply with the rules governing the legal system. If a practitioner decides to engage in significant criminal activities, as opposed to minor criminal breaches, and those criminal activities come to light, a practitioner may be prohibited from practising law and have their name, literally, removed from the roll of lawyers, on the basis that they are unable to provide fidelity (duty) to the law.

Other duties

Other obligations include:

- Duty to comply with civic obligations—legal practitioners are not permitted to ignore, or deliberately avoid, their obligations as citizens, such as by using bankruptcy laws to avoid paying significant income tax bills.
- Duty to honour undertakings—undertaking are promises provided by practitioners to each other to permit legal work to be conducted expeditiously. For instance, a practitioner may undertake to have a specified document delivered to the opposing practitioner as part of an urgent commercial transaction. This undertaking may be given so as to avoid the parties needing to go to court to have orders made for the document's delivery. If a practitioner fails to deliver the document in accordance with the terms of the undertaking, then that practitioner has, without proper excuse, engaged in misconduct.

Conclusion

There are myriad examples and rules and principles that could have been included here. We have focused on several of the main ones. We urge you to consider legal ethics very carefully, whether you intend to practise law or not. If you do intend to practise law, you must be aware that a breach of your legal ethical responsibilities may result in you being precluded from practice. If you do not intend to practise law, you should be aware that your law school will be applying the principles of ethical conduct for legal practitioners to your behaviour at law school. A breach of the broad principles of candour and honesty may result in academic misconduct proceedings (for more on this, see Chapter 12).

9

SOURCES OF LAW

There is a crucial difference between courts and legislators. It exists at the threshold of their respective activities. Courts do not choose their controversies. They do not entirely control the matters that they decide or the issues that they tackle. Many chance considerations affect the ascent of a controversy to a nation's highest court.

The Honourable Justice Michael Kirby.[1]

1 Kirby, The Hon. Justice M.D., 'Through the World's Eye' (Sydney: The Federation Press, 2000), at 93–4.

Introduction

Law comes from two sources: state, territory and federal parliaments; and, the courts. Parliamentary law is embodied in statutes also known as Acts of Parliament, or legislation, which are rules passed by the respective parliaments. Parliaments also delegate the power to make rules to certain persons or organisations and this sort of law is commonly called subordinate legislation. A typical example of subordinate legislation is the rules made by local councils. The second type of law is made by judges sitting in the various state or territory and Commonwealth courts. The law from courts is called common law, although these days it is more colloquially known as the general law, which embodies both common and equitable rules of law.

Law comes from either the parliament or the courts

The reason new laws, or amendments to old laws, come about is interesting and a crucial element of the system of democracy we cherish so much in Australia. Statutes sometimes come into existence, or are amended, because the community places political pressure on the various political parties that affects their chances of being elected. If enough members of the community want to see new or amended laws in place, they exert pressure on their local members of parliament or create lobby groups that attempt to coerce politicians into changing or introducing new laws. This process is crucial to the system of democracy because politicians should respond to the concerns of the community or act with the view of protecting or making the lives of members of the community better by enacting certain legislation.

Statutes are passed because of any number of pressures exerted on politicians

As to the general law, judges do not act with community concerns in mind. Judges act according to law. That is, they decide cases based on precedent, a concept discussed in Chapter 5. In other words, while judges are not bound by their own or the court's previous decisions, they are bound by the findings of a higher court within their own jurisdiction. For example, state and territory Supreme Courts are bound by the decisions of their respective Courts of Appeal, and although those Courts of Appeal do not bind themselves, they are bound by decisions of the High Court of Australia. Similarly, the High Court of Australia is not bound by its own previous decisions and may change the general law at any point in time that it feels justified to do so.

Courts are bound by the decisions of higher courts

The relationship between the parliament and the courts can be described by the concept of the 'separation of powers'. This means that the parliament and the courts are separate from each other and their functions and powers are mutually exclusive. Therefore, courts are not subjected to external political influence, which protects the application of justice for purely political motives. This is one of the hallmarks of a fair and just democracy and prevents the concentration of power within either the government or the judiciary. The separation of powers doctrine is derived by the layout of the constitution that describes the composition and powers of the executive government (cabinet), the legislature (parliament), and the judiciary as being separate from each other. It is argued that the line of separation between the executive government and the parliament is a little blurred under the Australian party political system. This is because the executive government is chosen from members of the political party with the most elected members in the House of Representatives that ultimately forms government by virtue of the fact that it enjoys the confidence of the House of Representatives. That is, it can defeat a vote of no confidence against it by virtue of having a majority of votes on the floor of the House of Representatives.

The Commonwealth constitution provides that the executive, the parliament, and the judiciary have separate powers

This notion of the separation of powers is a concept not widely understood, particularly by members of the media on occasions where in a high profile criminal case the accused is found guilty and receives what is perceived by the media to be a light sentence. The media call for judges to sentence according to community outcry when in fact it is the politicians who must pass sentencing legislation that reflects valid community concerns. Judges do not and should not respond to community concerns about these sorts of issues as they are matters for the public to take up with their elected members of parliament. If judges did decide cases and make judgments based on public outcry, then justice would be administered according to purely political motivations and not necessarily according to law. The danger of this would be inconsistent sentencing and law-making that responded in a 'knee jerk' way to whatever the latest public outcry may be. The proper process is to allow politicians to debate in a proper forum the positives and negatives of such changes to the law and formulate any changes in a reasoned and just way.

The separation of powers doctrine ensures that courts do not pass judgments under political pressure

It is important to understand the sources of law before understanding how to research it

This chapter considers these two sources of law in detail and discusses how they should be read and understood. As you need to understand the sources of law before seeking to understand how to research it, you should read this chapter prior to reading Chapter 10.

Primary and secondary sources of law

Primary sources of law are created by the courts deciding cases and the parliament passing legislation. That is, primary sources of law are law-making bodies that contribute to the creation of enforceable law. For example, in the case of legislation, political parties make law through the parliament according to their political agenda. Enforcement of legislation is carried out by the responsible prosecuting body generally set out in the legislation itself. For example, the enforcement and prosecution of matters under the respective criminal codes in each state and territory is carried out by the police and the Director of Public Prosecutions or their equivalents. Parliament may also delegate its law-making power to persons or bodies. Examples of such persons or organisations are the governor of each state or local councils. These people and bodies are empowered to make rules or regulations that are classed as being law so as to alleviate the burden on the parliament in having to make day-to-day or minor decisions. The enforcement of judge-made law proceeds through the courts, which apply the law as it has been created by the respective judge or judges.

Primary sources of law are those sources made by law-making bodies

Secondary sources of law are essentially commentaries on primary sources of law

Secondary sources of law include textbooks, journal articles, and law reform commission reports. They are those sources of law that are essentially commentaries on the primary sources of law and do not originate in the two law-making institutions of the courts or parliaments.

Courts are only bound by primary sources of law

It is important to note that courts are only bound by primary sources of law and generally must obey the law as set out by those sources of law. The one notable exception to that rule is where precedent (the legal principles created by case law) is distinguished or overruled by a court. However, secondary sources of law may be influential and judges frequently will be persuaded by academics and other commentators on the law to change their view on a certain legal issue based on scholarly research and opinion So, while secondary sources of law are not binding on courts, they may be persuasive. The remainder of this chapter deals with reading and understanding the two primary sources of law in Australia, cases and legislation.

Secondary sources, while not binding, may be influential on a court

Reading cases

Given that cases are classed as a primary source of law, you, as a law student and then as a lawyer, will read a vast number of them. In most black letter law subjects (those subjects that deal with the actual law and not a theoretical treatment of the law) your reading load while you are a student will require you to read at least ten cases per week per subject, sometimes more. Given such a workload, you need to ensure that you understand what you are reading and have a system of recording what you have read in order to use it more efficiently later on in learning opportunities and assessment. Cases reported in law reports are broken up into several parts:

You should understand and effectively record every case you read

a) Case name—including the legal role ascribed to the parties (for example, plaintiff/defendant or appellant/respondent).
b) Catchwords—describing the type of law raised by the issues in the case (for example, 'Contract-Consideration-Whether consideration was Sufficient').
c) Summary of the facts—that will generally not go into all the complex elements of the case.
d) What the court held—including the majority and individual reasoning of the judges and any dissenting judgments in summary form. Where appropriate, this part may split up the various judgments according to the different issues raised by the case. It may also refer you to the page numbers where the ratio is given by a particular judge or majority judgment.
e) History of the case—this is used more frequently to give a history of the appeal process and how the case found its way to the court.
f) Submissions of the plaintiff or appellant—including the legal argument supported by the relevant law.
g) Submissions of the defendant or respondent—including the legal argument supported by the relevant law.

h) Judgments—the majority judgment usually appears first, or the judgment of the chief judge of the relevant jurisdiction followed by any other judges hearing the case.
i) Orders—including any remedy or whether the case is to be returned to the court of original jurisdiction for hearing according to the established law as set out in the judgment.

The above description does not apply to computer-based judgments. Those judgments do not contain a detailed head note written by the law reporter. Therefore, such reports generally do not have a summary of the facts, other than those provided by each judge in the body of the judgment, and they will not have the submissions and the concomitant law as put by the parties to the case. They tend to just report the actual judgments as handed down by the respective judges.

Computer-reported judgments do not contain head notes

The term 'head note' is generally reserved for points a) to d) that provide a summary of the case and what the court held. There is a temptation for students to only read head notes of cases as a way to save time. You should not be satisfied with reading just the head notes of cases, the primary reason being that head notes are usually written by a barrister or solicitor commentator and do not form part of the judgment. The judgment begins with the first listed judge. Head notes do not set out the full reasoning of the court and they do not correlate the persuasive elements of the facts with the law. It is this correlation that is important in understanding case law. Today's law students have case books and a vast array of electronic databases and other resources that provide excerpts of these correlations while omitting the other parts of the judgment that are not directly related to the findings of the court. Therefore, your reading load is made a lot easier by the use of these resources. However, not all case books have every case you are required to read, so it is inevitable that you will be required to read at least some cases in the law reports or in loose leaf form or through the internet for unreported judgments, in which case the following comments should be of some significance.

Head notes do not set out the full reasoning of the court

Matters to note when reading cases

When reading cases, ensure you understand what you are reading

Dealing with the first issue of understanding what you are reading, there are several things to look out for that will ensure you have a better understanding of the case.

FACTS

It is very important to have a firm understanding of the facts in the case before the court. The reasoning of the court will come down to the facts before it, so understanding them is the first step to understanding the court's decision. The facts can be found in two places in the judgment. Usually whoever is the editor of the law report in which the case appears will give a summary of the facts under the case name in the head note. This will usually be an abbreviated version of the facts that will omit, depending on the case, a number of key elements of the fact pattern. However, it will give you an overview of the case. The best account of the facts is given by the judges themselves. A judge will usually begin her or his judgment with a fairly thorough account of the facts of the case. Where there is more than one judge on the bench, a designated judge will usually recite the facts and thereafter the other judges will just refer to the facts already recited. However, sometimes when the judges have not conferred with each other over the structure of the final judgment, you will read a repetition of the facts by more than one judge or a version of the facts that emphasises the difference in reasoning adopted by the respective judge or judges.

Your understanding of the facts is crucial to understanding the court's reasoning

The subject you are studying and the topic at hand will determine what facts are material to the decision made by the court. For example, in contract law cases where the issue may be the formation of a valid contract at law, the facts that relate to who said what and when may be material. The dates that people sent correspondence to each other could be important to establishing whether a valid offer has been validly accepted. Therefore, when reading the fact pattern of relevant cases you should pay particular attention to such details. In subjects involving consumer protection legislation, what a retailer said to a consumer or what was printed in an advertising brochure will be important to whether the court holds that the retailer misled or deceived the consumer. Such facts are material or relevant to the court's deliberations and therefore should be of importance to you when reading the facts of the case.

Discovering the relevant facts will be dependent on the issue before the court

You should actively seek out those facts that you think will help you understand what the court ultimately held and why they found the way they did. When it comes time to read the body of the judgment, a thorough understanding of the facts will assist you to quickly come to terms with why the judges

Understanding the relevant facts will assist you to understand the decision of the court

found the way they did and how they applied the prevailing law. In other words, understanding the facts of a case is the foundation for understanding the judgment of the court.

THE FINDINGS OF THE COURT

Once having understood the facts of the case, the next important step is to understand the findings of the court. The head note will give you the legal proposition derived from the case, but what is crucial to your ability to analyse and synthesise facts and law is to understand what elements of the facts before the court allowed the court to apply the law the way it did. It is the judges' reasoning that is important to understand when reading cases. You must read the judgments, or if using a case book, the extracts of the judgments, and determine what was the most persuasive factor, or factors, that led the judge to find the way that she or he did. An example of the persuasive elements of a case is given below when discussing the writing of case notes.

Discover the persuasive factors that led the court to its decision

Most judges will describe their findings in a way that will allow you to distil what the persuasive factor in the fact pattern before the court was. Like the legal problem-solving model discussed in Chapter 5, judges review the facts, state the issue or issues, preview the law that applies, argue the various sides of applying the law and then draw a conclusion and make orders. This is why some judgments can seem rather long—so that the judge can properly canvass the issues and the law. However, usually at some stage during the judgment, usually towards the end of the argument and when approaching the conclusion, the judge will express the persuasive factor in one or more sentences. This is called the *ratio decidendi* (ratio). The term is Latin and means the reason for deciding. The ratio is important for two reasons: first, it contains a very useful legal proposition that can be used when justifying the reference to a particular case; second, it sums up the case and the common law created or affirmed by the case.

Look for the ratio in the majority judgments

Another important element when reading a case is to note whether the findings of the court were unanimous or whether the decision of the court was a bare majority. In each state and territory the Courts of Appeal generally sit with three judges; similarly the full bench of the Federal Court will

Whether the decision of the court was unanimous or a bare majority can be important

sit with three judges and the High Court will generally sit with one, three, five, or the full seven justices. Usually where there is more than one judge sitting on the bench there will be an uneven number of judges so that there can never be a deadlock. So ascertaining whether the decision was, arrived at unanimously by the full bench of the High Court (7:0) or by a bare majority (4:3) can be of some importance. If three High Court judges disagree with the other four judges, then the case is not as clear cut as a majority decision and there is potential that the decision may be overturned at some time in the future depending on the future composition of the bench. Despite the potential of the decision being overturned in the future, you should also consider that three eminent legal minds have disagreed with the findings of four other eminent legal minds, and that in itself says something about the arguments raised in the case and the arguments you can use in your studies.

DISSENTING JUDGMENTS

Sometimes judges disagree on the outcome of a case. Those judges who disagree with the majority of judges are called 'dissentients'. While dissenting judgments do not carry any weight in terms of the case precedent, sometimes these judgments can be influential on later cases of a similar kind. Often you will read in judgments that a judge prefers the view of a dissenting judge over the view of the majority in a previously quoted case. Therefore, sometimes it is worthwhile noting the reasoning of the dissentients, particularly in cases where the ultimate decision was a bare majority.

Dissenting judgments can be influential in later cases

THE LEVEL OF THE COURT

Finally, you should note the level of the court handing down the decision. For example, a single judge of the Supreme Court is less persuasive than three judges of the Court of Appeal or, in turn, seven judges of the High Court of Australia. As previously discussed, the High Court is the highest court of appeal in Australia and its decisions are binding on all lower courts. However, be careful, because if the High Court, or the respective state or territory Court of Appeal, has not pronounced on an issue, then you may be left with a situation where two single judges of the respective Supreme Court disagree with each other—as occurred

Understand whether the judgment binds lower courts

in the cases of *Elizabeth Bay Developments Pty Ltd v Boral Building Services Pty Ltd* (1995) 36 NSWLR 709 and *Aiton Australia Pty Ltd v Transfield Pty Ltd* (1999) 153 FLR 236 where two single judges of the same court disagreed with each other on the issue of the enforceability of good faith negotiation in the performance of a contract. In such cases the law has not been settled and really requires a Court of Appeal or High Court decision on the matter.

Writing case notes

Reading a case and not writing a case note is a waste of time

Sometimes throughout your studies you will need a mental prompt to explain the significance of a certain case. Unless you have a photographic memory or have worked very hard to memorise the case, among the many cases you will have to read and understand, you will be stuck for an answer. In such circumstances the value of reading the case in the first place has been lost. You will only waste time if you have to go back and reread the case. Therefore, it makes sense to make a case note for every case you read. Writing a case note takes a little extra time at the time you read a case but pays dividends when it comes time to prepare for classes and assessment.

Work out a way to manage your case notes

There are many different ways of writing and managing case notes. Some students keep their case notes in an index card box in alphabetical order or in topic order devoting one index card only to each case. Some students keep their case notes alphabetically in a loose-leaf folder, again devoting a single A4 page to each case note. Some students keep their case notes on a computer database that can sort the cases in any number of ways depending on the fields created in the database. If cases are downloaded from case law databases, most storage software programs, such as Adobe Acrobat and Goodreader for Apple, provide facilities such as underlining, text shading or 'post-it-note' style comments where you can annotate cases just like writing notes on a hard copy of the case. These systems allow you to write case notes noting at the exact place in the judgment and saving in a variety of formats for future use.

Whichever way you keep your case notes, make sure they are easy to access and cases are easy to find when you need them. There is nothing worse than knowing you wrote a case note on a case and being unable to find it. To have to reread the case and write another case note is clearly time-wasting. Chapter 7 sets out the elements that you should consider including in your case notes.

Reading statutes

Courts are frequently called upon to interpret statutes that have been drafted by parliamentary drafters, who seek to put into words the sentiments of a parliament, which is composed of many different political and philosophical views. The task is not an easy one and a series of rules and maxims or methods has been developed by the court system, and parliaments, to assist lawyers and citizens in reading Acts of parliament, particularly when there is a sense of ambiguity. Over the years, parliaments have adopted certain rules to make the drafting of statutes easier and more similar in their form. The task still comes down to expressing the wishes of the prevailing government as accurately as possible.

Statutes reflect the sentiments of the parliament

The job of the parliamentary drafter is to take the intentions of the parliament and draft words that reflect those intentions. While there are state, territory and federal offices of parliamentary counsel that are responsible for drafting statutes, statutes all largely conform to a standard format that usually consists of the elements set out in Table 9.1.

TABLE 9.1 General form of a statute

Element	Content and purpose
Name of the statute—short title	The short title of the statute
Name of the statute—long title	The long title of the statute
Contents	The table of contents of the statute
Commencement	When the statute is to commence operation
Objects	The objects of the statute—what it hopes to achieve
Headings	Headings that break up the content of the statute but are not part of the statute
Sections	Numbered sections of the statute that break it up into logical chunks
Subsections	That take a section and expand upon it through further explanation
Paragraphs	That further explain the subsections
Subparagraphs	That further explain the paragraphs
Schedules	That provide an array of additional information about the statute such as: table of amendments; transitional arrangements; penalties; application of the statute
Dictionary or definitions	Some statutes leave the dictionary or definitions to last

Commonality among the states, territories, and the Commonwealth

Interpretation acts help explain how to read statutes

Each state and territory and the Commonwealth have interpretation acts that assist in the task of interpreting statutes. Some say that interpretation acts are themselves large dictionaries on how to interpret the statutes of a state, territory, or the Commonwealth. This description is partly true. Interpretation Acts seek to explain how to read statutes within a given jurisdiction. They cover a wide variety of issues but they also have many common sections that cover how to interpret statutes. For example, the various interpretation statutes in Australia all have provisions that allow for statutes drafted in one gender to import the other gender and for statutes that specify the singular to import the plural.

Methods of interpretation

The courts have developed various methods of interpreting statutes

The courts have developed various methods to interpret statutes. They are called methods as opposed to rules as it seems that not one method has authority over the other, except perhaps in the case of the purposive method discussed below. The following is a summary of the aforementioned methods.

THE LITERAL METHOD

Interpret statutes so that the words are applied according to their literal meaning

The literal method provides that judges will be bound by the words of the statute when those words clearly cover the facts before the court. That is, the words are literally applied according to their accepted meaning and nothing is added or taken away from that meaning. This is a foundational position for interpreting statutes in that the literal method applies when the statute is clear and unambiguous, and other methods of interpretation should not be used if the statute is clear in its meaning. In *Amalgamated Society of Engineers v Adelaide Steamship Co Ltd* (1920) 28 CLR 129, Higgins J sitting in the High Court defined the literal method of statutory interpretation when his Honour stated, at 161–2:

> The fundamental rule of interpretation … is that a statute is to be expounded according to the intent of the Parliament … and that

> intention has to be found by an examination of the language used in the statute as a whole. The question is, what does the language mean; and when we find out what the language means, in its ordinary and natural sense, it is our duty to obey that meaning …

An oft-quoted criticism of the literal method is that it assumes that words have one meaning only. Of course this is a falsehood. When people speak to each other they often use words in a certain context that allows another meaning of the word. For example, the word 'complex' can mean either something consisting of many parts, or a psychological condition, or a building. The meaning of the word depends upon its context. Such a shortcoming is one of the endearing features of the context method of interpretation that allows the word to be interpreted in the context of the section it appears within.

The literal method does not allow for different meanings of the same word

THE GOLDEN METHOD

The golden method of interpretation allows judges to interpret statutes with a sensible meaning as opposed to an absurd meaning, where both are possible from an interpretation point of view. In other words, where one interpretation would result in an absurd or inequitable finding by the court, the golden method allows the court to interpret the statute to produce a result that avoids the absurdity and inequity. Often an absurd or inequitable result will occur because there has been an error in the drafting of the statute that if interpreted literally would produce such a result. In such cases the golden rule is invoked to prevent the absurdity. Using the golden rule implies that the judge knows what is 'just' or 'equitable'.

Interpret statutes with a sensible meaning and not an absurd meaning

THE MISCHIEF METHOD

The mischief method requires the judges to look at the 'mischief' or problem or issue that the statute was introduced to prohibit, control or organise. To do this the judges need to consider the position of the common law, and society, before the statute existed and examine the statute in the light of the 'mischief' that the statute was meant to avoid. Then, the statute should be interpreted so as to prevent the mischief and consistent with the remedy provided by the statute itself. In other words, judges should interpret the statute consistent with fixing

Interpret statutes to prevent the mischief the statute was meant to avoid

the problem that the statute was first intended to solve. An important concept here is the notion that in many cases statutes were introduced in order to solve a problem, usually some form of inequity that existed in the common law. In such cases the parliament often steps in and passes legislation in order to remedy the problem and restore a sense of fairness in the application of the law. When applying the mischief method the judge will look closely at the language used by parliament when drafting the statute, and given the judge's experience and knowledge of applying the common law, she or he will be able to recognise the mischief sought to be avoided by the parliament and interpret the statute so as to avoid such mischief.

THE PURPOSE METHOD

The purpose method provides that the court will determine the purpose parliament had in passing the statute and ensure that the interpretation of the statute is consistent with that purpose. It is generally agreed that this method should only be used where the meaning of the words used in the statute are unclear. However, this method may also be invoked where the literal method produces a result that runs counter to parliament's purpose. The purpose method is similar to the mischief method and most commentators agree that the purpose method sprang from the mischief method because interpreting a statute to avoid the mischief the statute sought to prevent is very similar to interpreting a statute according to its purpose. Its purpose must generally seek to overcome the mischief that prevailed in the common law prior to the statute being enacted.

Interpret statutes consistent with the purpose of the statute

WHICH METHOD APPLIES?

It is important to note that there is no hard and fast rule as to which method should apply as it is generally a discretionary matter for the court. Some of the methods discussed in this chapter have been superseded by the amendment of the various interpretation Acts that endorse the purpose method. For example, in 2011 section 15AA was inserted into the *Acts Interpretation Act 1901* (Cth) and states:

Statutes now tend to promote the purpose method

> In interpreting a provision of an Act, the interpretation that would best achieve the purpose or object of the Act (whether or not that

> purpose or object is expressly stated in the Act) is to be preferred to each other interpretation.

Every state and territory of Australia has a similar provision that provides that when interpreting statutes in the respective state or territory, regard shall be had to the purpose and object of the statute. The statutes and their concomitant sections are as follows:

Each state and territory endorses the purpose method

- *Legislation Act 2001* (ACT)—s 139
- *Interpretation Act 1987* (NSW)—s 33
- *Interpretation Act* (NT)—s 62a
- *Acts Interpretation Act 1954* (Qld)—s 14a
- *Acts Interpretation Act 1915* (SA)—s 22
- *Acts Interpretation Act 1931* (Tas)—s 8a
- *Interpretation of Legislation Act 1984* (Vic)—s 35
- *Interpretation Act 1984* (WA)—s 18

So it seems that the purpose method is the statutorily endorsed method that provides that the purpose and object of the statute should be observed when interpreting statutes. The next question becomes, 'How do you determine the purpose and object of a statute?' The answer is quite simple. You just need to find out the purpose and object of the statute by looking at its long title or objectives section. For example, the New South Wales *Farm Debt Mediation Act 1994* lists its object in section 3 of the Act and states:

The purpose of a statute can be determined by its long title or its objectives section

> The object of this Act is to provide for the efficient and equitable resolution of farm debt disputes. Mediation is required before a creditor can take possession of property or other enforcement action under a farm mortgage.

Here the purpose and object of the Act can clearly be seen as being to promote the efficient and equitable resolution of farm debt disputes before a creditor may take action against a farmer to recover moneys under a farm mortgage. Therefore, under section 33 of the *Interpretation Act 1987* (NSW) the statute must be interpreted to promote that purpose and objective. Because of the Interpretation Acts, the purpose method of interpretation has been given pre-eminence over the other methods of interpretation.

Parliamentary draftspersons and courts will favour the purpose method of interpretation

However, there is not always a clear statement of purpose or objects in all legislation and the task of determining the purpose can result in multiple interpretations:

> Sometimes the purpose of the legislation is expressly stated; sometimes it can be discerned only by inference after an examination of the legislation as a whole; and sometimes it can be discerned only by reference to the history of the legislation and the state of the law when it was enacted. It need hardly be said that a particular Act may have many purposes.[2]

Maxims of interpretation

While it may seem clear that methods we have referred to make the task of statutory interpretation quite simple, the truth is that it is sometimes exceedingly complex. To assist in the interpretation of statutes there have been developed a series of maxims (often written in Latin) and guides to assist in interpreting certain limited statutory words and phrases. These rules and maxims may be seen as generalisations, so while they can be very useful they should be used with caution.

EJUSDEM GENERIS

'*Ejusdem generis*' means 'of the same kind'. If a statute lists a series of specific things and concludes the list with a general, catch-all phrase, this maxim can be used to assist in interpreting whether something not listed in the specific things can be caught by the catch-all phrase. For example, a section of an act may describe a vehicle as a 'car, truck, bus, motorcycle or any other mode of transport'. While a push-bike or a horse may possibly be considered a vehicle covered by this section (despite their not relying on motors to push them), would a submarine be covered?

NOSCITUR A SOCIIS

'*Noscitur a sociis*' means 'known by its associates'. It is a maxim that emphasises the context within which a word or phrase exists. This means that when trying

---

2 McHugh J in *Saraswati v The Queen* [1991] HCA 21 at para 7 of his Honour's judgment.

to interpret a word, phrase, or even a whole section of a statute, judges should look at the rest of the section in which the word or phrase appears or look at the whole of the division, part, or statute in order to obtain the meaning of the ambiguous word, phrase, or section. The context method highlights the fact that the same word appearing in a statute may carry different meanings depending on the context at the given point in the statute where the word appears. A specific example of *noscitur a sociis* is the case of *R v Ann Harris*,[3] where the defendant was charged pursuant to a section of an Act where the actions described within the section included: 'shoot ... stab, cut, or wound ... with intent to maim or disfigure ... shall be guilty of a felony'. The prisoner has bitten off the end of the nose of the victim. By applying *noscitur a sociis*, the court determined that the action of the prisoner was not consistent with the words specifically listed in the Act—'stab, cut or wound'. The prisoner could be found guilty of a different offence, but not for one under the Act in question.

EXPRESSIO UNIUS EST EXCLUSIO ALTERIUS

'*Expressio unius est exclusio alterius*' means 'the express reference to one thing excludes others'. This rule is designed to emphasise the fact that when parliament makes an express reference to one thing it may also be clearly excluding another. For example, if a prohibited place is defined as: 'a school, home, or church', a factory or shop, being expressly excluded from the list in the definition, would not be considered prohibited places.

Other general guidelines to interpretation of statutes

Without limiting the range of guidelines and maxims, the following are some of the other important general principles that apply to interpretation of statutes.

1 An Act should be read in its entirety in order to glean an understanding of its purpose and intent.
2 Later Acts impliedly amend earlier Acts to the extent of any inconsistency.
3 Later provisions within Acts that are general in nature do not impliedly amend earlier provisions within Acts that are specific in nature.

---

3 *R v Ann Harris* (1836) 173 ER 198.

4 In a definitions section, the operative word 'includes' indicates that the definition is not exhaustive. That is, the definition may be added to via judicial interpretation. In a definitions section, the operative word 'means' is considered to be all-encompassing. That is, courts will not imply other words into the definition when interpreting such definitions sections.
5 Acts of parliament do not operate retrospectively. Unless parliament clearly and unambiguously states otherwise, legislation takes effect from the day it becomes law. That is, an Act of parliament that comes into force today does not necessarily affect my behaviour from yesterday.
6 An Act is applicable to its jurisdiction only. That is, an Act only applies to the area or territory over which the parliament is sovereign.
7 Acts that impose a penalty, or empower arrest or detention, are typically narrowly read. In criminal legislation, an ambiguity within an Act will typically be read in favour of an accused where there is the prospect that a penalty or incarceration could result. Where the meaning is clear and unambiguous, or the intention of parliament can be clearly discerned, the rule narrow reading may not apply.

Intrinsic versus extrinsic materials

In determining the purpose of a statute, reference may be made to intrinsic and extrinsic materials. Intrinsic materials are literally parts of the Act within the body of the document. The intrinsic materials that may be used to assist in resolving ambiguities within an Act are: the Long Title, the Short Title, Preamble/Objects clause, Headings within the Act, Schedules. As a general rule these intrinsic materials can be used to resolve ambiguity but cannot be used if the meaning of a provision is plain. Please note that some parts of a printed Act are not considered intrinsic to the Act and cannot be used as above. These include margin notes, footnotes and endnotes.

Extrinsic materials are those materials not considered part of a statute, which may assist a court in determining the meaning of a word, phrase or provision. Extrinsic materials may be used in limited circumstances. Each jurisdiction provides guidance on the use of extrinsic materials consistent with the Commonwealth interpretation legislation.[4]

---

4 Section 15AB *Acts Interpretation Act 1901* (Cth).

S 15AB Use of extrinsic material in the interpretation of an Act

(1) Subject to subsection (3), in the interpretation of a provision of an Act, if any material not forming part of the Act is capable of assisting in the ascertainment of the meaning of the provision, consideration may be given to that material:
   (a) to confirm that the meaning of the provision is the ordinary meaning conveyed by the text of the provision taking into account its context in the Act and the purpose or object underlying the Act; or
   (b) to determine the meaning of the provision when:
      (i) the provision is ambiguous or obscure; or
      (ii) the ordinary meaning conveyed by the text of the provision taking into account its context in the Act and the purpose or object underlying the Act leads to a result that is manifestly absurd or is unreasonable.
(2) Without limiting the generality of subsection (1), the material that may be considered in accordance with that subsection in the interpretation of a provision of an Act includes:
   (a) all matters not forming part of the Act that are set out in the document containing the text of the Act as printed by the Government Printer;
   (b) any relevant report of a Royal Commission, Law Reform Commission, committee of inquiry or other similar body that was laid before either House of the Parliament before the time when the provision was enacted;
   (c) any relevant report of a committee of the Parliament or of either House of the Parliament that was made to the Parliament or that House of the Parliament before the time when the provision was enacted;
   (d) any treaty or other international agreement that is referred to in the Act;
   (e) any explanatory memorandum relating to the Bill containing the provision, or any other relevant document, that was laid before, or furnished to the members of, either House of the Parliament by a Minister before the time when the provision was enacted;

(f) the speech made to a House of the Parliament by a Minister on the occasion of the moving by that Minister of a motion that the Bill containing the provision be read a second time in that House;

(g) any document (whether or not a document to which a preceding paragraph applies) that is declared by the Act to be a relevant document for the purposes of this section; and

(h) any relevant material in the Journals of the Senate, in the Votes and Proceedings of the House of Representatives or in any official record of debates in the Parliament or either House of the Parliament.

(3) In determining whether consideration should be given to any material in accordance with subsection (1), or in considering the weight to be given to any such material, regard shall be had, in addition to any other relevant matters, to:

(a) the desirability of persons being able to rely on the ordinary meaning conveyed by the text of the provision taking into account its context in the Act and the purpose or object underlying the Act; and

(b) the need to avoid prolonging legal or other proceedings without compensating advantage.

10

RESEARCHING THE LAW

I like to do my principal research in bars, where people are more likely to tell the truth or, at least, lie less convincingly than they do in briefings and books.

P.J. O'Rourke[1]

1 P.J. O'Rourke, 'Holidays in Hell' (London: Picador, 1989).

Introduction

As carpenters need woodworking tools to successfully carry out their trade, lawyers need the ability to be able to research the law quickly and easily in order to successfully carry out their profession. One of the main tools of a lawyer is to know the law. A lawyer who knows the law is able to advise clients of their legal options and in turn clients can then give clear instructions to the lawyer about what course of action to take given the situation. Given that the law changes relatively frequently, knowing how to research those changes is an invaluable asset to the modern practising lawyer.

Researching is the basic tool of the lawyer

To succeed at law school it is vital to know the law. Knowing the law and being able to analyse and synthesise arguments based on a correct understanding of the law is crucial to earning a law degree. Knowing how to research the law enables you to find the answers to essay and tutorial questions efficiently. It allows you to broaden your research net and capture sources of information that help you to succeed in assessment tasks. Most importantly, good research skills enable you to finish your degree as a well-informed graduate of law and be an effective researcher in your chosen field of work.

Good research skills will enable you to become an informed law graduate

This chapter gives you key pointers on becoming a good legal researcher but you should note that you will not become a good legal researcher unless you plan your research and practise the skills of a good researcher and develop your own techniques. Good legal research skills can sometimes be a matter of trial and error. Sometimes a path of enquiry can lead you to find other paths that you did not first anticipate. Allocate reasonable amounts of time to research in order to follow as many paths of research as are feasible for the project at hand.

Good legal research requires practice

Most references in this chapter are to sources freely available from most law libraries where you are a student. However, you should note that there are some very good databases that you need to pay for if you do not have free access to by virtue of being a law student at your home university. One of the more such worthwhile databases is LexisNexis, which offers access to United States primary and secondary sources of legal material as well as British, French, and Canadian law. It also has a thorough database of specialist and generalist legal materials from Australia, New Zealand, the United Kingdom,

This chapter will try to make reference to sources available from your law school library

and Ireland. You should note that LexisNexis is particularly good on United States case law, which can often be hard to find in hard-copy form in Australian law libraries.

Planning your research

Many of you reading this book will be comfortable with the idea of writing an essay plan before you commence writing your essay or assignment. When writing a plan to answer a legal problem you may well adopt the structure suggested in Chapter 5 of this book. When it comes to researching the law, you should similarly write a short plan that will help guide you through the process of researching and ensure you achieve the outcomes you have set yourself without being diverted into irrelevant areas of research or duplicating research.

Understand the question and what it is asking you to do

Read the question a few times to make sure you understand what the assessment is asking of you. If you do not understand any part of the question, ask your tutor, lecturer or subject convener. Be conscious of what the actual question is. The question may set out a legal problem that requires you to advise a client or it may be a statement from a judgment with the instruction to simply 'discuss'. It is most important to understand what you are actually required to do. In fact, you should revisit the question several times while you are conducting research to ensure you are staying on point and not straying into areas that are irrelevant and will waste your time.

Once you read the question it should be apparent what area or areas of the law are being raised. If this is not apparent then you may need to cast your research net a little wider than first anticipated until you understand which area of the law the subject convener wishes you to address. Do not panic if you do not immediately understand the question. Sometimes it takes some preliminary research to accurately identify the area of the law it raises. Whether you identify it at the start or mid-way through the research stage of your assessment task you need to be clear about the area of law you are being assessed on in order to better understand what the question requires you to do.

Be clear on what research is required to answer the question

Whatever the subject and the type of question, you need to be clear on what is required in order to complete the assessed task. Is the question asking you to research the case law in order to answer a problem-based question? Is the question asking you to research the commentary on a particular issue? Is the question asking you to research both and if so what is the balance of case law versus commentary?

Based on the answers to these questions, you need to decide what type of research is required in order to complete the assessed task. The answers will also point you to where you need to start and probably spend most of your research time. For example, if the question requires you to provide advice on the likely outcome of a problem-based fact pattern, then you are going to need to consult the latest law—both statute and case law. This will mean accessing certain databases (discussed below). It is unlikely that you will be spending huge amounts of research time searching out secondary sources; rather, primary sources of law will provide you with the necessary leading cases to enable you to prepare an accurate answer to the question posed.

Set parameters to your research (where, when and what)

Most research tasks start by casting the research net wide; that is, you tend to think about a wide variety of resources to help answer the question set in the assessment task. This is not a bad way to start thinking about research; however, it can be fraught with problems if you allow the research to take over from achieving the objective of answering the question. To avoid this, you need to set parameters for your research. You need to ensure that the task of researching is manageable. A way to do this is to consider: what you need to capture in your research; where the persuasive research will come from in terms of jurisdiction or, if it is commentary, from what reputable sources; and, how far back you wish to research in order to ensure your answer reflects current case law or thinking on the issue at hand.

You may like to draw a rough diagram of your research parameters to help guide you through the task. Figure 10.1 shows a basic diagram to research a basic legal problem-based question.

FIGURE 10.1 Setting research parameters

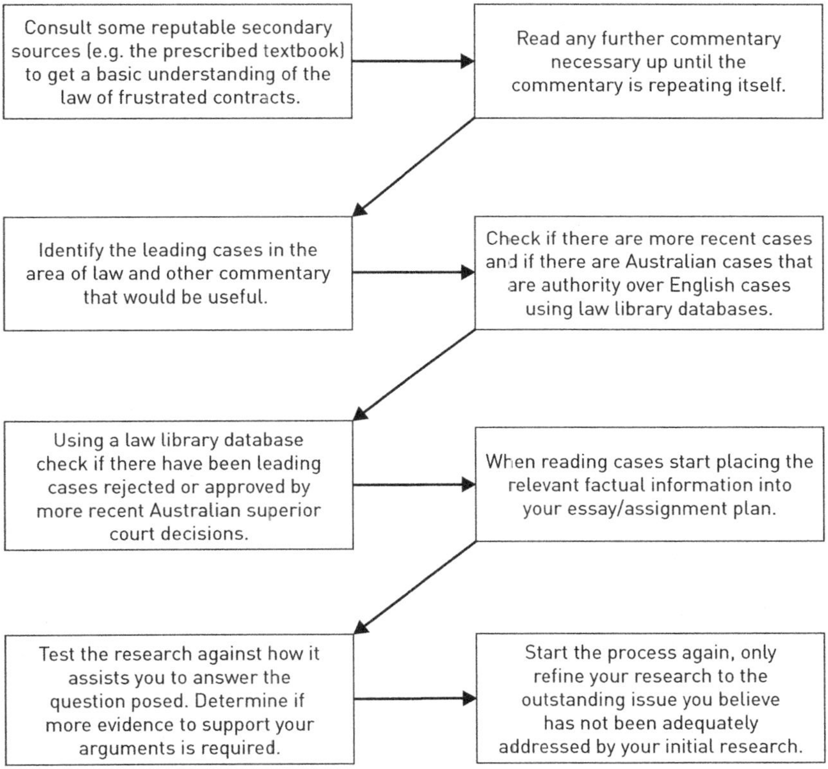

Plan how you will discover relevant research (search terms to use)

Before starting to trawl the databases offered by your university, government and private libraries, you need to be familiar with the language that search engines use to ensure you optimise your research efforts. How you use database search engines will determine the value of the return you receive on the time you invest in research. Often key research and writing in the area you are researching is lost simply because you failed to ask the search engine the right question. In other words, the words you use to ask the search engine to find information can often make or break the effectiveness of your research.

The first step is to develop a list of key words. For example, if you were searching for information (both commentary and cases) on the subject of the discharge of a contract for frustration simply typing into a search engine "contract" will yield millions of results (522,000,000 in 0.23 seconds using a basic Google search to be precise). Even typing in the words "frustrated contract" would yield millions of responses (5,650,000 in 0.17 seconds). Of course it is impossible to check so many sources and sifting the reliable from the unreliable sources could burn a lot of useful research time. A more refined search would be something like, "contract law, frustration, supervening illegality" (which still yielded 38,200 results in 0.27 seconds). An even more refined search would be, "contract law, frustration, supervening illegality, czamikow v rolimplex" (which yielded 41 results in 0.31 seconds). So by narrowing down the search on databases using specific key words, you can yield a manageable number of research sources that will allow you to quickly sift the good from the bad and start you on the way to completing your assignment.

Most university law libraries have quite sophisticated databases that allow you to use different search options to assist the effectiveness of your research. For example, all law libraries have access to the Australasian Legal Information Institute (AustLII), which is a partnership between the University of NSW and the University of Technology Sydney and is the key player in the provision of free internet access to Australian and, through its affiliates, overseas legal materials. AustLII's search operators are shown in Table 10.1 (found at http://www.austlii.edu.au/austlii/help/operators.html).

Know when to stop researching

Knowing when to stop researching is an important skill to develop. Often the key reason to stop researching will be time. At university, assessment tasks have to be submitted by a due date and the time you allocate to researching the question and then writing up your research will be limited. When planning your approach you should be clear on what amounts of time you can allocate to researching the question and drafting the assignment. Try not to go over your allocated research time as you will be cutting into the time it takes to draft the assignment and that may mean you end up submitting an inferior piece of work.

TABLE 10.1 AustLII database search operators chart

Operator	Example(s)	Explanation
word • Plural matching is automatic • Case insensitive	copyright	Returns all documents containing that word. Note that plural words are matched with singular words automatically (and vice versa). So searching for "contract" includes searching for "contracts" and "strategy" is considered the same as "strategies". Words and phrases are case insensitive. So "bob" is the same as "Bob" or "BOB".
wildcards • An asterisk * matches any string (including none) • A question mark ? matches any single character	tax* licen?e	Returns all documents containing a word beginning with tax—this would include: tax, taxes, taxi, taxicab, taxation, taxable, taxing, taxidermy. Note: using the asterisk slows down searching significantly. Returns all documents containing the word "licence" or "license" including the plurals of those words.
phrase • Use double quotation marks for phrases (see explanation at right)	"moral rights" "crime #and punishment"	Returns all documents containing that phrase. If the phrase contains a common word, for example "crime and punishment" (with the double quotation marks), you must add a hash character (#) or a plus sign (+) to search for that exact phrase (i.e. the phrase becomes "crime #and punishment"). Without the double quotation marks the search will be for all documents with crime that also contain the word punishment (the two words not necessarily appearing next to each other). Without the # or +, the common word "and" will become a placeholder for *any* other word. Note: excessive use of quotation marks slows down the search significantly.
AND • Boolean operator • Document must have both words (or both phrases) • Can be written "AND" or "and" • Synonyms: &, &&, +	copyright AND moral rights	Returns all documents that contain both the first term and the second term. A "term" can be a single word or complete phrase (no quotes are necessary around a phrase). Only works when your search is set to Boolean mode.

(continued)

TABLE 10.1 AustLII database search operators chart (*continued*)

Operator	Example(s)	Explanation
OR • Boolean operator • Document can have either word (or either phrase) • Can be written "OR" or "or" • Synonyms: |, ||, comma	treaties OR conventions	Returns all documents that contain either the first term or the second term or both. A "term" can be a single word or complete phrase. Only works when your search is set to Boolean mode. Most useful when searching for synonyms of words.
NOT • Boolean operator • Document must have first term. Must not have second • Can be written "NOT" or "not"	love NOT war	Finds documents that contain the first word, but do not contain the second. Occasionally useful to exclude irrelevant documents that contain unique words or titles. Only works in Boolean mode. You can also use "and not", for example "love and not war" (without the quotes of course).
NEAR • Proximity operator • Synonym for w/50 (see below) • Words or phrases must be within 50 words of each other • Order of terms not important	mabo NEAR queensland	Returns all documents where the first term appears nearby the second term. "Near" corresponds to 50 words, which is intended to be roughly the size of a paragraph. If two words are close together, then the chance of them being related is increased. Only works when your search is set to Boolean mode. Useful when searching for references to case names.
W/*n* • Proximity operator • Can use any number after slash (1 to 1000) • Order of terms not important (i.e. "a w/5 b" same as "b w/5 a")	mabo w/5 queensland	Returns all documents where the first term appears within *n* words of the second term, where *n* is a number you specify. So you could use "mabo w/10 queensland", "mabo w/50 queensland" (same as using near) or "mabo w/100 queensland". If two words are close together, then the chance of them being related is increased. Only works when your search is set to Boolean mode. Useful when searching for references to case names.
PRE/*n* • Proximity operator • Can use any number after slash (1 to 1000) • Order of terms important (i.e. "a pre/5 b" is different to "b pre/5 a")	sentencing pre/5 statistics	Returns all documents where the first term precedes the second term by no more than *n* words, where *n* is a number you specify. This means that the first term must come before the second term in the document, separated by no more than *n* words. Examples might be "sentencing pre/10 statistics", "sentencing pre/50 statistics" or "sentencing pre/100 statistics". Only works in Boolean mode.

Operator	Example(s)	Explanation
/n/ • Proximity operator • Same as W/*n* operator (above) • Emulated *STATUS* operator	smith/10/brown	Finds documents where words and phrases appear within *n* words of each other (as in the old *STATUS* system), where *n* is a number you specify. Similar in function to W/*n* (see above).
/m,n/ • Proximity operator • Finer control than W/*n* (above) • Emulated *STATUS* operator	smith/-10,10/ brown smith/1,10/ brown	Finds documents where words and phrases appear somewhere within *m* to *n* words of each other. You can use a negative value for *m* to mean "this many words before the second" and a positive value to mean "this many words after the second".
TITLE(...) • Field operator • Limit search to title of document • Also limits to case names • Also limits to section and regulation names for legislation	Title (commonwealth) commonwealth@ title *But use:* title (commonwealth bank) *and not:* commonwealth bank@title	Limits the search to document titles only. The example will find all those files with the word "commonwealth" in the title. This only works in Boolean mode, and can be combined with other operators. The text inside the title can contain other operators as well. This is a valid search: "title(westpac OR suncorp) AND title(australian taxation office OR ATO)".
punctuation • Replace all punctuation with a space in searches (unless using the # or + characters to ensure a common word is searched for) • Only use double quotation marks for phrases	[ ] { } ^ + - ,	See Full SINO Documentation for information on the special meaning of many symbols. As a general rule, omit all punctuation in your searches by replacing it with space characters, since some characters have a special meaning that could yield unpredictable results.
Precedence		
Default precedence rules: • *word* • (*terms*) *phrase* • w/n pre/n w/seg */n/* */m,n/* @ *name* (terms) • or & && • and not ^ || | , ;	(crime and punishment) or jail	Normally, searches are evaluated left to right. There is a default precedence order (see SINO Precedence), but it is a good idea to force parts of your search to be evaluated first using round brackets. Note that the following searches are all different: "journalist AND defamation OR publish", "journalist AND (defamation OR publish)" and "(journalist AND defamation) OR publish".

If you have cast the research net too wide and cannot manage the volume of research collected, you need to stop and rethink the research outcomes you are seeking and refine them to a point where the research task is manageable within the time and resource constraints you have set.

Another indicator that you have exhausted your research is when information is becoming repetitive. This commonly occurs with secondary sources but you should also be aware of this when researching primary sources. For example, if several recent cases in superior courts all quote with authority the same one or two cases, then you can feel comfortable knowing that those cases represent the current status of the law on the particular subject matter. Some databases are very good in listing where a landmark decision has been used and how it has been used by other courts. For example, in LexisNexis once you have entered the search operator for a case and found the case, you will sometimes have the option of viewing the CaseBase data entry that provides a list of cases where the case in question has been mentioned. The entry will list how the case in question was treated by the court along the following lines:

- Applied;
- Cited;
- Considered;
- Disapproved;
- Distinguished;
- Followed; or,
- Referred to.

Depending on the above classification, the data entry will also provide the judgment of the editors as to whether the case received a:

- Neutral treatment;
- Positive treatment;
- Cautionary treatment;
- Negative treatment; or,
- Citation only (no real treatment of the case).

The entry for a case in CaseBase will also list relevant articles and complete journal citations that the case has featured in as well as legislation considered by the case.

Know what to do with your research

As you complete certain parts of your research, you should record your findings for easy reference and incorporation into whatever form the assessed task will need to finally take. Placing a short-form reference (such as a case or author name) and page number into your final written piece will save you having to go back and check wads of printed or handwritten notes and will make the writing process a lot easier. You may find it useful to write small vignettes (up to one short paragraph) from research that has been conducted in the draft assignment so that you can see how the research fits into the argument being proposed.

Most importantly, you must weave the research conducted into your assessment task to create an authoritative piece of work that is well supported and persuasively argued because of the research you did. Striking the balance between your research and your own analysis of the research is critical. Too many students do not seek feedback from their tutors, lecturers or subject conveners on striking the right balance. Most law assessments do not require an exhaustive account of other people's views or quotations from case judgments. Most law assessments require that you display your own thoughts on what the research is and how it affects the question being asked. Chapter 5 of this book emphasises the balance between analysis (your interpretation of the materials) and synthesis (your argument). This chapter emphasises the balance between the research acquired and your analysis and synthesis. Your assessment should not be just a summary of the research with little of your own analysis and synthesis. Nor should it be full of your own unsubstantiated opinions and light on the research that gives weight to your arguments.

Resources available to law students

Resources for legal research continue to improve with the advances in educational technologies. Most legal research now takes place via the internet and accessible overseas sources of law have never been more available than they are now. For example, within two hours of a decision being handed down by the High Court in Canberra or the English House of Lords in London, you can have a copy of the judgment available through the internet.

Most legal research takes place via the internet

Online legal databases now link material for easy access and cloud computing allows large volumes of material to be stored for personal use. Specialist databases that list journals make the old-fashioned job of thumbing through the index of journals a bygone activity. Such databases open up many thousands of overseas journals that Australian libraries could not afford to subscribe to. Some of these journal databases can provide downloadable copies of articles making the researcher's task even easier. What is particularly attractive to law students is that most of these computer-based resources can be obtained for free through the law school library. Law students do not even need to have a computer themselves, provided they have access to a library computer linked to the internet.

Some databases allow you to download journal articles

Even the use of case books has made legal research easier as students are given a collection of the most relevant cases acting as precedents in the chosen areas of the law being studied. These potted versions of case precedents cut down the amount of time you need to spend researching them and free you to conduct more in-depth research. Not many law students will ever have to thumb through a 200-page High Court judgment to extract the ratio; rather, case books extract the relevant sections of the judgment that apply to the area of law the case deals with—the only exception being very recent cases not yet appearing in case books.

Case books provide summaries of cases that reduce your research time

The other recent arrival, courtesy of the same publishers that produce text and case books, is the ability to access fully integrated resource packages. These electronic packages are usually enabled for wireless access from mobile devices and will often feature one or more of the following elements:

- an electronic text and case book that can be annotated;
- access to a range of legal databases with the ability to annotate downloaded files and to cut-and-paste excerpts from relevant information;
- podcasts on specific topics, often from well-known people who are an authority on the subject matter;
- example assessment tasks including sample answers;
- access to online tutors;
- academic literacy and numeracy modules; and
- automated connections to external websites with further resources.

Usually a specific subject or program of study will purchase an integrated package of resources for your use as an enrolled student in a specific subject or course; however, it is possible to pay for access yourself to some of these packages.

Using Google and Wikipedia is okay

When Google and Wikipedia first arrived, academics generally discouraged students from using these databases as research tools. Today, while some academics still take the same view, many do not and see these and other sources of information as an acceptable 'first start' to the task of researching, particularly for undergraduate students. According to Wikipedia's own website, 'Serious researchers can often find a wide range of vigorously or thoughtfully advocated viewpoints not present in the consensus article. As with any source, information should be checked'.[2] Information appearing on Wikipedia is written by anyone who wishes to contribute to the body of knowledge in the database. In answer to the question, 'How do you know if the information is correct?', Wikipedia states:

> Given that anyone can *edit* any article, it is, of course, possible for biased, out-of-date, or incorrect information to be posted. However, because there are so many other people reading the articles and monitoring contributions using the Recent Changes page, incorrect information is usually corrected quickly. Thus, the overall accuracy of the encyclopedia is improving all the time. You are encouraged to help by correcting articles, validating content, and providing useful references.[3]

As with all sources of information, you should be satisfied as to such information's accuracy before using it and, if in doubt, you should check from other sources the accuracy of the information.

Legislation

Australia

Legislation starts its life as a Bill. A Bill is a proposal for a new law or a change to an existing law. In parliaments with two houses, Bills are generally introduced into the lower houses of parliament for discussion and then if approved pass to the upper houses for further discussion and possible amendment. If a Bill is amended in the upper house it has to go back to the lower house to be passed again with the amendment or amendments. Sometimes Bills can originate in the

---

2 http://en.wikipedia.org/wiki/Wikipedia:About#Strengths.2C_weaknesses.2C_and_article_quality_in_Wikipedia (accessed 18 June 2013).

3 http://en.wikipedia.org/wiki/Wikipedia:FAQ/Overview (accessed 18 June 2013).

upper house but all Bills must be passed through both houses. Bills are usually sponsored by the government, opposition, or minority parties but can also be introduced by individual members of either house in which case the Bill is called a 'private member's Bill'. Once Bills are passed by both houses, or, in the case of a single house (as in Queensland), by that house of parliament, and have assent by the Queen's representative, they become legislation.

Bills are passed by the parliament before receiving royal assent

In states other than Queensland, the houses of parliament are called the 'legislative assembly' (lower house) and the 'legislative council' (upper house) and legislation has to pass through both houses of parliament in order for it to proceed to royal assent by the respective state governors. In the two territories of Australia there is only one house of parliament, a legislative assembly, and Bills are not given royal assent; rather, Bills become legislation by virtue of the Clerk of the Assembly certifying a copy as a true copy of the Bill as passed, and then the Speaker of the House presenting the Act to the Chief Minister for notification in the respective Territory Legislation Register. Once an Act is notified it becomes law. In Queensland, legislation still needs royal assent, but Bills merely pass through the single house, the legislative assembly. The Commonwealth system operates the same as the states, except the lower house is called the House of Representatives and the upper house is called the Senate and legislation is presented to the Governor-General for royal assent.

In the territories Bills are certified and do not need royal assent

Royal assent signifies the passing of legislation into law. However, because of the way government business is managed the date of assent is not necessarily when the legislation commences. In some jurisdictions in Australia, legislation commences from the date of assent. In others, it will be 14 or 28 days after assent before the legislation commences. Further, you should carefully check the specific piece of legislation as the statute itself may specify the commencement date.

Finding legislation is made very easy today through AustLII and its free access affiliates, which hold legislation for the following jurisdictions:

AustLII legislation holdings

- Commonwealth of Australia (at http://www.austlii.edu.au/)
- ACT (at http://www.austlii.edu.au/)
- New South Wales (at http://www.austlii.edu.au/)
- Northern Territory (at http://www.austlii.edu.au/)

- Queensland (at http://www.austlii.edu.au/)
- South Australia (at http://www.austlii.edu.au/)
- Tasmania (at http://www.austlii.edu.au/)
- Victoria (at http://www.austlii.edu.au/)
- Western Australia (at http://www.austlii.edu.au/)

Using AustLII, legislation may be searched in a number of ways. Legislation may be searched by title, that is, by selecting the jurisdiction from the home page and then conducting an alphabetical search of the title of the legislation. AustLII now archives legislation not currently on the statute books using the 'Point-in-time' search engine thereby allowing access to any statute that has been passed by a state, territory or federal parliament at any time.

Legislation on AustLII can be searched by title

If you do not know the title of the legislation, you may initiate a full form search from the home page, which will allow you to search all the legislation databases or just jurisdiction-specific legislation databases using key words. Commonly used words or phrases can turn up extraordinarily large results that may not help you to narrow down the piece of legislation you actually require. However, AustLII allows you to refine your search using keyword combinations that will lead you to the legislation you are seeking (see above for the search operators chart).

Where you do not know the title, legislation on AustLII can be searched by key words

There are many other internet sites that offer electronic versions of current legislation. For example, Australian legislation and related material such as Gazette notifications (on assent dates of legislation) are available on the federal government funded 'ComLaw' (at http://www.comlaw.gov.au/). State and territory legislation can be found through the various state and territory government sponsored websites. The following is a list of those sites:[4]

- Australian Capital Territory—http://www.austlii.edu.au
- New South Wales—http://www.legislation.nsw.gov.au
- Northern Territory—http://dcm.nt.gov.au/strong_service_delivery/supporting_government/current_northern_territory_legislation_database
- Queensland—http://www.legislation.qld.gov.au

4 All accessed on 18 June 2013.

- South Australia—http://www.parliament.sa.gov.au/Legislation/Pages/LegislationHome.aspx
- Tasmania—http://www.thelaw.tas.gov.au
- Victoria—http://www.parliament.vic.gov.au/legislation
- Western Australia—http://www.slp.wa.gov.au/legislation/statutes.nsf/default.html

Overseas

Not all law libraries carry hard copies of legislation for overseas jurisdictions. The cost is too great and the space to carry such information is too vast for most university law schools. However, again thanks to technology, a great deal of overseas legislation is available electronically. The following is a list of those sources available just through AustLII and its free access affiliates.

Overseas legislation is best found through the Internet

- Alberta (at http://www.canlii.org)
- American Samoa (at http://www.paclii.org)
- Bangladesh (at http://www.commonlii.org/)
- Britain (at http://www.bailii.org)
- British Columbia (at http://www.canlii.org)
- Brunei (at http://www.commonlii.org/)
- Canada (CanLii at http://www.canlii.org)
- Cook Islands Cases (at http://www.paclii.org)
- Cyprus (at http://www.cylaw.org/)
- East Timor (at http://www.austlii.edu.au)
- France (at http://www.droit.org/)
- Fiji Case law (at http://www.paclii.org)
- Federated States of Micronesia Legislation (at http://www.paclii.org)
- Germany (at http://www.jura.uni-saarland.de/)
- Hong Kong (at http://www.hklii.org)
- India (at http://www.liiofindia.org/)
- Ireland (at http://www.ucc.ie/law/irlii/index.php)
- Italy (at http://www.ittig.cnr.it/IndexEng.htm)
- Kenya (at http://www.kenyalaw.org/klr/index.php)

- Kiribati Cases (at http://www.paclii.org)
- Korea (at http://www.klri.re.kr/kor/main.do)
- Marshall Islands (at http://www.paclii.org)
- Mexico (at http://info.juridicas.unam.mx/)
- Nauru (at http://www.paclii.org)
- New Brunswick (at http://www.canlii.org)
- New Zealand (at http://www.nzlii.org)
- Niue (at http://www.paclii.org)
- Northwest Territories (at http://www.canlii.org)
- Nova Scotia (at http://www.canlii.org)
- Nunavit (at http://www.canlii.org)
- Ontario (at http://www.canlii.org)
- Philippines (at http://www.lawphil.net/)
- Quebec (at http://www.canlii.org)
- Samoa (at http://www.paclii.org)
- Singapore (at http://www.commonlii.org/)
- Solomon Islands (at http://www.paclii.org)
- Sri Lanka (at http://www.commonlii.org/)
- South Africa (at http://www.saflii.org)
- Thailand (at http://www.lawreform.go.th/)
- Tokelau (at http://www.paclii.org)
- Tonga (at http://www.paclii.org)
- Tuvalu (at http://www.paclii.org)
- Uganda (at http://www.ulii.org/)
- Vanuatu (at http://www.paclii.org)
- Yukon (at http://www.canlii.org)

One of the more recent innovations from AustLII is the advent of WorldLII (at <http://www.worldlii.org>) that provides primary and secondary materials from many countries of the world and the list is growing day by day. Not every jurisdiction is covered and some are covered but not in any great detail; however, the information is growing steadily and soon anything you need in terms of legal research will be available through AustLII and its free access affiliated databases.

Subordinate legislation

Subordinate legislation is made under delegated authority by non-government persons or organisations

Subordinate or delegated legislation is made by persons or bodies other than the parliament. The most common persons or bodies that have such power delegated to them by the parliament are the Governor-General; the state Governors; Commonwealth, state, and territory Ministers of the Crown; and local government bodies. Subordinate legislation takes the form of rules, regulations, by-laws, orders, and ordinances.

Most legislation contains the power to make subordinate legislation

Most legislation contains enabling sections for subordinate legislation to be made. For example, section 315 of the *Bankruptcy Act 1966* (Cth) states:

> (1) The Governor-General may make regulations prescribing matters:
> (a) required or permitted by this Act to be prescribed; or
> (b) necessary or convenient to be prescribed for carrying out or giving effect to this Act.
>
> (2) In particular, the regulations may:
> (a) (l) (lists many things that regulations can achieve)

Enabling powers specify the delegated authority and the extent of the power

So the legislative enabling powers may not only specify the person or body that may make subordinate legislation, as in section 315(1) above, but may also specify the types of matters the delegated person or body may make subordinate legislation regarding, as in section 315(2)(a)-(l) above.

Another reason subordinate legislation comes into existence is when, for example, fees and levies for government services are involved that will rise on a regular basis. It is easier to have these sorts of issues embodied in subordinate legislation that can be changed quickly and easily rather than enacting a new statute or amendment for each change. In such cases the legislation is drafted by the government and presented to the Governor-General (in the case of Commonwealth legislation) and the Governor (in the case of state legislation) for signature. Once signed by the Queen's representative, the legislation is published in the respective government *Gazette*, after which it is tabled in the respective parliament and, provided there is no motion for disallowance within a prescribed number of days, the subordinate legislation becomes law. The government

Subordinate legislation must be published in the government *Gazette*

Gazette is a weekly publication that publishes, among other things, various different kinds of government activity including the passing of all legislation.

Unless otherwise stated, subordinate legislation comes into effect on the day of notification, which is the same day that the legislation was passed. Like primary legislation, subordinate legislation can be easily found through the various legal databases mentioned above, such as AustLII and ComLaw and the above mentioned state and territory websites.

Subordinate legislation usually comes into effect on the day of notification

Cases

Cases that create new law or more clearly define existing law are generally reported in the numerous published law reports. In other words, not all cases are reported; rather, only those cases that communicate something important about the law find their way into the law reports. Cases may be reported in a series of law reports that only report cases from a particular court, such as the Commonwealth Law Reports that report only High Court of Australia cases. Other series will report cases from numerous courts, such as the Federal Law Reports that publish decisions from State and Territory Supreme Courts exercising Federal jurisdiction, the Family Court of Australia, the Federal Magistrates Court and Federal tribunals. There are also series of law reports that report on specified subjects such as the Australian Tax Cases or Australian Criminal Reports.

Only cases that communicate something important are reported in the law reports

Law reports may be authorised or unauthorised. Authorised law reports contain judgments approved by the court that decided the case and are approved by that court prior to publication in the respective law report. Further, authorised law reports are published by an official law reporting authority. For example, the NSW Law Reports are authorised law reports of the Supreme Court of NSW published by the Council of Law Reporting for NSW.

Authorised law reports are approved by the court

Hard copies

A significant feature of the modern law library is its collection of law reports. Although technology is making the need for hard copies of law reports less significant, copies of some older cases are not available through electronic means and hence the need for the hard copies. Case law has traditionally been reported in bound books called case reports. While the internet has now served to modify how we retrieve and store the law, the reporting of cases still relies heavily on the established system of abbreviations and formats. So how do you read the report abbreviations? Let us start with the following example:

STOLLERY V GREYHOUND RACING CONTROL BOARD (1972) 128 CLR 509

- The case is a High Court case as the CLR abbreviation indicates, to an experienced reader of case reports, the specific jurisdiction—the High Court—is reported in that report series.
- Stollery is the applicant before the High Court—if the case was a case at first instance, like a trial, then Stollery would be called the plaintiff.
- Greyhound Racing Board (GRB) is the respondent before the High Court—if the case was a case at first instance then GRB would be the defendant.
- (1972) is the year that the report was published.
- 128 is the volume number for the report series.
- CLR is the abbreviation of the report series where the case can be found—in this case it is the Commonwealth Law Reports.
- 509 is the page number within the report where this case begins.

Older cases may only be available via hard-copy law reports

Most good law dictionaries provide you with a list of most of the report abbreviations commonly used within the jurisdiction where the book is sold. Table 10.2 sets out a brief list of the more popular ones used in Australian law schools.

TABLE 10.2 Commonly used law reports

Report/Journal Abbreviation	Report/Journal Full title	Jurisdiction	Authorised	Square brackets*
AAR	Administrative Appeals Reports	Aust	No	No
AC	Appeal Cases	UK	Yes	Yes
ACLC	Australian Company Law Cases	Aust	No	No
A Crim R	Australian Criminal Reports	Aust	No	No

Report/Journal Abbreviation	Report/Journal Full title	Jurisdiction	Authorised	Square brackets*
ACTR	Australian Capital Territory Reports	ACT	No	No
ALJ	Australian Law Journal	Aust	No	No
ALJR	Australian Law Journal Reports	Aust	No	No
All ER	All England Reports	UK	No	Yes
ALR	Australian Law Reports	High Court, Federal Court and ACT	No	No
ATC	Australian Tax Cases	Aust	No	No
ATPR	Australian Trade Practices Reports	Aust	No	No
BCL	Building and Construction Law	Aust	No	No
Ch	Chancery	UK	Yes	Yes
CLR	Commonwealth Law Reports	High Court	Yes	No
Crim LR	Criminal Law Review	UK	No	Yes
ER	English Reports	UK	No	No
Fam LR	Family Law Reports	UK	No	No
FCR	Federal Court Reports	Aust	Yes	No
FLR	Federal Law Reports	Aust	No	No
KB	King's Bench	UK	No	Yes
LQR	Law Quarterly Review	UK	No	Yes
MqLR	Macquarie Law Review	Aust	No	No
MULR	Melbourne University Law Review		No	No
MonLR	Monash University Law Review	Aust	No	No

(continued)

TABLE 10.2 Commonly used law reports (*continued*)

Report/Journal Abbreviation	Report/Journal Full title	Jurisdiction	Authorised	Square brackets*
NSWLR	New South Law Reports	NSW	Yes	Yes to 1984
NSWR	New South Wales Reports	NSW	Yes	Yes
NTLR	Northern Territory Law Reports		Yes	No
NTR	Northern Territory Reports	NT	No	No
NZLR	New Zealand Law Reports	NZ	No	Yes from 1973
QB	Queen's Bench	UK	Yes	Yes
Qd R	Queensland Law Reports	Qld	Yes	Yes
QLR	Queensland Law Reports	Qld	No	No
QULJ	Queensland University Law Journal	Aust	No	No
SALR	South Australian Law Reports	SA		
SASR	South Australian State Reports	SA	Yes	Yes to 1971
SR (NSW)	State Reports New South Wales	NSW	Yes 1901–60	Yes from 1961–1963
St R Qd	Queensland State Reports	Qld	No	Yes
SR (WA)	State Reports Western Australia	WA	No	No
Tas LR	Tasmanian Law Reports	Tas	No	No
Tas R	Tasmanian Reports	Tas	Yes	No
Tas SR	Tasmanian State Reports	Tas	Yes	Yes
Syd LR	Sydney Law Review	Aust	No	No
UNSWLJ	University of New South Wales Law Journal	Aust	No	No
Univ TLR	University of Tasmania Law Review	Aust	No	No

Report/Journal Abbreviation	Report/Journal Full title	Jurisdiction	Authorised	Square brackets*
Univ WALR	University of Western Australia Law Review	Aust	No	No
UWSLR	University of Western Sydney Law Review	Aust	No	No
VLR	Victorian Law Reports	Vic	Yes	Yes from 1905–1956
VR	Victorian Reports	Vic	Yes	Yes from 1957
WALR	Western Australian Law Reports	WA	No	No
WAR	Western Australian Reports	WA	Yes	Yes from 1960–1990
WLR	Weekly Law Reports	UK	No	Yes

On occasions it is useful to be able to search for cases according to their subject. This is made simple by using the *Australian Digest* and the *Australian Case Citator* both published by Thomson Reuters. The great benefit of using these publications is that they list each case under multiple subject headings covering different areas of law raised by the case. This can be very useful if you are unsure of how the editors of the digest classified a particular case by subject. In other words, with most cases having multiple entries, you have more chance of finding the right case to suit your needs. The same information in these services is also available electronically via *FirstPoint* also published by Thomson Reuters.

The *Australian Digest* allows you to search cases by subject

Electronic copies

The same information in the abovementioned *Australian Digest* and *Case Citator* is available electronically via *FirstPoint* also published by Thomson Reuters. As with statutes, one of the best collections of case law is available electronically through AustLII, which holds cases from every state and territory in Australia for most courts and tribunals. You should check what jurisdictions are covered by AustLII for reference.

AustLII has substantial holdings of Australian case law

United Kingdom and the United States of America: Hard copies

As in Australia, there are many different law reports that cover key case law from the most authoritative jurisdictions within the United Kingdom and the United States of America. The following is a non-exhaustive list of the key law reports. English report abbreviations are the same as Australian abbreviations. American report abbreviations are different from Australian abbreviations; therefore, two examples are given below.

Key law reports for the UK and USA report decisions from superior courts

a) England
   - Appeal Cases [AC] (House of Lords and Privy Council)
   - Queen's Bench [QB] (or King's Bench depending on the applicable reigning monarch) (Queen's Bench Division of the High Court and appeal cases)
   - Chancery Division [Ch] (Chancery Division of the High Court and appeal cases)
   - Weekly Law Reports [WLR] (variety of higher courts)
   - All England Law Reports [All ER] (variety of higher courts).

b) United States of America
   - US Supreme Court Reports Lawyers' Edition [US L Ed 2d] (Supreme Court of the United States)
   - Supreme Court Reporter [Sup CT] (Supreme Court of the United States)
   - Federal Reporter (Circuit Courts of Appeal)—for example, 92 F.3d 57 (2d Cir 1996):
     - '92' pertains to the volume number;
     - 'F' tells you it is the Federal Reporter;
     - '3d' [pertains to the series number (all cases after 1993 are in the 3rd series);
     - '57' pertains to the page number in the volume;
     - '(2d Cir)' relates to the circuit number of the appeal. America is divided up into 13 regional groups of States that each have a circuit court of appeal; and,
     - '1996' pertains to the year of the appeal.

- Federal Supplement (District Court)—for example, 931 F.Supp 159 (EDNY 1996):
  - '931' pertains to the volume number;
  - 'F.Supp' tells you it is the Federal Supplement;
  - '159' pertains to the page number;
  - 'EDNY' pertains to the Eastern District of the District of New York (some Districts have more than one District Court distinguished by their geographical location); and,
  - '1996' pertains to the year of the case.

Overseas—Electronic copies

AustLII and its subsidiary overseas legal databases provide a good starting point to researching overseas jurisdictions for case law. Again, you should check the jurisdictions available electronically early in your law school life as you can save yourself the time of having to source hard-copy versions of law reports that are available electronically.

AustLII subsidiaries have significant holdings of overseas case law

Secondary sources

When you are given an assignment at law school, it is often difficult to know where to start your research. Once you have started, the difficulty usually becomes knowing when to stop. Frequently, assignments at law school will lead you down a path where you discover too much information and the job then becomes a question of filtering information down to what is going to be useful and relevant to answering the assigned question.

Having too much information is problematic when researching an assignment

Where the question deals with a substantive law issue, such as a legal problem, the temptation is to merely look at primary sources of law. However, you should also look at secondary sources of law as often there has been some useful commentary on the introduction of legislation or the handing down of a case precedent that can help you understand the motivations of the parliament and the court. Such commentary may disclose a useful and well-argued point of view that you had not previously considered.

Secondary sources can provide valuable commentary on primary sources

Where the question is more theoretical, then the use of secondary sources is obviously vital as you will be required to bring together the various arguments that have emerged from consideration of the question by lecturers, jurists, and others. In such a case it is important to consider how widely to cast your research net and whether the question calls for extensive references to overseas material. As stated previously, you should ask your tutors or lecturers about their expectations in relation to the extent of research required for any assignment. Some lecturers mark students down for excessive referenced work, while others encourage it—you need to strike the right balance.

When answering theory questions, secondary sources are vital

Finding useful secondary sources is like entering a lottery. Sometimes you do not know whether the research will produce a tangible result. Like a lottery ticket that does not win, your research using some sources may not bear fruit. However, by about the end of your first year at law school, you will start to understand which secondary sources consistently bear fruit and you will come to rely on those sources frequently. But a word of warning: research, like most disciplines, requires you to try out new ideas and new sources, so do not rely on the same research sources all the time—try to test new sources of research to uncover new material and new authors. Some of the secondary sources you should encounter in your time at law school are included in the following non-exhaustive list:

Try to determine which secondary sources yield good research

- textbooks and other monographs
- lecture, seminar, workshop, and tutorial notes
- current law services
- legal encyclopaedias
- legal databases
- internet websites
- podcasts, for example iTunesU
- massive open online courses (MOOCs) offered by reputable overseas and Australian universities whose content is generally free of charge
- journals
- newspapers
- media in general, for example online sources such as crikey.com

While not all of the above sources will be discussed, the major sources will be discussed in more detail below. We have already discussed some secondary sources such as the various subject indexes to search legislation and cases. But before discussing other such sources you should consider consulting a detailed legal dictionary such as the *Australian Law Dictionary* published by Oxford University Press to clearly define the area of law you intend to research and to get a summary of the relevant primary and, on occasions, secondary sources. This dictionary will give you a basic understanding of the area of law you intend to research and generally a few sources of law with which to commence your research.

Start your research by consulting a comprehensive legal dictionary

Textbooks

Textbooks, whether hard copy or electronic, are a good starting point for research of secondary sources. They are generally written by experts in the area of law they seek to cover and are sometimes written with a student audience in mind. Beware of textbooks that are not written in a student friendly manner as they may be more of a hindrance than a help. Also, be conscious of the fact that the lead time between the author finishing the manuscript and the publication of the textbook can be up to one year or more. Therefore, sometimes some of the law in the textbook may be out of date—check the publication date inside the front cover.

Textbooks are a good starting point but parts of them may be out of date

Where textbooks are written by lecturers, often they write them according to the topics covered in a university course they teach. Therefore, the textbook may not cover everything in the particular subject that you are studying. Often the topics are covered in too great detail, for example where a lecturer teaches a full-year subject and your university teaches the same subject in one semester. In such cases some textbooks can be too detailed in some areas and lacking detail in other areas. To overcome this problem, it may be advisable to invest in an introductory book that briefly explains the issues surrounding the particular area of law. You will find that there will be introductory books in just about every area of law available for study. For a small investment you can have a text that helps explain the more complex text and might possibly give short case notes to help you understand at a glance some of the case law surrounding the area of law you are studying.

Introductory books are a good way to understand complex issues set out in textbooks

Current law services

There are two key current law services that record new or amended legislation and influential decisions from the courts. They seek to keep the profession up to date with the latest law on a monthly basis. The *Australian Legal Monthly Digest*, published by Thomson Reuters and available in both hard copy and electronic version, is very easy to navigate. It lists legislation alphabetically and by the date it passed the parliament, as well as Bills and subordinate legislation. Case lists are extensive, with appeals to the High Court also being listed.

Current law services have good indexes of cases and legislation

Australian Current Law, available in electronic form and hard copy, is a rival publication published by LexisNexis and like its rival is easy to navigate. It lists legislation alphabetically and chronologically and also includes Bills and subordinate legislation. The cases section contains a cumulative table as well as a table of cases judicially considered. It delivers fast notifications of superior court decisions and legislative changes. It also contains a section on books, articles, and other materials that may be a useful source of secondary materials.

Some current law services contain secondary source materials

Legal encyclopaedias

Like the current law services there are two major works in Australia that seek to summarise the law. They summarise the law in a narrative form that sets out relevant legal proposition. They do this in a succinct fashion with extensive footnotes that cite the relevant cases and legislation that establish the aforementioned legal propositions. These encyclopaedias give you a summary of the current law in the area you are researching then back it up with the authorities. In this respect they are a good starting point for research on a selected topic but are not sufficient on their own.

Legal encyclopaedias give you a summary of the law and extensive references

Both *The Laws of Australia* published by Thomson Reuters and *Halsbury's Laws of Australia* published by LexisNexis, come in numerous volumes and are split up alphabetically by subject. They both have very powerful search engines and you can narrow your search down to the exact area of law you are researching with ample authorities to either confirm or conclude your research brief or to lead you to further avenues of investigation. Most law school libraries will give you access to these powerful research tools as part of your enrolment as a student.

Legal databases

Legal databases allow you to cast your research net quite wide to include overseas sources

Legal databases are of great use in researching legal problems and theoretical questions at law school. Some of the more popular legal and non-legal databases are listed below.

- AGIS (Australian Attorney-General's Information Service—http://www.informit.com.au/agis.html)—this database will enable users to access articles from key Australian journals in full text, including pictures, diagrams, and charts. The articles can then be viewed, downloaded and printed
- APAIS (Australian Public Affairs Information Service—http://www.informit.com.au/apaft.html or http://www.nla.gov.au/apais)—this database will enable users to access articles from key Australian journals in full text, including pictures, diagrams, and charts. The articles can then be viewed, downloaded and printed
- AustLII (Australasian Legal Information Institute—http://www.austlii.edu.au)—large database of Australian and overseas case law, legislation, journals and links to other relevant websites
- Australian Law Reform Commission (Commonwealth Government—http://www.alrc.gov.au)—all discussion papers, reports and recommendations on a wide variety of law reform issues (see also the various state law reform commissions)
- Heinonline (http://heinonline.org/HOL/)—American and Canadian law, British reports, treaties and more
- LexisNexis (http://wwwlexisnexis.com.au) case law including some unreported judgments and legislation, *Halsbury's Laws of Australia* and journals
- ComLaw (Commonwealth Government—http://www.comlaw.gov.au)—all Commonwealth primary legislation and supporting information
- Law and Justice Foundation (NSW Law Foundation—http://www.lawfoundation.net.au)—legislation, practice collections, publications and reports and other links to legal databases
- LawLink (NSW Government—http://www.lawlink.nsw.gov.au)—an excellent database that will link to all courts and tribunals in Australia as well as information for the community, media and students
- Laws of Australia (http://www.westlaw.com.au/maf/api/tocectory?ndd=1&ao=o.AUNZ_TOC||anzencycloAU&stnew=true&srb=fulltext#advs-showless)—cases, legislation and commentary

- Legaltrac (http://go.galegroup.com/ps/start.do?p=LT&u=acuni&authCount=1)—legal publications, major law reviews, legal newspapers, bar association journals and international legal journals
- Oxford Journals (http://www.oxfordjournals.org/subject/law/)—all the major law jurnals
- Oxford Reference (http://www.oxfordreference.com/browse?t1=ORO:LAW00010) —reference book library with over 2 million entries
- United Nations (http://www.un.org/en/law/)—international law, treaties and conventions
- Westlaw Au (http://www.westlaw.com.au/maf/wlau/app/homepage)—cases, legislation and commentary, journals, encyclopaedia and news and current awareness
- WorldLII (http://www.worldlii.org)—provides primary and secondary materials from many countries of the world

Among the very first things you should do upon starting law school is speak to your law liaison librarian (a position that exists at most universities) and find out what legal databases are available at your university. Most universities have guided tours of the library for new students and you should make sure that you sign up for one of those tours and find out the sorts of research resources your library has to offer. Spending a small amount of time at the start of your law school life on a library tour will pay dividends when you have to conduct research for assessment tasks.

Become well acquainted with the law library—take a tour!

Journals

Journals, also known as periodicals, are a great source of information and commentary on primary sources, theory, and philosophy of law. There are literally hundreds of law journals in publication in Australia and overseas. There are two types of journals: those that cover the law very widely and those that cover a specific area of the law. For example, the *Australian Law Journal* published by Thomson Reuters covers a variety of topics including regular columns on current issues; property law; advocacy; family law; international law; and recent cases. The journal also records most of the significant High Court decisions and at the

Journals are a good source of commentary on the primary sources of law

end of each year is bound in two volumes, one being the journal and the other being the law reports.

The second type of journal is the subject-specific journal such as the *Journal of Contract Law* published by LexisNexis. Obviously this type of journal deals with specific subject matter and only publishes articles on those areas of the law. These journals often contain case notes of significant cases and are therefore of use when you are seeking to understand a particularly complex judgment or piece of legislation. Most journals publish an index at the end of each year so you may search each volume by article name or subject or, in some cases, by author.

Subject-specific journals can target your research more directly

The challenge in sourcing journal material is to know how to search journals according to a subject. If you have a reference to a certain journal article, then chances are you have the full citation of the article and searching becomes simply a matter of finding which law collection holds that specific journal. When you want to search journals for a particular topic, you need secondary sources that will allow you to access such materials without knowing the author or the article title.

It is possible to source journals by subject

Publications such as the *Index to Legal Periodicals* (USA, Canada, Britain, Australia and others) and the *Current Law Index* (United States, Canada, the United Kingdom, Ireland, Australia and New Zealand) are good starting points if you are trying to find journal articles by subject. Both are available electronically and if accessed via university websites are particularly powerful to the point where many journals give you access not just to the references but to the actual article you are searching for. However, not all databases allow this sort of access and you may walk away with a list of journal articles for which you will have to source hard copies.

Another very popular journal index is the Attorney-General's Information Service or AGIS for short. This index is administered by the Commonwealth Attorney-General's Department and is particularly good on Australian journal articles relating to the law.

AGIS targets Australian journals

You can access a vast array of journals easily through most of the law school library catalogues. Most law libraries have special journal search functions for their own collection. As well, many of the law libraries have a link to other law school libraries that will allow you to search library collections outside your home university. Your law liaison librarian should have a list of all legal periodicals held in the library's collection. You should obtain a copy of this list as some useful journals will be obvious from just reading the list. AustLII is the host to over 100 Australian journals with the full text available to most articles.

Become familiar with your library's catalogue and obtain a list of journals

A warning: Beware of the internet!

Beware of the accuracy of information on the internet. When using internet sources you need to check the accuracy of the information. In particular, try and find out who is responsible for the site and who has written the information, and use your judgment as to whether you think the information is reliable. Simply because it is on the internet does not mean the information is correct and true.

A number of reliable sites have been set up to counter the unreliability of information currently available on the internet. One of the best is located at the University of California Berkeley at http://www.lib.berkeley.edu/TeachingLib/Guides/Internet/Evaluate.html. This site contains some very important information about evaluating websites and how to verify whether information is correct or fraudulent.

11

ASSIGNMENTS: TYPES AND TIPS

Law school taught me one thing: how to take two situations that are exactly the same and show how they are different.

Hart Pomerantz, Canadian Attorney[1]

1 http://survivelaw.com/index.php/blogs/procrastination/704-legally-witty-funny-law-quotes.

Introduction

Assignments, of one form or another, are critical and obligatory activities. They are obligatory because you find them in all units of study. They are critical because they serve a number of important ends. If you are interested in the law and properly engage in your studies you will find that doing and completing those assignments can be enjoyable. In a properly designed program of study, assignments are a means by which you are able to fulfil the learning objectives and achieve the outcomes set for your unit (as discussed in Chapter 4 these outcomes are typically linked to your graduate attributes). That is, you can use the assignments, in conjunction with other learning activities, to be active in your own learning and gauge how well you are learning the law and related skills. Additionally, assignments are a way for your lecturer to determine whether you have undertaken the learning set in the objectives and have attained the unit outcomes. From the university's perspective this allows the lecturer to give you a mark and grade for the unit.

The type of intellectual difficulty within and permutations between assignments means that we cannot adequately describe all the assignments that you might come across in law school here. What we do in this chapter is provide you with an overview of the types typically used in law schools. Whatever the assignment, always read the full instructions for any assessment task and ensure that you understand the criteria by which the assessment task will be marked or graded. You cannot properly understand what it is you are required to do unless you understand what the purpose of the task is and how the things you do to complete the task are evaluated. A final point: it is also worthwhile considering what the personal predilections are of the person who will mark your work. For the same piece of work, a lecturer with a more practical focus may be looking more for professional skills development and application through the task than a lecturer with a more theoretical focus who might be looking at the same task with an eye to your ability to consider and criticise certain philosophical or policy positions. Of course, there are many combinations and permutations of lecturers' backgrounds and interests, and we do not wish to presuppose that certain lecturers are more or less practical, theoretical or professional than others simply because of that background. However, the personal biases of your lecturers will become apparent and you might benefit from considering who your 'audience' is when presenting orally or submitting written work.

Assignments allow you to meet unit and course learning objectives

Class participation and presentation

Class participation, tutorials and seminars are discussed in Chapter 6. We mention class participation here because it can often include components that are more than 'merely' reading and preparing for class by answering questions, or considering problems. Class participation typically requires you to actively engage in a discussion with your class colleagues about particular issues and problems. Class participation does not generally equate with turning up to class and occupying a seat. It is not simply about asking questions, speaking a lot, or conversely contributing monosyllabic answers to questions. Class participation may usually be assessed by either the quality of the ad hoc contributions you make to a discussion—as shown by the level of detail of those contributions and the level of research that underpins those contributions—or by way of a presentation. Whether you are simply adding to the discussion as part of a learning activity in a class, or presenting to the class as part of an assessment, you need to bear one important point in mind: always speak clearly and with a view to developing your communication skills to a professional level. Specifically, we consider that the development of your oral communication skills is a vital part of any university course, but particularly so in a discipline such as law where there is a significant chance that you may become a legal professional.

Communicating clearly and professionally means several things. It means:

- enunciating words unambiguously—do not mumble;
- using words that you know the meaning of in an appropriate way—do not use words that you think have a particular meaning unless you are sure about that meaning, that is, speak within your limits;
- speaking respectfully to all members of a class at all times—never speak angrily or sarcastically;
- learning the jargon of the discipline and when, and when not, to use it;
- not using colloquial language unless you are quoting something—leave the social talk for social settings;
- understanding that simplicity is more effective than verbosity;
- appreciating that winning an argument or debate does not necessarily require greater emotion or volume.

Where a class presentation is the assessment method for class activities it is essential that you adopt a mindset appropriate for the task. You should consider the directions given in relation to how and why you are presenting. Where those directions are brief it often pays to consider yourself in the position of a lecturer for the day and prepare to teach your colleagues about an area in which you (will) have significant expertise. Where you have the opportunity to use a computer or tablet to assist your presentation we urge you to be mindful of our comments in Chapter 4 and use the technology wisely. While programs like PowerPoint are excellent tools for helping to get a message across they do not make up for poor preparation and planning. Indeed, one of the easiest ways to reduce an audience's interest is to simply read all the words that have been crammed into a presentation slide or overhead projector slide. Do not think that your lecturer will be bamboozled by the light show either! Simply reading prepared slides need not mean that you have fulfilled the assessment criteria—which might include dynamism!

Class participation is more than just turning up

Here are nine tips for presenting material in class that will help you to use the process to learn and achieve good results.

1 Answer the question or fulfil the set task

You must answer the specific questions asked of you

Students often do not do well in class presentations because they do not actually answer the question, or do what is asked of them. Instead, poorly prepared students will skirt around the issue or issues in the hope that what they are saying will be sufficient to pass the assessed presentation. The other reason they do this is to avoid being quizzed on the actual issue that may have an uncertain answer. Remember the law is about exploring the grey areas of facts and precedents and arguing persuasively for your own opinion. This is hard work and requires a certain threshold of research. Do not be afraid of expressing your view based on your research. If you have not completed enough research to be confident about your answer, then do more research until you are confident to argue your opinion. If you do not understand an issue raised by your research, then speak to your lecturer prior to the presentation in order to resolve your misunderstanding. The lecturer is keen for the whole class to get as much benefit from your presentation as possible. Remember, your lecturer is placing substantial responsibility on students to present information to other students and will be keen for you to present the right information and reach a justifiable conclusion. Therefore, you should not feel awkward speaking to your lecturer before the presentation.

Another trap for law students is casting the research net too wide. This results in gathering too much information that in turn becomes impossible to assemble correctly in time for the presentation. If there is too much information to be included in your presentation, make a forensic decision about what you are going to include and what you are going to exclude. A good presentation informs and challenges your audience. Again, if you are concerned about your choices, run them past your lecturer to ensure that you are raising the issues that she or he wants you to raise in class.

Cull your research findings to a manageable level

Given all of the above, it is important to plan your presentation meticulously. Write out the issue or issues to be resolved and write a plan similar to an essay plan setting out how the presentation will flow from topic to topic. Work out whether to deal with the theory or practice, common law or statute first, and carefully plan any audio-visual aids and note where they are to appear. Try not to write a script, rather, use dot points for your notes. You will be surprised that after having completed the research how much of the information your mind will have retained. Use key words to jog your memory about, for example, case facts where relevant. Rehearse it well and double check at the end that you have actually answered the question.

Dot points and key words are good ways to remember your speech

2 Do not discuss irrelevancies

If you have planned well and are focused on answering the question, you will not fall into the trap of discussing irrelevancies. When researching a legal problem or theory question, there are usually a lot of published opinions and relevant cases. Your job, in part, is to sort out the relevant from the irrelevant. You need only raise those cases and commentaries that are relevant to answering the question. In this respect a question you should continually ask when considering whether to include certain material is, 'Is this information relevant to answering the question?' If it is not relevant, then dispense with it. It is inevitable that some cases and commentary will lead you down the path of an obscure but perhaps persuasive argument. In such cases, feel free to follow the argument; just make sure you can always link it back to the central issue and state the link clearly and concisely for your audience before you commence arguing it in your presentation.

Your job is to sort out the relevant from the irrelevant

3 Use the legal problem-solving model if appropriate

There are at least two great benefits of using the legal problem-solving model discussed in Chapter 5. First, it forces you to focus on the question and the likely answer. It does not allow you to stray into irrelevant areas or to discuss issues that might be persuasive but not relevant because they are not properly linked to the question. Listing the issue or issues raised by the question means you will not apply a 'scatter gun' approach to the answer raising allied areas of the law in the hope that they will be on point.

Where appropriate structure your presentation using the legal problem-solving model

Next, previewing the relevant law means you will only use authorities that will help you answer the actual question rather than randomly trying to apply authorities that may not assist you to answer the question. The third step of stating your argument will be straightforward and always relevant if you have followed the first two steps properly. Your argument should be focused given the foundations of having listed the issue or issues and having previewed the relevant law. Finally, making your conclusion will once again focus your mind on where you started, how you argued, and what sort of conclusion you should draw.

Make sure that you always link your arguments to the question

Second, it provides a structure to your presentation that is logical and does not allow you to miss any important issues. When presenting answers to legal problems or theory questions it is important to have a structure within which to present. Legal issues are usually complex and most questions put before you in law school are multi-issue questions. Therefore having a structure to fashion your answer upon is of great assistance not only when preparing the answer, but also for the audience when listening to your presentation. A structure such as the legal problem-solving model is logical in its approach and makes for an excellent template within which to present legal issues.

The legal problem-solving model provides a structure to your presentation

4 Use audio-visual aids where they help the presentation

Audio-visual aids should only be used to emphasise important points

Audio-visual aids should only be used where they help the audience understand a point you are making. For example, in a contract law case where the topic is express terms, or uncertainty or exclusion clauses, it would be advantageous to show the audience the words used in the actual contract and then to refer to the particular words that influenced the court to find the way it did in the case precedent guiding the discussion. Where you want to make several critical points and address each point in order it can be useful to list the points so the audience can follow you more closely. Other examples of the usefulness of audio-visual aids are where there is a photograph or diagram that will be easier to explain with a copy of it on a big screen. Where a conversation can be played back to provide an example of something said or a taped interview with a person material to the discussions at hand can all be moments where an audio or video tape can have a high impact on the audience. You should always go back to the basic proposition of only using audio-visual aids where it will help the audience understand your point more vividly.

One last piece of advice: if you intend to use audio-visual aids always check and double check that the equipment needed to use the aid will be available in the room you are presenting in. Most lecturers can tell you stories of students who assumed that the room was fitted with a data projector only to find out on the day of the presentation that they could not access their PowerPoint presentation after all. Similarly, it is easy to forget to bring a charger for an iPad, or to bring printed notes in case your hardware simply fails to work. Always have a backup plan in event of equipment failure.

Think of contingency plans for audio-visual failures

5 Consider an abbreviated hand-out

Where you are dealing with a lot of complex material and making arguments that are linked together in a cohesive single case, you should consider a simple one-page hand-out so that the audience can follow the discussion and how you are developing the points you wish to make. It can also help if you are quoting several cases as you will avoid having to stop the flow of the presentation to read out case citations or write them on the white board. Audiences like hand-outs as they tell the audience where the presentation is at any point in time. It also saves the audience having to take copious notes and asking you to repeat something just said because they did not get the point down in time. The extent to which you can make listening to the presentation easier will be

An abbreviated handout can assist the class better understand your presentation

repaid in the level of attentiveness of the audience and the level of engagement you can expect when asking questions of your audience.

6 Consider engaging the class by asking questions

Engaging the audience keeps their attention on what you have to say

Engaging the audience is very important in any presentation. Asking the audience questions is a way to keep their attention and to broaden the discussion by seeking different views. It is far more interesting to be able to engage the audience rather than having you as the constant focus of attention. It also tests the audience's knowledge of the materials and highlights those members of the audience who have read the materials and prepared for the class—a piece of information very useful for your lecturers.

However, you need to be sure that when you seek to engage the audience that they will be able to competently participate in the discussion. This means crafting the questions carefully so that they come at the right time in the presentation and so that they will be within the realms of the audience's knowledge. Also, if someone answers a question incorrectly try not to belittle that person by stating they are wrong. Rather, say something positive about the answer and seek further answers. If you do not handle answers from the audience in a positive way you risk alienating your audience and you will not get another contribution from them for the rest of the presentation. It is also important to consider that you may be a member of an audience in the future and would want your answer to be respected by the presenter.

Treat audience involvement positively to encourage further involvement

7 Find out what the lecturer wants out of the presentation

This is the easiest way to succeed at law school, yet few students avail themselves of the opportunity to find out what the lecturer wants in terms of the assessed and non-assessed tasks. This tip should be used for all tasks and if approached correctly is the simplest way to ensure a good mark in any assessed task. Most of your lecturers are very approachable; however, they are also busy people who not only teach, but also research and write, sit on various university committees, and may be completing

Ask your lecturer what level of presentation she or he is seeking

a higher degree. Therefore, your question needs to be brief, precise and pointed directly at the answer you need. General questions like 'What extent of detail do you want in this presentation?' are useless and from a lecturer's point of view disconcerting. It shows that the student has not yet thought about the presentation and is just fishing for ideas. A better type of question would be, using a contract law example, 'Do you want me to restrict my comments to 'offer' only or do you want me to discuss 'acceptance' as well?' This question shows that the student has done some research and that she or he has determined that there is potentially more than one issue involved in the question.

Lecturers will normally be happy to help a student in any piece of work when it is clear that the student has already done some work towards finding the answer or structuring the presentation. It is the student who comes to see the lecturer looking for the answer or a starting point that most concerns lecturers. Remember, university is a place of adult education and that means taking responsibility for your own learning.

Show your lecturer that you have tried to find the answer before asking for assistance

8 Feel free to be creative

As opposed to simply answering a question or addressing a topic, by standing in front of an audience and talking or using a PowerPoint presentation, it is frequently permissible to 'think outside the square' and do something completely different. For example, if you are required to consider and present a fact scenario where there are several parties and issues and if you are presenting as part of a small group you could consider presenting the facts, issues and law by way of role plays and theatre. For instance, you could have a narrator, explain who the role players are, have the role players indicate their facts and issues, and then have the narrator explaining the relevant law that does or could apply as the role play unfolds.

9 Do not read your presentation

Unless you are quoting something it is imperative that you do not read your oral presentation. As we will highlight below, in the context of mooting, you need to ensure that you have engaged your audience and that they are listening to you, are being persuaded by you, or at the least are being entertained by you. If you are reading a script then you will bore your audience, you will not be able to determine what their reactions to your points are, and you will frustrate many (including your lecturer) who could just as easily have read your script in their own time as have you read it to them.

Discussion board contributions

The increasing use of online and blending technologies means that you will most likely be required to engage in synchronous or asynchronous online learning at some point during your studies. Here your lecturer will establish a part of a virtual learning area dedicated to discussing a particular topic. In order to successfully contribute to a discussion board, and receive marks that may be allocated to it, you will need to have completed and understood the preparatory readings. If the discussion board is operated in a synchronised fashion you will be required to make a contribution during a set period of time—usually an hour or two at an allocated date and time. If the discussion board contribution is asynchronous then you will be able to make contributions over longer periods of time. In this latter approach, you will have an opportunity to read and reflect on what your lecturer and other students say before you upload your submission.

A critical aspect of an assessable discussion board is to be prepared for the time allocated for making contributions. If the contribution period is time-limited you need to be able to quickly and efficiently make your submissions. The process here is not unlike an examination. If the contribution period is longer and less time restricted you will profit from being an early contributor. Waiting, and reading others' contributions, may be enriching but you may find that waiting to submit, particularly because you had not prepared adequately, may result in someone else writing what you were hoping to contribute.

Discussion boards need not be assessable events and are frequently used by lecturers as a means of encouraging interactions between students about: important, but peripheral, topics; current events; assignment preparation; and general feedback on the learning activities and readings within the unit.

Essays

Aside from written examinations, essays are one of the most popular forms of written communication that your lecturers will use to assess you during your law studies. As the word limit is usually somewhere from 1000 to 5000 words, essays are a means by which you can develop research skills, ideas, and arguments in an extended way. There are two main types of essays: the theoretically based essay and the problem-style essay. You should note that some essay topics may be a combination of the two.

Theoretically based essays

Theoretically based essays give you a chance to criticise the law

The theoretically based essay is one that asks you to consider prompting material such as a recent case, new piece of legislation, a Bill, a quote, a question or an idea and to then evaluate that prompting material in some way. Usually this will be by some direction such as to discuss the new law in the light of the pre-existing law or to criticise an idea or law reform proposal in the light of jurisprudential concepts about what the law should be. Sometimes your lecturers may ask you to take a side in an argument (for example about anti-terrorism legislation and policy, or sentencing reform) and write your essay as an advocate for one side in a submission to a law reform commission. Other lecturers may ask you to select a topic yourself based upon your readings and interests—although this option tends to occur more in later years than in the initial years of law studies.

Theoretically based essays help you consider the law in a broader societal context

Theoretically based essays tend to provide you with more opportunity than problem based essays to consider the relationships of the law to wider society. Whether that relationship is examined by way of economics, cultural, moral, or other filters the theoretically based essay will cause you to examine the law beyond a simple analysis of the words of the law itself. In theoretically based essays you have greater scope to read and consider areas of your choosing when compared to a more problem-style essay. Finally, while a theoretically based essay topic may be quite narrowly drafted, thus leaving you with a fairly narrow area within which to write, such essays do not generally have a single correct answer. That is, you may deal with issues and research differently from other students and yet still meet the assessment criteria applicable to that essay.

Problem-style essays

There is usually a 'correct' answer in problem-style essays

Problem-style essays are those that are based upon a fact scenario, or problem, which you are required to analyse and advise upon. Problem-style essays have problems similar to those referred to in Chapters 5 and 13. You should refer to each of them for a consideration of how to solve problems generally and the specific issue of dealing with problem scenarios in examinations. An essay that is based on a problem is one that requires careful consideration. Because it is an essay, the lecturer will expect more than evidence of being able to follow a problem-solving method suitable for lawyers. Your lecturer will also expect you to have successfully recognised the issues that arise in the problem as well as properly analysing them with reference to relevant law. Further, your lecturer may also expect you to write your paper as though you were formally advising a party to, or a person interested in, the problem. Finally, problem-style essays are generally written so that there is a dominant, more persuasive, or more likely correct answer and therefore you should ensure that you properly understand the applicable law so that you are able to show your understanding of that better response. As we noted in Chapter 5, writing a problem-style essay in a form that shows that you have been logical and methodical in your approach to the facts, law, and policy will go a long way to satisfying the assessment criteria for this form of assignment.

Essay directions and instructional words

Your lecturer will normally provide certain clear directions about how and when an essay is to be submitted. You must follow those directions, or seek clarification if you do not understand them.

Typical directions include:

- the time, date, and place, or manner, of submission
- whether the essay should have a cover sheet or folder, or be submitted electronically
- what page length or word limit should be adhered to
- whether there are any penalties for breaching directions (for example, if you submit your essay late or go over the word limit).

The instructional words are those used within the essay topic itself. These are the words, or phrases, used by your lecturer to give you guidance as to the broad parameters of the essay. It is essential that you pay proper attention to these instructional words before beginning your research. Instructional words have specific meanings and they are used to cause you to do specific things.

Carefully consider directions and instructive words

Typical examples of instructional words and phrases are set out in Table 11.1.

TABLE 11.1 Instructional words and phrases

Instructional word or phrase	Meaning
Advise	To consider a scenario, explain the way the law applies to the scenario, and make a recommendation; usually found in problem questions
Analyse	To explain component parts of a scenario, quote, or law and explain how those parts link to each other and what ramifications or recommendations may arise
Compare and contrast	To point out similarities and differences between facts, laws, theories, or policies
Criticise	To analyse; compare and contrast; discuss; examine or explain a problem, law, policy, or theory at a meta-level of understanding; to undertake a deeper level of analysis by the application of theory, reflection, or other criteria
Discuss	To identify issues pertaining to a problem law, theory, or policy and then to analyse; compare and contrast; evaluate or explain those issues with reference to particular law, theory, or policy
Evaluate	To consider a law, problem, or theory in the light of competing arguments, laws, or ideas and to then come to some conclusion about it
Examine	To dissect elements of a problem, law, or theory by explaining those elements
Explain	To describe a scenario, or its ramifications, usually with reference to a particular point of view, theory, or legal interpretation. Explanation and examination (or description) are rarely used as instructional words in essays due to the lower level of knowledge and understanding required to comply with them

What is the process of writing essays?

Understand your topic as well as you can before beginning your research and reading

Before any writing takes place you need to understand your topic. To do this you need to take into account the instructional words or directions used by your lecturer as mentioned above. You also need to gain an idea about the possible boundaries to your assignment. If your essay is properly designed, and thus forces you to learn by doing, then it is most likely that after you conduct your research you should know quite clearly where the limits of your paper lie. However, you should begin your research with an idea about where you are headed—the internet and library bookshelves are full of wonderful resources that are interesting to read but not always relevant to your assignment. So you should begin by reading relevant parts of your textbook, or unit notes, to see if you can narrow the area of research you are about to undertake. If this does not help then you should consider what the key words and topics in your essay question are and consider examining those.

Once you have a better idea of where your research is to be directed then you should go about the process of researching and reading the law and associated materials. In Chapter 10 we explain some of the tools that can assist you in this task. For the purpose of essays, researching involves more than simply finding things. It involves marshalling the materials in an organised and usable way. This may be by borrowing books, photocopying articles, or downloading material from the internet but always with an idea of why those materials are useful for your assignment. To help you on this aspect of the task it is useful to keep a logbook of what you have gathered, and why, plus a record of where you have been to find those materials. The record allows you to understand the links between pieces of information and enables you to avoid redoing searches, particularly internet searches, which may be quite time-consuming.

Collecting resources does not mean you have read them!

During your research you should be reading material, even if cursorily, so as to determine its relevance. The big danger that many students fail to see is that this part of the essay writing process is about researching and reading. This latter point is often overlooked during the satisfying locate, borrow, or photocopy stage. That is, you should be aware of the danger of thinking that simply because you have a large pile of books or photocopies that you now have that information in your head, let alone properly understood. The point we are making here is that you need to ensure you have adequate time to read all the material that you have deemed to be relevant—otherwise what is the point of gathering it?

After you have read the researched material you should make time to:

- consider it carefully and reflect on what it says;
- ask how different parts of the materials are different from, or the same as, each other; and
- make notes about how it might be practically used in your assignment.

Read, reflect, and then plan

This is part of developing a writing plan. This plan, if buttressed by good research and carefully developed, can assist you in moving methodically through the different stages of writing. Your plan should include:

- a beginning that sets the tone for the paper (possibly a statement of introduction or intent, a point of view that you wish to assert and vindicate, a question that you are to answer, an overriding purpose for your essay, or the nature of the argument that you are going to justify;
- a place for the identification and discussion of the issues, problems, or ideas as detected in the initial phase of essay production and which you now know to be relevant;
- a clear articulation of how your issues, problems, or ideas link to each other and the beginning statement; and
- an ending that brings your earlier writing together in a conclusion, decision, or answer to the beginning statement.

Computer technology now means that there is no excuse for submitting inferior quality work to your lecturer. Depending on your approach to writing, most students will make a number of drafts of their essay before handing it in. The first, or rough, draft is used to get your main ideas down on paper. This gives you a chance to see how those ideas link to each other and what you need in broad terms to make your paper more cohesive. A second draft is useful for starting to fill in the gaps that you have identified in the first draft. The second draft might be the place where you also begin to fill in details of references that you will have in your footnotes, or work out where you have gaps in those references (see Chapter 12 for a fuller discussion of referencing). A third draft is useful to determine whether the essay reads well and for the creation of bibliographies, tables of cases and statutes, and cover pages where necessary. A final draft is one that is properly checked for spelling and grammatical errors. It is good practice to allow a non-law student (like a parent, spouse or friend) to read your paper at this stage to assess it for comprehensibility. If you are not a person who uses multiple drafts of your work, because you 'edit as you type', you should at least ensure that you have time to consider your final draft from the readability, spelling, grammar, and consistency perspectives.

Whether you make multiple drafts or whether you 'type as you go' ensure that you do not deliberately or inadvertently plagiarise the work of another. Please see our discussion of plagiarism in the next chapter. Of importance to note is that many law schools are now using plagiarism detection software, such as Turnitin, to detect poor referencing and academic misconduct. Given that there are very few people who do not use computers to produce their papers, many law schools now require any and all written work to be submitted via the plagiarism detection programs.

In our experience there is rarely any piece of writing that cannot be improved if looked upon with a constructively critical eye. Before you submit any essay always ensure that you proofread it carefully. We do not recommend that you proofread any assignment immediately after you have finished typing it. We also do not endorse proofreading 10 minutes before the submission deadline passes. If you have planned your time we suggest that you proofread your essay a day after you believe you have finished typing it. This will give you an opportunity to put some 'distance' between yourself and your document so that when you read it again, you come to it a little fresh. The difficulty of proofreading something that has just been typed is that you are more psychologically prone to missing mistakes.

Ensure that you proofread any essay

The following is a brief list of things to do and not do when submitting any form of essay or written paper:

- Avoid overusing one source, particularly a secondary one, when one of the purposes of your paper may be for you to have done some research beyond the textbook.
- We deal with referencing in Chapter 12, but you should note that when you submit a paper you should make sure that your references are accurate and complete. A complete lack of referencing will obviously suggest

plagiarism unless you have been requested to draft a completely unique document. Incomplete footnoting, particularly of cases, may suggest to the reader that you have sourced the information from a secondary source and have not properly noted the primary source.

- Make sure your footnote number positions, where used, appear after the punctuation marks.
- Avoid using different referencing systems in the one paper. Always use the recognised referencing system adopted by your school. One such system is discussed in Chapter 12.
- Avoid using secondary resources instead of going to the primary sources when your paper really requires you to use primary sources. Using primary resources frequently gives you insights that a paraphrased summary in a secondary source simply cannot.
- Ensure your footnotes are on the correct page (that is, the same page as the superscripted footnote call out number).
- Ensure correct placement of your footnote numbers. They should, usually, appear after relevant quotes and names, not at the beginning of the sentence.
- Always indicate the date on which you visited certain website addresses.
- Always proofread your document before submission. An excellent way to do this is to read it aloud. The way it sounds when spoken can give you an idea as to whether your sentences are too long, or whether something is grammatically incorrect.
- Check that any technical word you are using is in fact the correct one in that situation. Many students erroneously use 'section' instead of 'sub-section', 'clause', or 'regulation'.
- Avoid contracting words like 'don't' in formal papers—unless you are quoting someone else.
- Do your spell check with an Australian English spellchecker—turn off the US spellchecker.
- Avoid using 'we'/'us' when the paper is by you ('I'/'me').
- Use capital letters for proper nouns.
- Do not capitalise words that are not proper nouns or the first word of a sentence just to make them look more important.

- Avoid using archaic language when plain English will express what you intend.
- Regardless of sub-divisions that may be made within the various primary and secondary sources you use, make sure your bibliography items are in alphabetical order.
- Generally it is appropriate to capitalise the word Act when referring to a statute.
- Italicise or underline case names.
- Understand that some words sound pretty much the same but are spelt differently, so be sure about which one it is that you wish to use. Here are some examples of words sometimes confused and misused:

adverse/averse	its/it's	their/there/they're
advice/advise	lose/loose	to/too/two
affect/effect	practice/practise	wave/waive/waver
council/counsel	prescribe/proscribe	whose/who's
enquiry/inquiry	principle/principal	

A final point is in order on essays. While we explain traditional research theses briefly below it is the case that most regular essays are opportunities for you to argue a view or adopt a perspective or present a 'thesis' about the question or issues in dispute. That is, unless the directions indicate otherwise, most essays, whether theoretically oriented or problem based, give you the opportunity to develop 'your' argument or thesis buttressed by the positive law or policy or theory. Many good essays, which simply answer the question asked by referring to the relevant materials and addressing the identifiable issues, could become great essays if the students writing them had more clearly and forcefully argued their own position or thesis. It is our experience that the students who have more fully researched an area, thought about it deeply, and set about answering the question (or addressing the problem issues) in the light of their own view or thesis, are the ones who consistently achieve higher grades. This is because the development of one's own thesis, which is properly supported by the relevant research materials, requires the use of higher-level thinking skills than 'simply' answering a question.

Field-trip reports

An exciting opportunity for legal contextual learning occurs when you have the opportunity to attend a field trip. Field trips may be to the offices of legal practitioners, police stations, prisons, court or tribunal complexes, community legal centres, government departments, legal support services or just into the community. But wherever they occur there are usually a number of matters to consider. First, you should always do some background reading to understand the environment that you are about to enter. There may be procedures and behavioural protocols that you need to comply with. You should also read and carefully consider what the objectives of the field trip are. What is it that your lecturer wants you to experience by attending the field trip? On a field trip, you need to be focused on the experience and make relevant observations, or, (where possible), take good notes. This can be enhanced by using smartphones and other devices to take photographs and recordings where permissible.

Having been out of the confines of the law school you will hopefully have learnt a great deal about the practice of law, or the context in which an aspect of law is used in society. But what you learnt will need to be translated into a written report for assessment. The directions in your learning guide as to what to write about are important. Some lecturers will ask you to engage in research to buttress your observations. Others will be seeking to elicit from you more subjective statements about your experience on the field trip. Importantly, you need to make sure you write in a logical and structured manner in answering the requirements for the report. Following the guidance we provided in relation to essays is usually consistent with report writing.

Reflective journals

Reflective journals, also known as learning logs, daily diaries and learning journals, are devices that allow you to record, ponder, and evaluate your reactions to nominated experiences. Reflective journals are used in practice-oriented contexts, like clinical placements and alternative dispute resolution activities. But they can also be used in more theoretical contexts to provide insight into how students have responded to an essay question, classroom problem, visiting speaker or reading. In this more theoretically oriented approach you might be asked to reflect on how and why you made the decisions you did in relation to researching a particular topic that you then wrote up as an essay or report.

Reflective journals sound like easy-to-produce, subjective, and random collections of thoughts. Do not be deceived. While such journals require you to make some subjective submissions, the link to research literature and the need to be critical of what you are recording is usually a significant part of the task. Simply, you need to be able to pull apart the subjective materials and consider why you thought, felt and believed the way you did. Typically, you will be required to briefly describe your experiences, emotions and understandings. Then you will need to consider those perspectives from different viewpoints. What was the process you were in or adopted? How was what you experienced consistent with theory or the stated experiences of others? What does the similarity or difference you perceive say about you, others and the theory? What have you learnt about yourself, or a particular situation, or an area of legal practice?

Again, it is recommended, subject to particular guidance you might be given, that you follow the logic and advice provided in relation to essay writing in relation to prose, referencing and presentation.

Mooting and the viva voce examination

Moots and viva voce examinations are two forms of oral assessment. They are generally considered by students to be quite stressful exercises due to the public speaking requirements of the tasks.

Moots

Mooting is an integral part of many law school units. Mooting is an intellectual and practical activity that involves the blending of many skills. Mooting involves you as a student advocate arguing points of law before a judge, or judges (usually real ones) in a mock court. Normally moots are arguments based on how a case is argued in an appeal court. Thus you will not be examining witnesses or speaking to a jury (the typical courtroom fare on television programs). Rather, you will be

Mooting means engaging in mock court

making submissions about the law and how it should be interpreted or changed, to appellate judges. Mooting requires you to analyse a given fact situation, identify the issue(s), research the law pertaining to those issues, and then produce arguments supporting the case for your client. The analysis and research involved in a moot is extensive, and good preparation will assist your submissions. By being thoroughly familiar with the facts and law of your case you will be better able to assist the court in coming to a decision. In addition you will ensure that you are performing to the expectations of mooting examiners.

In moots you submit arguments to judges

The presentation of arguments usually involves both oral and written submissions. Good preparation ensures that written submissions are complete and accurate. A complete understanding of your case allows you, as advocate, to be able to think quickly on your feet and answer questions that are asked by the bench. You must have complete familiarity with any case, statute, document or reference that you refer to in a moot. It is important for you to note that judges will ask questions of you and therefore good preparation allows you to predict questions that may be asked and deal with those questions in an appropriate and competent manner.

OVERVIEW OF MOOT PROCEDURE

Mooting is a group activity

Moots are conducted in the following manner. Teams of students are provided with a set of agreed facts or a common law precedent. In teams, you are required to develop arguments for a hearing in your university's moot court, classroom, or occasionally a genuine court. Students in each team are usually divided into those who will be acting as counsel for their client—and will need to prepare oral and written arguments for the court and for assessment purposes—and those acting as non-advocates—who normally have a greater responsibility for written submissions. The division of arguments or issues in the case and respective workloads is a decision for the team, or the lecturer. Where there are two or more advocates in a team the senior and junior counsel are usually expected to speak for similar periods of time. The time limits vary from university to university and can be between 15 and 40 minutes per speaker.

PREPARATION FOR MOOTS

Agreed facts

Determine the parameters of your problem

The facts of each moot are known as 'agreed' facts. Facts are 'agreed' because each party has consented to the consistent version of events that led to the case being examined in the mock appeal court. These facts should not be altered by you without the prior permission of the relevant mooting coordinator. Initial preparation requires you to meet with your moot partners; sometimes they are your regular law school colleagues and sometimes they are complete strangers. When you all come together for the first time you will be required to master the facts of the case. Often an initial meeting of all students (that is, your team and your opponents) is helpful in determining the limits of the facts of a case—including jurisdictional questions. Having fully comprehended the agreed facts, you, with the rest of your team, should determine the different interpretations available to all parties to the dispute. It is not until you are familiar with the facts of the case and the opposing views of those facts that you will be able to successfully identify the relevant legal issues and research the law. Having identified the issues, you, with the rest of your team, should begin to formulate arguments that may be used on behalf of your client. Issues and arguments should be ordered chronologically or in order of strength—the key is to have some logical system to the arguments you are to research and develop. Unless chronological order is really necessary to use, good advocates will generally ensure that the strongest arguments are submitted first, even if these are not in order of time. The arguments developed will be the basis of submissions that you will present to the court to resolve the case in favour of your client. Before engaging in extensive library research, try to develop arguments from your understanding of the facts and (initial) limited knowledge of the law. Arguments may be based on: commonsense notions of what the law is and what justice would require; authorities and case law that you already know may be relevant; arguments by analogy to like situations; arguments that are typically used in these types of cases; the effect of a decision both for and against your client; and, arguments affecting public policy. Further research will allow you to expand on these ideas.

CONDUCTING THE RESEARCH

After identifying initial arguments and the remedy that your client desires, you should establish which court is available to grant that remedy. Then proceed to determine the basic principles of law that may apply to that case. Initial research should involve an examination of secondary materials followed by an extensive review of primary materials (cases, legislation, Bills, treaties, and then those same materials in other jurisdictions). Frequently you will find that there is no one piece of legislation or case that provides all the answers to your client's issues. Therefore you will need to fully research the area of law in dispute. For this, you should consider the notes on legal research skills in Chapter 10. Relying on reported decisions of the High Court or your Supreme Court alone is not always adequate preparation for a moot. You will be expected, where appropriate, to research unreported decisions and decisions from other jurisdictions. Decisions of the superior courts in Canada, England, and New Zealand are generally well respected and persuasive when comparable fact and law situations arise. Sometimes you may be able to find a precedent that appears to have a similar fact situation to that of the moot problem. You should be careful in relying on just that precedent as usually that case may be distinguished from your case on the facts, or it may not be binding on the court in which you are to appear. Additionally, you should not be attempting to find that 'one' particular case that is determinative of the law in question. Moot problems are normally designed to take you past the known boundaries of the decided law with a view to making you submit arguments as to how particular precedents may be utilised to positive effect on the moot problem.

Mooting research requires consideration of jurisdictions

DEVELOPING SUBMISSIONS

The key to effective submissions will be your ability to relate the legal arguments to the specific fact situations. Constantly apply the law to the facts to determine the worth of your research. Oral and written submissions each have distinct roles in the process of attempting to influence the decision of the court. Oral arguments are an opportunity to test and explain the written submissions upon which the court will strongly rely. By arguing orally you have an opportunity to gauge the reaction of the judge to your ideas and modify them accordingly. Oral argument presents an opportunity for you to quickly respond to the arguments of opposing counsel and to clarify or enhance areas in your written submissions that you feel are not being well received.

Written submissions

Your written submission is the basis of your oral arguments and a referent for the judges when your oral arguments are not as persuasive as they would have liked. Your written submissions should be a brief, clear, and systematic presentation of the arguments that you believe the court should adopt. These arguments must clearly indicate relevant legal authorities. The written submissions should be a progressive series of points that you consider should lead the court to a decision in favour of your client. Having determined the relevant issues and arguments and researched the applicable law, you should begin to formulate submissions. Writing the submission will often require you (individually and in your team) to assemble a chronology of facts and a list of issues and arguments that have arisen from the facts (including those that do not favour your client's arguments). Specific submissions must be developed in relation to the facts and arguments. Your submissions must be supported by legal authorities. After you have developed a number of arguments, it is wise to test your submissions with your mooting partners. This is best done by playing 'devil's advocate' and questioning every statement made. It is essential that you consider every word that you place in a written submission. Analyse it for legal appropriateness and tactical advantage.

Writing submissions

Unlike oral submissions, where you are able to explain the choice of word or phrase used, your written submissions must be accurate and complete when printed and submitted or tendered. As you may be required to present separate oral arguments in court, and separate written submissions for assessment, it is wise to develop separate written documents as a final part of a process. Written submissions should be an outline of the arguments that you intend to use in the moot. They should be logically organised and should not be a list of the facts or a list of *rationes decidendi* from the cases. Submissions should be combinations of fact and law that provide the court with the legal and factual reasons your arguments should be adopted by the court. Written submissions should have appropriate legal references within them and should refer to page numbers of judgments cited. Unless your moot is informal, your written submissions should be typewritten. Once you have completed your personal written submissions, ensure that you proofread the document from start to finish and check your partner's written submissions. In preparation for the oral submission, you will also need to make an outline of the key points of your submission.

Consolidated list of authorities

Normally you are required to provide the court with a consolidated list of authorities. Frequently these will be required by the judges and lecturer in advance of the date of the moot. These should be listed chronologically by jurisdiction. Ensure you speak with your opposing team early in the event to ensure that the consolidated list is truly one list for both teams.

MOOT COURT PROCEDURE AND COURTESIES

You should be sitting at the Bar table well in advance of the time for the moot. You should gain instructions from your lecturer as to which side of the Bar table each team should sit. Different courts have different approaches but a general rule is that counsel for the prosecution/plaintiff/applicant/appellant normally sit on the left-hand side of the Bar table (the right-hand side from the judge's perspective). Counsel for the defence/respondent sit on the right-hand side of the Bar table. You should be well prepared and have organised your file and notes, drinking water, lectern, and, where necessary, library resources prior to the moot beginning. Where your moot court does not hold all the physical resources within it that may need to be used by the judge, you should ensure that you have organised copies (through your library) of all the case reports, statutes, and other primary legal documents well in advance. Alternatively, you may be allowed to use electronic resources if your court and judge are equally well-equipped to use them.

Court protocol

The court officer (if at university a student appointed for the role on the day) will ask everyone to stand before the judge makes her or his entrance. As the judge takes a seat, everyone should bow to her or him. Once the judge is seated, the court officer should announce the name of the case and then take a seat in front of the judge

Stand upon entrance of the judge

and assist with the passage of documents during the moot. Counsel should be prepared to announce appearances as soon as the judge is settled. Sometimes the judge will ask for appearances but frequently the judge will just look towards counsel for the prosecution/plaintiff/applicant/appellant. Senior counsel for the prosecution/plaintiff/applicant/appellant should stand and introduce himself or herself and the junior and indicate who they are representing. For instance: 'Your Honour, my name is Georgia Lillian and I am assisted by Giselle Celeste. We represent XYZ Pty Ltd, the appellant in this matter.' Counsel should then sit and wait for the rest of the appearances. Senior counsel for the defendant/respondent should then stand and introduce the opposing team in a similar fashion.

Counsel should always stand when speaking or being spoken to. In the event that opposing counsel speak while you are still on your feet, sit until they have finished. This enables the judge to have a conversation with one person at a time. By sitting you allow yourself time to collect your thoughts and take a break from the questioning of the judge—normally the judge will be addressing the person left standing.

Oral argument

Upon the completion of introductions by all counsel, senior counsel for the prosecution/plaintiff/applicant/appellant should then stand and provide the court with a brief overview of the case for the appellant, and an indication of the respective roles of senior and junior counsel (that is, the division of labour). In some moots, the senior counsel for the opposition will also be given a brief opportunity to outline their case—but sometimes upon giving the overview of the case for the appellant, senior counsel will then begin their detailed address to the court.

No matter how confident you are at speaking in public, engaging in moots can cause you to be nervous. In fact, if you are not nervous you probably have not prepared properly! How do you deal with nerves? The easiest way to deal with nerves associated with moots is to be well organised and prepared. If you have considered all the issues, researched the relevant law, communicated well with your moot partner(s), and practised your speech then you should be in a position to tell yourself that you have all the resources you need to complete the task. Other things to consider are: get to the venue early, locate the toilet, ensure you have a drink and some snacks, and make sure your notes are organised. Also consider the following three points. Even the most senior barristers or advocates are nervous before heading into a trial or appeal. When you start talking you will gain confidence and should be able to relax—time will seem to fly once you enter the mooting 'zone'. Understand that the moot court judge is simply another human being to whom you are making a submission (talking). Like any oral communication process this can be made simpler if you listen and answer the judge's questions (as opposed to what you 'want' the question to be), and you speak using plain and precise language.

Generally, counsel should begin any address to the court with the phrase 'If it pleases the court …' or 'May it please the court …'. These phrases signify the respect that should be accorded the judge and provide an opportunity for counsel to start their address without having to use exotic phraseology. The use of such phrases during the course of the moot, usually to preface new points, also provides counsel with an opportunity to collect their thoughts if they are rushing or as a 'gap-filler' instead of 'um'. You should not be reticent about using such phrases often during your oral submission. Counsel should never just read their written submissions. It is expected that counsel will maintain eye contact with the judge for most of the session and only refer to notes as an aid to memory or for case citations or quotes. To assist you in maintaining eye contact it is recommended that the summary sheet and list of authorities be kept on the lectern so that a quick glance at them does not require large head movements down to the Bar table. In addition to assisting with eye contact, having brief notes on the lectern enables you to keep your head up, which should help you to project your voice across to the bench.

You should always bear in mind that counsel's task is to assist the judge in coming to a decision about the case. While you will be putting forward views consistent with your client's wishes it is essential to make sure that what you have to say is heard and understood. Many students are nervous about speaking in a public forum and tend to speak too quickly. Do not attempt to finish your submission in as short a time as possible. You are advised to allow the spoken word to be properly heard. Therefore you must project your voice and allow it to be understood by the judge—slow down and speak in a measured tone. Do not mistake a moot for a debate or television courtroom advocacy. While theatrics sometimes have their place, a moot requires a systematic and comprehensive progression through your arguments. Do not move from your position at the Bar table and always use court staff to ferry documents back and forth to the bench.

Always indicate that you are submitting an argument on behalf of a client, not a personal opinion. For instance it is correct to say 'I submit …', 'It is my submission …', or 'It is submitted …'. Never say 'I think …' or 'In my opinion …' or 'I believe …'. The judge is not interested in personal opinions of counsel but rather the arguments you place before the court on behalf of a client. Should the judge ask you for your 'personal' opinion about the present state of the law in question, or your private view of the facts, you are entitled to 'think'; however it is recommended that you preface your response with the phrase 'I submit …' or 'In my humble submission …' Further, it is grammatically incorrect to continually refer to 'We submit' when it is you, an individual, making the submissions. 'We' is often used by students as a psychological defence mechanism, as a means of sharing responsibility for your arguments with the rest of your team. Unfortunately, when so used, it is usually used incorrectly.

You should expect questions from the bench. While mooting can be stressful, particularly if you are a nervous public speaker, questions from the bench should be looked upon without fear. Questions are an opportunity for you to demonstrate your ability to synthesise your arguments into a cohesive whole and a chance to validate the arguments you have been progressing through. Remember that the judge is interested in testing your arguments as a way of clarifying his or her thoughts on the issue. If you do not react confidently and persuasively to the judge's questions you may be doing yourself and your client a disservice.

Always allow the judge to complete her or his question or statement before answering or responding. Good advocates will be aware of attempts by judicial officers to interrupt, or question or make a statement quite simply because they are good communicators. Part of the multifaceted task of acting as an advocate is to be completely aware of the person to whom you are communicating your message and to understand that good communication does not occur if the recipient does not effectively receive that message.

Always answer the question being asked—do not answer the question you wish you had been asked or the question you anticipate may come in the future. In the event that you do not understand a question from the judge, politely ask for it to be repeated. If you find that the question itself is still not clear ask for it to be clarified. When answering the question it is important to do so from the perspective of the research you have undertaken. That is, base your response to judicial questions on the research that you have undertaken for the hearing and the insights you have gained from judicial input during the moot.

In the event of being corrected or 'educated' by a judge always respond with 'If the court pleases' or 'As your Honour pleases'. If you believe that the judge is in error or is under a misapprehension then you should preface any response with the phrase 'With respect, your Honour …'. You are entitled, indeed sometimes expected, to push a point with the bench. Do so forcefully but respectfully and if you have lost the point politely concede.

Importantly, be aware that you are the mouthpiece for your client and as such should never become emotionally involved in the arguments you place before the court. Never personalise an argument or react unprofessionally to an adverse decision by the Bench.

Whenever you refer to the judge it is always 'Your Honour', whenever referring to opposing counsel you should use the phrase 'My learned friend'. Should you ever need to confer with opposing counsel, perhaps to inspect a case reference that they may have, always seek permission from the bench: 'Your Honour, may I briefly confer with my learned friend …'. When you have completed your submission you should indicate the same to the judge: 'Your Honour, that completes my submission(s).' You may find that the judge wishes to ask a question of you before you take a break so be prepared.

Once senior counsel has completed the address for the prosecution/plaintiff/applicant/appellant, junior counsel should stand and continue the appellant's case. Following this, the senior counsel for the defendant/respondent should address the court, followed by junior counsel for the defendant/respondent. Some mooting assessments give the first team an opportunity to make a further brief submission based upon its response to the second team's submissions. However, regardless of whether you have this opportunity you should note that a well prepared team will already have addressed its opponent's arguments during their initial submissions. This arises because you have been compelled to swap arguments prior to the moot, or, more importantly, you have prepared comprehensively enough that you have dealt with such arguments already.

As mentioned earlier, different universities run mooting assessments differently. However, you should normally expect to speak anywhere from 15 to 40 minutes. You should factor into this time period the questions and interactions from the bench. That is, do not think that you will be able to deliver a lecture without interruption for the time allocated. If you know that you will be answering questions quite regularly throughout your oral submission then you should realise that you will probably not be able to put everything before the court that you would if you had the full time totally at your disposal. Thus, you should arrange your material to make sure that you have, at the least, made the more important or crucial submissions at the beginning—in case you run out of time.

At the end of these questions and submissions by both teams the judge will deliver judgment.

Citation of cases during oral submissions

Cases are not described orally in the manner they are read on a page. A citation such as *R v Brown* (1996) 150 CLR 209 at 211 is not spoken as 'Are vee Brown round brackets nineteen ninety six one-fifty see-ell-are two hundred and nine at two hundred and eleven.' The manner of description is 'Crown against Brown Commonwealth Law Reports, volume one hundred and fifty, page two hundred and nine at two-eleven.' Note: the 'v' is pronounced 'against' in criminal cases and 'and' in civil cases. The abbreviation CLR is spoken in full (know all the report abbreviations that you will use). The year reference is not necessary as the year is surrounded by round brackets indicating that the volume number is sufficient. Should this have been a square bracket series (i.e., the year is important) the year would be spoken after the name of the report series—the judge's associate or judge who needs to locate the case being referred to from the collection of authorities to be used by both teams will need to know the report series before locating the year or volume number. The switch in order between the report series/title and the volume when written or spoken (it is written with the volume first but when speaking the volume is said second) is because when a judge, or their associate, is reaching for 'volume 150' they must wait until you have indicated the report series before obtaining the required volume 150—there may be more than one volume 150. If you indicate the report series/title first then the volume or year number is the next logical piece of information the judge requires to find the reference to which you are referring.

When referring to the judgment of a particular judge always say 'Justice McHugh' not 'McHugh Jay'. If referring to a Chief Justice of a particular court, do not say 'Chief Justice Gleeson' or 'Gleeson Cee-Jay', say 'Justice Gleeson, Chief Justice of the High Court' or 'The Chief Justice, Justice Gleeson'. If it is necessary to refer the judge to a specific passage on the page of a judgment, do so by making use of any margin indicators in the report series. For example, the printed hard copy form of the Commonwealth Law Reports uses margin indicators A through to E down the page. If the report series does not have margin indicators, you should make use of the 'decimal-point' system. That is, you imagine the page is divided into tenths and indicate the passage by reference to the nearest tenth. For example, 'Your Honour, that passage may be found at point 7 on the page.' Always allow the judge time to read and digest the passage to which you have referred. Generally, the judge will require you to address her or him about the relevance and importance of the passage (otherwise why would you be making the point) and may only glance at the passage before asking you to discuss it. Most electronic, and citation neutral, case systems use paragraph numbers to assist students, practitioners and judges find the relevant text quickly.

You should understand that oral submissions are about verbal communication in a one-to-one situation. If you smile, where appropriate, and have a positive demeanour the judge will be more disposed to you on a personal level than if you are frowning or angry. This will never take the place of excellent oral arguments, but judges are human and like to have some humanity in their courts. Humour will appear in a moot from time to time. If a judge makes a joke, a polite laugh is appropriate, but never attempt to make a comedy routine part of your submissions.

Judges may be distracted from your arguments if you overuse your hands in flourishing gestures or fiddle with your notes or pen. Additionally, do not lean on the Bar table—try to keep your hands together and grasp the lectern if you have a habit of talking with your hands. We are not saying that advocates should not use hand or bodily gestures to make significant points but we recognise that overuse renders gestures ineffective when you really need to emphasise a point.

Legal ethics

Counsel is required to comply with the relevant advocacy rules as provided in the professional ethics rules in your jurisdiction. You should refer to the websites of your jurisdiction's bar association or law society. Across all the jurisdictions the chief rules are:

1 Counsel must not mislead the court as to the law or facts—you cannot lie, or otherwise misrepresent anything in court, no matter how much benefit you or your 'client' may receive by so doing.
2 Counsel must bring relevant authorities to the attention of the court, even if those authorities are against your client's interest. Dealing effectively with the adverse authority is one way of showing the court and examiners that you have a full grasp of the law, and may allow you to place the authority in a less positive light than your opponents probably would have—this is consistent with the view that a legal professional's duty to the court is higher than their duty to the client.

Individual unit learning guides may have specific administrative requirements for your moot. Please read them in conjunction with this chapter and remember that your unit outline is the primary document regarding the requirements for that unit.

Viva voce examinations

A viva voce is an oral examination where you present an argument, defend a position, or discuss other materials in front of an examiner or panel of examiners. The viva voce is discussed in some detail in Chapter 13, as it is typically referred to as a form of examination. For the purpose of this chapter it is relevant to note that viva voce examinations may be an assignment that you undertake during the course of a semester. This is because a viva voce may be a formative learning exercise. That is, it is not simply an examination designed to show what you know and understand, but is also a form of feedback on how well you know a given topic, what you may still need to learn, and how effective your oral communication skills are. A viva voce examination is simply an opportunity for you to show the depth of your learning by discussing a case, legal topic, or theory with your lecturer.

Preparation for a viva voce examination is similar to a moot in the sense that you need to:

- read and comfortably understand the material you are to be examined on;
- be prepared to orally defend your understanding, or position;
- demonstrate an ability to speak as an advocate in court (in some forms of such examinations);
- consider, without notice, competing ideas, or fact situations and how they might relate to your topic.

Viva voce examinations are great opportunities for students who enjoy communicating orally to show their comprehension and grasp of certain subject matter. For those less comfortable with oral tests, the viva voce should be seen as an opportunity to develop new skills that will be useful in any professional environment.

Research papers and theses

Research papers are highly refined arguments

Research papers are essay-style assignments that might also be labelled mini-theses. These papers compel the writer to undertake more advanced research and create more finely tuned arguments than would normally be expected in a standard essay. This is because the nature of the assignment is more narrowly focused than is normally the case with typical essay topics. Research papers and theses, if genuinely research based, are usually undertaken in later years of a law program. The exception that you might encounter is that you might have to do a 'research paper' in an introductory law unit. Such a research paper is really a research skills-oriented assignment. That is, the 'research paper' is simply a method of causing you to become familiar with research methods and legal resources. It is not research in the sense of a narrowly confined topic where you might be developing a unique view about a legal problem or theory.

Typically, the topic of a true research paper will be chosen by the student and will need approval by the lecturer. Undertaking research papers and theses requires interaction with your lecturer or supervisor as mentor (on a regular basis) and is a specialist research process beyond the scope of this book. If you do undertake a research paper, or thesis, you need to follow similar approaches to those suggested above for essay production.

Importantly you need to:

- Develop an argument (or thesis)—most research papers require the writer to hold or develop an opinion or point of view and then justify it.
- Keep the focus of your paper very narrow—a broad topic will generally not fit within the available word limit for the assignment.
- Continually check to consider how what you are writing is consistent with your thesis.
- Consider materials beyond those normally referred to when doing essays—for example, by considering what occurs in other jurisdictions (even where your general topic is arguably jurisdiction-specific), and what other academic disciplines have to say about related issues.

Research papers normally acquire formal supervision

A thesis or research project is not something that most students write unless they are engaged in honours or postgraduate studies. However, the principles that underpin a thesis are commonly referred to by lecturers in essays and other forms of written work. Additionally, you might find the prospect of undertaking this form of research appealing, so we touch upon it briefly here.

So what is a thesis? A thesis, in its basic form, is an extended essay that delves into a particular area of law to a depth considerably greater than a typical essay. A thesis will be distinguishable from an essay in two main ways. First, a thesis will examine a much narrower topic than a standard undergraduate essay. Second, a thesis will have a much more refined argument than would be expected in an essay and that argument must be maintained throughout the paper. If you undertake a thesis, or research project, you should consider two main things. What is the position or argument that you are holding? And what are the strengths and weaknesses of your thesis? Let's briefly consider these two areas.

The thesis statement

The thesis statement is the focal part of your paper

The thesis statement is the position or argument that you are maintaining and justifying throughout your paper. This statement is often very difficult to develop and requires a significant amount of pre-reading and thinking. A thesis statement, in draft form, is often required before you will be given permission to undertake the writing of a thesis or research project. The statement needs to be suitably narrow so as to allow you to focus in on the issue or issues that derive from a close consideration of it. A thesis statement is also the point about which the rest of your writing will centre. And while it is flexible and may change as a result of your further research and writing, the statement in final form is the core of your paper. Therefore you need to consider it very carefully when first thinking about engaging in such research. And you also need to ensure that the research that you ultimately undertake actually results in an answer to the question or justifies the position to which your thesis statement refers. Many students engaging in this form of research often struggle with a thesis statement that does not accurately represent the direction in which the research they are doing has proceeded.

Clearly, having a good thesis supervisor, or supervising lecturer, enables you to discuss issues about your thesis and the direction of your research—so use the expertise on offer if you engage in this form of legal writing. There are two main steps to developing a useful thesis statement. First, you need to find something that is new and different in some respect. That is, you need to have an angle or view of a particular area of research that is in some way unique. The best way to find the difference required for a thesis is to undertake significant background research. By examining journal articles, relevant court cases, conference proceedings, law reform commission reports, and media reports you will be in a position to know what the limits of a particular area of study are, and thus where the 'new' and different areas may be. Clearly, speaking with your supervisor can give you a head start in this process. Second, you need to ensure that what you intend to research is relevant, necessary, and achievable. To do this you will need to develop some form of justification for the thesis statement itself—'this is an important area of enquiry because …'—as well as the process you are going to follow in order to achieve the task of answering your question or justifying your position.

There is no point undertaking a thesis if it is not deemed to be different enough from existing knowledge or if the means proposed to complete the research are practically impossible—for instance, because the relevant literature is in another country, or the financial costs or time factors are too great for the time allocated to the thesis.

Strengths and weaknesses of your thesis

A thesis must, word by word, sentence by sentence, paragraph by paragraph, heading by heading, and chapter by chapter, show any reader that your thesis is one that is logical, rational, and strongly defended. To this end you must ensure that everything you place in your paper goes towards showing that your argument is well maintained. Thus you cannot afford to write a thesis with an eye primarily on reaching a word limit. Such an approach leaves you open to using filler material that is irrelevant or simply wasting valuable space in your paper. A thesis should be considered a form of written advocacy to the extent that you are attempting to persuade a reader that your argument is strong and thus should be accepted. Therefore you need to make it very clear to the reader that you have some persuasive and powerful arguments that support your thesis. Equally, the academic process and academic integrity require you to consider and reduce or eliminate arguments that may run counter to your thesis. Where you have engaged in some original research, whether empirical or theoretical, you will need to justify the reasons you took the research path that you did. For example, simply because a particular series of questions was easy to develop or ask is not, in and of itself, a good reason for that series. You would need to have some theoretical, practical, economic, or other justification to satisfy academic judges of your work.

A thesis must be internally consistent

Finally, ensure that in your efforts to produce an excellent argument you do not deliberately or inadvertently use another person's views without proper referencing. Please consider the material on plagiarism in the Chapter 12.

Late assignments and misadventure

If you adopt our advice in Chapter 7, you will be unlikely to submit an assignment late or have resort to university or school regulations relating to misadventure. However, as carefully as you may plan, there may be times when the unexpected arises and you are compelled to submit an assignment late, or ask for special consideration based on some misadventure you have suffered. We recommend that you become very familiar with your university's and law school's rules about late and missing assignments as well as provisions dealing with misadventure. As discussed in Chapter 7, and as reprised in Chapter 14, you should always try to give your lecturers notice about lateness or misadventure so as to maximise your chance of avoiding a penalty.

12

ASSIGNMENTS: REFERENCING/CITING AND PLAGIARISM

I hate like death the situation of the plagiarist; the glass I drink from is not large, but at least it is my own.

Alfred de Musset[1]

1 Alfred de Musset (1810–57), 'La Coupe et les Lèvres' (1832), 'The Oxford Dictionary of Quotations'.

Introduction

When making an oral presentation, whether in a moot, viva voce, seminar, or other activity you may be asked to justify your statements by way of explaining the source of ideas you are using. For example, as discussed in Chapter 11, participants in a moot may be asked, by the presiding judge, to provide details of the law that is being cited. Similarly in written assignments you are compelled to explain the source of your ideas. Unlike oral presentations, where in the absence of disclosure you may be asked to provide the source of an idea, written assignments place the emphasis on you to disclose your sources without any prompting. In this chapter we will explain how to reference and the ramifications for you if you do not properly reference.

The importance of correct referencing

Referencing is an integral part of the academic process in that it assists any author, as you will become, to explain how and why you have reached certain conclusions about something. Referencing assists you in justifying your arguments because the works you use as references lend weight to, or support, your argument. Referencing is important for your lecturers because it allows them to see the path that you have followed in researching and discussing an area of law.

If you have researched well, the lecturer will be able to see evidence of that research in your footnotes or other referencing method. Thus, referencing is a positive way of reinforcing your arguments and showing support for your views. A well-referenced paper will make it easier for your lecturer to understand the position or argument you hold and will assist you in clarifying your thoughts. But there is a downside to referencing if it is not done adequately. If you have researched well, but have failed to show correct evidence of it in your paper—and most lecturers want to know that you have read relevantly and widely in relation to such tasks—then you will suffer in four possible ways. First, your lecturer cannot give you marks that may be allocated for research. Second, unless your arguments are unique, the lack of correct references may be viewed by your lecturer as your having appropriated someone else's ideas. Third, if the lecturer develops a suspicion that you have not written your own work you may suffer the pain of having to answer charges of plagiarism, a form of academic misconduct. Plagiarism is the most serious form of

Referencing is essential to written assignments

Referencing provides evidence of your research

academic misconduct in the university learning system. Fourth, if you are found guilty of plagiarism, and should you wish to practise law, you will be required to disclose any finding of academic misconduct to your legal profession admitting authority when you apply to become a practitioner.

To reiterate our earlier point, referencing and citation are very important to academics and lawyers and thus to you. If you reference your paper correctly then you will have created a better paper with sound intellectual support. Because of this, many law schools have developed their own style guides for essays that include direction on a number of the matters related to the presentation and referencing of written papers. You should examine your school's guide carefully. In the event that you need more information than your school's style guide provides, you should refer to one of the many comprehensive referencing and citation guides. One guide that is increasingly popular among academics and utilised by many law schools and law school reviews is the Melbourne University publication *Australian Guide to Legal Citation*. While it is not a perfect system of referencing, its popularity across Australian law schools compels us to utilise aspects of it in parts of the following discussion.

Find your law school's style guide

What do I put in my references?

In order to understand what needs to be referenced and when it is essential, it is necessary to understand what materials should be referred to in your assignments and how you cite those different forms of materials. Regardless of what materials you cite you must ensure that you have read the materials being referred to. If you have not read the materials directly, but have gained the information through another source then you should state that fact.

Primary sources

In legal research primary sources are all those documents either being law (for example, case reports and legislation) or possibly becoming law (for example, Bills before Parliament). Primary sources are typically created by the organs of the law, the Courts and Parliament. Primary materials include those set out in Table 12.1, which provides a list of the most commonly used primary materials and the manner in which they would normally be referred to in a piece of legal writing.

Primary materials are the basic components of your reading and research

TABLE 12.1 Primary materials[2]

Primary materials	Method of citation		Example
Decisions from the courts and tribunals—whether state/territory or federal	Reported	Parties or case name (italicised), year, volume number, report series, starting page number, pinpoint reference (where required).	*Ousley v R* (1997) 192 CLR 69, 70.
	Unreported	[Where the court uses a court-based, medium-neutral citation system] Parties or case name (italicised), [year], court identifier, judgment number (Date of judgment) pinpoint reference (where required).	*R v Favero* [1999] NSWCCA 320 (19 October 1999) para 5.
		[Where a medium-neutral citation system is not used] Parties or case name (italicised), (Unreported status), (court, judge(s), date) pinpoint reference where required.	*R v Favero* (Unreported, Supreme Court of New South Wales, Court of Criminal Appeal), Sully J, 19 October 1999), para 5.
	Overseas	Some jurisdictions, such as the USA, use a different order for the component parts of a citation. Parties or Case name (italicised) Volume, Report series and series number, Starting page, Pinpoint reference (where required), (Jurisdiction & Court, Year).	*US v Simpson* 979 F 2d 1282 (8th Cir, 1992).
Parliament—whether state/territory or federal	Name of Act or title (italicised), year, jurisdiction, pinpoint reference where required.		*Crimes Act* 1914 (Cth) s 5.

2 The citation method here is based upon that used in the 3rd edition (2010) of the 'Australian Guide to Legal Citation' produced by the Melbourne University Law Review Association Inc.

Primary materials	Method of citation	Example
Delegated or subordinate legislation—as made by government departments and local government	Name or title of rule/regulation/by-law (in italics), year (in italics), (jurisdiction), pinpoint reference if required.	*Summary Offences Regulation 2000* (NSW) reg 4.
Bills—that may or may not become legislation	Name of Bill (not italicised), year, jurisdiction.	Bail Amendment (Repeat Offenders) Bill 2003 (NSW).
Hansard—parliamentary debates	Jurisdiction, Parliamentary Debates (italicised), Chamber of Parliament, full date, pinpoint reference (such as speech title) speaker's name.	Commonwealth, *Parliamentary* Debates, House of Representatives, 28 May 2003, National Handgun Buyback Bill 2003, Second Reading, Daryl Williams, Attorney General.
Treaties—even those treaties that do not form part of the law of Australia	Treaty name, Parties names (where necessary), Date opened for signature or signed, Treaty Series Citation, Date of entry into force, Pinpoint reference (where required).	Rome Statute of the International Criminal Court, 17 July 1998, UNTS 2187, 1 July 2002, art 8.

Secondary sources or materials

The term primary sources should be distinguished from what we might call secondary sources of law. Secondary sources are materials that have as their basis the description, discussion, analysis, or evaluation of primary sources. Your law textbooks, or journal articles, are examples of secondary materials in that they are usually designed to provide you with some commentary about the primary source of interest to you and your lecturer. The reason that these materials are referred to as secondary sources is that they usually came into existence after the creation of the primary source. Secondary sources are also created by a person, organisation, one step removed from the law-makers, who make the primary materials. That is, secondary materials are created not by judges and parliamentarians, but by law reform commissions, academics, and journalists. The information provided by secondary sources may sometimes include contextual material missing from the primary material. In this sense the secondary material can be extremely valuable for your understanding of the law. Frequently a secondary source commentary about the law by an expert will be easier to understand than the primary material. However, in one sense, secondary sources have a lesser status than the primary material. Except in an international law context, where the work of jurists has some significant weight, secondary materials cannot be legally binding, no matter how correct, just, or clear they are. Many secondary materials are extremely valuable and we do not wish to imply that they should be relegated to some lesser intellectual status. Indeed, many articles brilliantly analyse the benefits and deficiencies of the primary source law. The courts may also refer to such secondary sources in the course of developing a judgment—a primary source. However, we urge you to always consider the primary source when writing any paper or completing any oral assignment. This is because you should 'always' refer to the text of any primary source if you are referring to the law. Secondary sources, with the exception of international law, are not the law.

Secondary materials are commentaries and analyses of primary materials

Typical examples of secondary materials that you might consider using in any assignment are set out in the following table.

Table 12.2 provides a list of the most commonly used secondary materials and the manner in which they would normally be referred to in a piece of legal writing.

TABLE 12.2 Secondary materials[3]

Secondary material	Method of citation	Example
Textbooks and books generally	Author(s), book title (italicised), (Publisher, edition, year), pinpoint reference (where required).	David Spencer and Michael Brogan, *Mediation Law and Practice*, (Cambridge University Press, 2006) p 76.
Journal articles	Author(s), article name or title, (year of journal), volume of journal, journal name, starting page, pinpoint reference (where required).	David Spencer, 'To what degree of certainty must a dispute resolution clause be drafted?' (2003) 14 *Australasian Dispute Resolution Journal* 153, 157.
Legal encyclopaedias	Publisher, encyclopaedia title (italicised), volume number, (at date of retrieval), title number, name of title, 'chapter number, name of chapter' [paragraph number].	Law Book Company, *The Laws of Australia*, (at 12 March 2007) 27: Professional Liability, [27.1.3].].
Loose-leaf services	Publisher, Title (italicised), volume number (where relevant), (at most recent service number for pinpoint reference), pinpoint reference.	Butterworths, *Local Court Criminal Practice NSW*, Service 27, para 2.105.
Explanatory memoranda to Bills	Explanatory Memorandum, title of Bill (not italicised), year, jurisdiction, pinpoint reference (where required).	Explanatory Memorandum, Bail Amendment (Repeat Offenders) Bill 2003 (NSW).
Law reform commission reports	Law reform commission, report title (italicised), report/discussion title, number (year) pinpoint reference (where required).	Law Reform Commission of Victoria, *Rape: Reform of Law and Procedure*, Report No 43 (1991).
Internet material	Author name, title of document (italicised), (full date of last page update), website name, uniform resource locator. Note where the uniform resource locator (web address) is large or cumbersome the general website address may be used.	Sir Ninian Stephen, *Restorative Justice*, Law Council of Australia, http://www.lawcouncil.asn.au/read/2003/2378925531.
Newspaper articles	Author (where signed), title of article, newspaper name (italicised), place of publication, full date of publication, pinpoint reference.	P. E. Corcoran, 'Our rude parliamentarians are just victims, too', *Sydney Morning Herald*, 24 August 1995, p 7.

3 The citation method here is based upon that used in the 3rd edition (2010) of the 'Australian Guide to Legal Citation' produced by the Melbourne University Law Review Association Inc.

Referencing or citation methods

There are several ways of citing materials in an assignment. In law essays, reports, and journals the most frequently used method of citation of references is the footnote system. Alternative systems sometimes used in law include the endnote system, or those adopted in the social sciences, such as the Harvard System or the American Psychological Association. Each of these systems attempts to provide a convenient method for the reader to quickly and conveniently find the source of an idea, quote, or other piece of information that a writer has referred to in their writing. These systems also provide the user of the system with a way of avoiding claims of plagiarism.

Do not combine systems

While our personal preference, and that of many of our colleagues, is for law students to use the footnoting system, we acknowledge that there are other lecturers, particularly those with a social science or business background, who may have a preference for another system. Important points to note about using a referencing system are:

- In the absence of a law school policy on referencing and citation, always find out what your individual lecturer prefers—it is not much use using one system if your lecturer desires or mandates another.
- If you are not compelled to use a particular system, ensure that you use one and stick to it—consistency is one of the key attributes of a referencing system.
- If you have choice over what system to use try to use that which provides the reader with the most comprehensive information while still being easy to use. We note that all systems take a bit of getting used to but suggest that the footnote system is generally the one that provides the most information at a glance.

The footnote system (AGLC)

This method uses footnotes at the bottom of the page (or less frequently endnotes at the end of a paper) as a means of storing the relevant information about materials you have referred to in your paper. Whenever you use footnotes the full bibliographic information about an item (as provided in Table 12.2) should be included in the first reference to that material. Footnotes also provide you with a space not too far from the main body of your paper in which you can supply extra information to your reader. Such extra information includes relevant side-issues that might detract from the flow of the argument in the body of your paper but are important to note nonetheless. Footnotes are also an opportunity to make reference to alternative or opposing points to those you make in the body of your paper.

So how do they work? All wordprocessing programs have advanced features that allow you to insert a footnote at a relevant point in your document. Relevant points are immediately after you have mentioned a case name, inserted a quote, used an idea of another person, or wish to make a non-essential, yet important notation about a point you have just made in the body of your text.

Footnotes are useful information tools

As a general rule footnotes should be inserted at the closest point to the text that needs to have such a reference attached. Where the footnote needs to be inserted at the end of a sentence or quote, the footnote should always fall after the punctuation mark, usually a full-stop.

Footnotes should follow the punctuation marks

When you need to use one reference a number of times in your paper you will need to footnote it every time. We mentioned above that you should provide the full bibliographic information about a referenced item within the footnote when it is first referred to. But what do you do for second and subsequent references as indicated here? One approach is to take advantage of the copy and paste facility within your computer's word processor and simply duplicate the footnote, making alterations as to differing page or paragraph numbers (within the reference) as you go. This approach is useful, especially in the early draft stages of any paper, because it allows you to keep proper track of the connection between the footnote and the text in the main body of your paper to which it refers. The problem of not having full bibliographic details in every footnote—at least at the draft stage of your paper—is that if you use an abbreviation method, such as that endorsed by the *Australian Guide to Legal Citation*, you might find that the text you transfer to another part of your paper takes only an abbreviated footnote with it. Other alternatives to using full bibliographic details every time include using Latin abbreviations and the pure note number system. We also refer to those systems in Table 12.3 and Table 12.4 below. What follows is the footnoting system used in the *Australian Guide to Legal Citation*.

These are the main types of footnoting systems

TABLE 12.3 The *Australian Guide to Legal Citation* footnoting system[4]

Rule	Example (where necessary)
The first citation to a source should be given in full. Legislation should be cited in full every time it is footnoted.	1. David Spencer and Michael Brogan, *Mediation Law and Practice* (Cambridge University Press 2006) p 76. 1. *Crimes Act 1914* (Cth), s 5. 2. *Crimes Act 1914* (Cth), s 5.
Where a source is referred to again in the immediately following footnote use 'ibid' (Latin for in the same place), except for legislation.	1. David Spencer and Michael Brogan, *Mediation Law and Practice* (Cambridge University Press 2006) p 76. 2. Ibid.
Where a source is referred to again in the immediately following footnote but the page is different use 'ibid' followed by the new page reference.	1. David Spencer and Michael Brogan, *Mediation Law and Practice* (Cambridge University Press 2006) p 76. 2. Ibid p 90.
Where a secondary source (other than legislation, a case or a treaty) is referred to again in a subsequent footnote (but not to one that it immediately follows), or where the immediately preceding footnote contains more than one authority, 'above' and the relevant footnote number should be used.	1. David Spencer and Michael Brogan, *Mediation Law and Practice* (2006) p 76. 2. *Crimes Act 1914* (Cth), s 5. 3. Spencer and Brogan, above n 1. Or 1. David Spencer and Michael Brogan, *Mediation Law and Practice* (2006) p 77; *Crimes Act 1900* (NSW), s 18. 2. Spencer and Brogan, above n 12.
Where a source is legislation, a case or treaty and is referred to again in a subsequent footnote (but not to one that it immediately follows) the source should be repeated in full.	1. *Crimes Act 1900* (NSW), s 18. 2. *Crimes Act 1914* (Cth). 3. *Crimes Act 1900* (NSW), s 18.

4 The material in this table is based upon parts of Chapter 1 of the 'Australian Guide to Legal Citation', (2010) pp 1–35.

EXPRESSIONS USED IN FOOTNOTES

Use 'See' where the source provides qualified support for a point being made.
Use 'See, eg,' where the source is one of several that supports a point being made.
Use 'See also' where the source provides additional support for the point being made.
Use 'See especially' to indicate a source that is the strongest of several that support an idea in the text.
Use 'See generally' for sources that provide background information.
Use 'But see' for a source that shows partial disagreement with a point made in the text.
Use 'Cf' where the source can be used to compare and contrast with the point made in the text.
Use '*Contra*' where the source cited contradicts the point in the text.[5]

The Latin system

The use of Latin abbreviations in footnotes is quite common in law. This is due, in part, to the traditionally strong links between the court system and legal practice with the Latin language: you will note that many of the terms you use in many of your law units are derived from Latin (for example—*ab initio*, *bona fide*, *coram*, *de minimis*, *ejusdem generis*, habeas corpus, *non est factum*, prima facie, *quantum meruit*, *sui generis*, *umberrima fides*, *volenti non fit injuria*, and of course *ratio decidendi*). It also reflects the experience of many of your law lecturers and their interest in the history of law and its Latin connection. While we enjoy the use of the Latin abbreviations we recognise that the continued development of plain English in the law means that over time the note number system (or variants of it as discussed above) will likely prevail as the dominant system. The Latin abbreviations that are often used in footnotes include those listed in Table 12.4.

Latin-based references within footnotes are still popular in law

Importantly, these abbreviations are never used when referring to cases and statutes. When referring to cases and statutes always repeat the citation details in full in every footnote.

Always repeat case and statute citations in full

5 Australian Guide to Legal Citation (2010) pp 5–6.

TABLE 12.4 Latin abbreviations used in footnotes[6]

Latin abbreviation	Meaning	Use	Example
Ibid	In the same place	To show that the footnote where ibid is used has the exact same information as the immediately preceding one.	Spencer, D., 'To what degree of certainty must a dispute resolution clause be drafted?' (2003) 14 *ADRJ* 153–164 at 157. Ibid.
Id	As above	To show the same as the immediately preceding footnote but with a minor change such as a page or paragraph number.	Spencer, D., 'To what degree of certainty must a dispute resolution clause be drafted?' (2003) 14 *ADRJ* 153–164 at 157. Id at 162.
Op cit	In the work cited	Preceded by the author's surname, op cit sends the reader back to a previous reference to that author's work but with a changed page or paragraph number.	Brogan, M., 'An Introduction to the International Criminal Court by William A. Schabas', [2001] *Aust ILJ* 297–304 at 298. Sher, A., 'Can lawyers save the rainforest?' (1993) 17 *Harvard Environmental Law Review* 151. Brogan *op cit* at 301.
Loc cit	In the place cited	Preceded by the author's surname, *loc cit* sends the reader back to the previous reference to that author's work without modification to that previous reference.	Brogan, M., 'An Introduction to the International Criminal Court by William A. Schabas', [2001] *Aust ILJ* 297–304 at 298. Sher, A., 'Can lawyers save the rainforest?' (1993) 17 *Harvard Environmental Law Review* 151. Brogan *loc cit*.
Supra	Above	Used to refer a reader to an earlier section of the main body of the paper.	
Infra	Below	Used to refer a reader to a later section of the main body of the paper.	

6 In this table and the next the author details appear as surname followed by initial. This is consistent with normal bibliographic practices but not that used for footnoting by the 'Australian Guide to Legal Citation'—refer to Table 12.3 for the footnoting system used by the 'Australian Guide to Legal Citation'.

The note number system

Like the Latin system the note number system is an abbreviation system for use with footnotes. It works by simply using cross-references to previous footnote numbers. The system is easy to use—you simply need to know where a previous reference is (by its footnote number) to cross refer to it—and efficient in that you do not have to enter much more than the number of the previous footnote to complete your reference. The disadvantage of this system is that readers are forced to return to the earlier footnote, sometimes many pages back, if they wish to work out what the reference is.

The benefit of the Latin abbreviation system is that at a brief glance the reader can quickly see what the abbreviated reference is referring to as the Latin abbreviation either immediately follows the full citation being referred to, or it provides the author's name where that citation appears more than one footnote back.

The note number system has found increasing support in legal journals.

In Table 12.5 we use the examples from the preceding table but this time use a note number abbreviation system.

Again, note number abbreviations are never used when referring to cases and statutes. When referring to cases and statutes always repeat the citation details in full in every footnote.

Other systems

The Harvard system, the Vancouver system, the American Psychological Association system, and the Modern Language Association system are all variants on a theme. These referencing systems do not use footnotes but parentheses for identifying sources of in-text citations. Within the parentheses is the author name and the year of publication, and if a quote, the page number(s), for example (Kirby 2003 pp 146–210). The advantage of this system is that, despite a few intricacies not listed, the system is quick and easy to use. A disadvantage, especially from a law perspective, is that a reader is required to examine the bibliography in order to obtain the full citation details—this precludes having a quick glance at the source conveniently listed at the bottom of a footnoted page. Also, if you leave drafting your bibliography to the end of your assignment then you may become confused about which reference goes with

Social science and other referencing systems fit sources cited in the body of the text

TABLE 12.5 The number abbreviation system[7]

Latin abbreviation	Latin example	Note number example
Ibid	Spencer, D., 'To what degree of certainty must a dispute resolution clause be drafted?' (2003) 14 *ADRJ* 153–164 at 157. *Ibid.*	Spencer, D., 'To what degree of certainty must a dispute resolution clause be drafted?' (2003) 14 *ADRJ* 153–164 at 157. Note 1.
Id	Spencer, D., 'To what degree of certainty must a dispute resolution clause be drafted?' (2003) 14 *ADRJ* 153–164 at 157. *Id* at 162.	Spencer, D., 'To what degree of certainty must a dispute resolution clause be drafted?' (2003) 14 *ADRJ* 153–164 at 157. Note 1 at 162.
Op cit	Brogan, M., 'An Introduction to the International Criminal Court by William A. Schabas', [2001] *Aust ILJ* 297–304 at 298. Sher, A., 'Can lawyers save the rainforest?' (1993) 17 *Harvard Environmental Law Review* 151. Brogan *op cit* at 301.	Brogan, M., 'An Introduction to the International Criminal Court by William A. Schabas', [2001] *Aust ILJ* 297–304 at 298. Sher, A., 'Can lawyers save the rainforest?' (1993) 17 *Harvard Environmental Law Review* 151. Note 1 at 301.
Loc cit	Brogan, M., 'An Introduction to the International Criminal Court by William A. Schabas', [2001] *Aust ILJ* 297–304 at 298. Sher, A., 'Can lawyers save the rainforest?' (1993) 17 *Harvard Environmental Law Review* 151. Brogan *loc cit.*	Brogan, M., 'An Introduction to the International Criminal Court by William A. Schabas', [2001] *Aust ILJ* 297–304 at 298. Sher, A., 'Can lawyers save the rainforest?' (1993) 17 *Harvard Environmental Law Review* 151. Note 1.

which material when the author has published multiple times in a given year. It is this possibility for imprecision in research and difficulty in determining detail quickly that causes most lawyers to use the footnote systems.

Other general rules

For consistency use the following rules adopted directly from the *Australian Guide to Legal Citation* and set out in Table 12.6.

7 In this table the author details appear as surname followed by initial. This is consistent with normal bibliographic practices but as far as a footnoting system is concerned is not that used by the 'Australian Guide to Legal Citation'—refer to Table 12.3 for the footnoting system used by the 'Australian Guide to Legal Citation'.

TABLE 12.6 Miscellaneous rules to assist with written work in law[8]

Where a quotation is three lines or less it should be placed within single quotation marks and incorporated directly into the body of your text. Where a quotation is more than three lines long it should appear in its own paragraph, indented, in a smaller font and without quotation marks.
Ellipses (...) should be used to indicate that words within a sentence or between sentences have been omitted from a quote.
[Sic] should be used to indicate that there is an error in the material being quoted, or that the quoted material is discriminatory.
Where there are multiple quotations within a quoted piece of text use single quotation marks, followed by double quotation marks, and if necessary further use of single quotation marks.
Spelling should be checked and comply with that provided by the *Australian Oxford Dictionary*.
Grammar should be checked and should comply with *Fowler's Modern English Usage*.
Numbers up to nine should be written in words, those from 10 up should appear as numerals—except where you are referring to section numbers (where numerals should always be used).
Dates should follow the format of DD Month YYYY, for example 26 July 1980.
Judges writing curially should be referred to by their judicial title. The word judge or justice should be used to start a sentence but an abbreviation used where the judge is referred to within a sentence (for example 'Justice Baston stated ...' or '... according to Baston J.'

Bibliographies and tables of cases and statutes[9]

At the end of any paper you are normally required to include a bibliography of all materials referred to in your paper. A bibliography will typically include a full list of the following items and in the following order.

- Articles, books, and reports referred to in the body of your paper. Articles, books and reports read but not used in your paper should not be included in your bibliography as their entry in the bibliography may lead a reader to think that you have used the ideas within them but not properly referenced them. Your list should be in alphabetical order but (unlike the footnote

8 'Australian Guide to Legal Citation' pp 8–24.

9 The bibliographic order referred to here is based upon that used in the 2006 edition of the 'Australian Guide to Legal Citation' produced by the Melbourne University Law Review Association Inc.

references noted in Table 12.3 and Table 12.4) with the surname of the author first and the author's initials following.

- Cases listed in alphabetical order and by jurisdiction. Normally the different jurisdictions are headed by the Commonwealth and then followed in constitutional order.
- Legislation (whether primary or delegated) in alphabetical order and by jurisdiction. Jurisdictional order is the same as for cases.
- Treaties in alphabetical order.
- Other sources such as Hansard and internet sites in alphabetical order.

The dangers of plagiarism

Academic misconduct is a generic term that covers all manner of behaviours from cheating in examinations, tampering with class work, acquiring or attempting to acquire confidential assignment papers or marking guides, impersonation of other students, to plagiarism. Unfortunately plagiarism is the commonest, and most serious, form of academic misconduct because of the relative ease with which a person can engage in it. The only way to avoid unintentionally plagiarising is to develop and maintain excellent referencing and citation practices.

Referencing and citation allow you to avoid plagiarism

Examples of plagiarism and academic misconduct

Plagiarism takes many forms and includes conduct that many may not perceive to be wrong. Here we provide some guidance but stress that you should check the details of your university and law school's academic misconduct policy as soon as you are able. We take a strict approach here but indicate where we think there may be some opportunity for divergence of opinion. In the context of submitting a written assignment that is designed to be your work and no-one else's, the types of activities that may constitute plagiarism include the following.

- Taking someone else's words and using them in your paper but not acknowledging that the words are not yours.
- Paraphrasing someone else's words or ideas and using them in your paper but not acknowledging that the words or ideas are not yours.

- Using someone else's words or ideas, whether paraphrased or not, in your paper and making reference to them by a footnote or annotation at the end of a paragraph. The problem here is that there is ambiguity about what it is that the footnote or annotation is referring to. As noted above, referencing needs to be clear and precise.
- Using someone else's idea, such as the detailed structure of an essay, or means of analysing a problem or fact situation, and representing it to be your original thinking.
- Speaking with someone about the way in which an essay should be written—particularly where the lecturer wants everyone to come to their own conclusions about materials and problems.
- Assisting someone to locate the materials they need to complete an assignment—particularly where the lecturer has incorporated individual legal research into an assessment task.

Plagiarism and admission to the legal profession

As is clear from the above, plagiarism is unacceptable conduct for any person involved in an academic pursuit. The particular problem for persons studying law is that plagiarism could, and in our opinion should, create difficulties for anyone seeking admission to the practice of law. If we accept that plagiarism is an example of dishonest behaviour, then it is apparent that a person guilty of plagiarism, or any other form of academic misconduct, cannot claim to be a good or honest person. The ramification is that in each state and territory the rules for admission of persons to legal practice requires that the applicant be recognised as a person of 'good fame and character', or words to that effect. A person who has committed academic misconduct, such as plagiarism, is unable to represent to the Supreme Court, or admitting authority, of their state or territory that they are, without qualification, a person of good fame and character. At the very least a person who has been found guilty of some form of academic misconduct should disclose this fact to the Supreme Court, or admitting authority, of their state or territory. After such a disclosure the admitting authorities may refuse the admission of the applicant.

Plagiarism may mean that a person is not of 'good fame and character'

So why should I disclose if it might result in my not being admitted to the profession? The reason for disclosure of such matters is that the rules for admission throughout the country obligate persons seeking admission to be of 'good fame and character'. By not disclosing academic misconduct an applicant for admission may, by reason of that non-disclosure alone, be exhibiting behaviour that is not consistent with the requirement of good fame and character. If the matter is declared to an admitting authority and that authority accepts the applicant's remorse and subsequent good behaviour as true then the applicant will usually be admitted. A decision to disclose negative matters will be in the best interest of an intending applicant.

A person not of 'good fame and character' will not be admitted to practise law

In *Ex parte Lenehan* (1948) 77 CLR 403 the High Court had to consider the application for admission of a man who had been involved in dishonest activities while working as a clerk in a legal firm some 20 years before. Lenehan disclosed his acts of dishonesty. Lenehan was allowed to be enrolled as a solicitor. While there is more to this case than this simple précis allows, the result appears to indicate that an applicant for admission will be rewarded, at the least, for candour about past misdeeds. Should a person seeking admission fail to declare a relevant fact, discovery of that fact may lead the legal profession to make an application to have such a person removed from the roll of practitioners. In the case of *In re Davis* (1947) 75 CLR 409 Davis failed to disclose his conviction for break, enter, and steal at the time he was admitted to the Bar. This conviction was subsequently discovered and Davis was removed from the roll of practitioners. The High Court per Dixon J stated:

> The Bar is no ordinary profession or occupation. The duties and privileges of advocacy are such that, for their proper exercise and effective performance, counsel must command the personal confidence, not only of lay and professional clients, but of other members of the Bar and of judges. It would also seem to go without saying that conviction of a crime of dishonesty of so grave a kind ... is incompatible with the existence in the candidate for admission to the Bar of the reputation and the more enduring qualities denoted by the expression 'good fame and character', which describe the test of his ethical fitness for the profession.

On the issue of non-disclosure Dixon J stated:

> ... a prerequisite, in any case, would be a complete realization by the party concerned of his [sic] obligation to the court in which he desired to serve as an agent of justice. The fulfilment of that

> obligation of candour with its attendant risks proved too painful for the appellant [Davis], and when he applied to the Board for his certificate he withheld the fact that he had been convicted. In those circumstances, the conclusion that he is not a fit and proper person to be made a member of the Bar is confirmed.

We argue that it is better for an applicant to disclose even minor matters that may have a bearing on an applicant's good fame and character. As was noted in the case of *Re Del Castillo* (1998) 136 ACTR 1, where the applicant for admission failed to declare having been charged but acquitted of a murder charge:

> ... applicants have a duty of frankness. An attitude that begrudges information which may raise eyebrows, whether logically it ought to raise them, is not consistent with such an attitude. It is common throughout Australia for applicants for admission to legal practice to disclose quite minor charges. Those standards are to be encouraged. Applicants need not fear that the court will seek to substitute a demand for perfection for the requirement that fitness to practise be demonstrated by showing good fame and character.

Non-disclosure may be grounds for removal from the roll of practitioners

In South Australia the admitting authority has the right to check the academic record of candidates for admission to practise law. This effectively ensures that candidates disclose relevant information such as academic misconduct. The *Supreme Court Admission Rules* 1999 of South Australia require an applicant to disclose, among other things, whether the applicant has been found to have engaged in academic dishonesty such as plagiarism.

PLAGIARISM: CASE STUDY 1

In one Australian Supreme Court decision the position of a recently admitted practitioner (here referred to as the student) was examined after it was alleged that the student, at the time of his application for admission to the profession, failed to disclose relevant matters arising while he was a law student. Specifically the student failed to inform the admitting authorities that an allegation of academic misconduct had been found proven against him by a University Academic Misconduct Committee.

During the course of a unit of study, the student was to complete an assignment, which involved some drafting. The student was alleged to have near identical answers to those of another student. In addition, the student had included a disclaimer that 'this assignment, to the best of my knowledge, contains no material previously published or written by another person except where due reference is made in the text'.

Before the University Academic Misconduct Committee, the student gave evidence that when completing his assignment he discussed the assignment with his mother who was a legal practitioner. The student's mother provided the student with a copy of a relevant precedent and together they identified relevant parts of it. The student completed part of his assignment with his mother's assistance. This behaviour was, strangely, not questioned. The student also explained that he and another student sat down and talked about the assignment but that he had done all the work on the assignment, including making notes on his draft. The other student was allowed to take a photocopy of his draft at the conclusion of the discussion. There was no evidence that the student had used the other student's ideas. This was the behaviour that resulted in the finding of academic misconduct by the University Academic Misconduct Committee. A University Discipline Appeals Committee later allowed the student's appeal and set aside the decision of the University Academic Misconduct Committee, primarily because of a failure to comply with administrative procedures thereby denying the student 'natural justice'. Even with this information the local Law Society continued its application to have the student, now a practitioner, removed from the roll of practitioners because it implicitly held the view that whether the student was successful in his appeal or not, the mere fact that he had been the subject of such an inquiry should have been disclosed upon his application for admission.

Owing to various ambiguities in the University processes and on the evidence, in relation to the reasons for the student's failure to disclose the University misconduct charges and hearing, the Court concluded:

> The most severe criticism that arguably may be made against [the student] is that he made an error of judgment, a mistake, based largely on the advice of two experienced practitioners who were also his parents. Even if it is valid, it is no justification for removing his name from the roll. His fitness to practise, his honesty, character

> and trustworthiness have not been adversely affected by his failure to make the relevant disclosure. I am satisfied that at no time did he intend to mislead the Court.

Disclosure of academic misconduct does not guarantee admission

The point that needs to be drawn from this case is that the University took the prospect of academic misconduct seriously such that the student had to endure two formal committees in assessing his conduct. Further, the State Law Society considered the failure to disclose the academic misconduct matter to be worth pursuing. The result was that the student's place in the profession was seriously questioned. Had the student not discussed his individual assignment with another student then he would not have been subject to an inquiry by his University. Had the student disclosed the matter to the admitting authorities at the outset it is arguable that he would not have found himself subject to such opposition by that Law Society. While further details of the case serve to justify the decision we respectfully note that, in the absence of administrative ambiguities within university regulations and procedures, allegations of academic misconduct may be avoided if you determine exactly what opportunities you have for discussing assignments with others. Further, while there are a number of views regarding what should or should not be disclosed to admitting authorities we strongly recommend that anyone involved in a formal academic misconduct matter take a conservative approach and disclose the matter to the admitting authorities of their respective state or territory. Finally, we find this case a little odd in that even with the ambiguity in university regulations as to what academic misconduct was, the fact that the student was assisted in his assignment by his mother, albeit briefly, should have drawn some comment.

PLAGIARISM: CASE STUDY 2

That case may be contrasted with *Re Liveri* [2006] QCA 152 where a student disclosed a finding of academic misconduct but was not admitted to the profession. Here Liveri had submitted a paper, written by a professor of law and published on the internet, as her paper for a unit dealing with the law

Plagiarism does not need to be within the Law School program

of trusts. The student denied wrongdoing and claimed that the submission was accidental. In addition, it was subsequently discovered that the student had plagiarised in two further units of study. Only after some time did the student appear to acknowledge any form of wrongdoing. The Court took the view that given that the professor's internet-based paper, which had been formatted into a word-processing document and included a personalised cover sheet from the student, was significant misconduct. The Court also found that the student was guilty of:

> serious plagiarism, committed more than once. At relevant times, she was a person of mature years—25 and 27 years old. Her unwillingness, subsequently, to acknowledge that misconduct, establishes a lack of genuine insight into its gravity and significance: for present purposes, where the Court is concerned with fitness to practise, that aspect is at least as significant as the academic dishonesty itself. It could not presently be concluded the applicant is fit for admission as a legal practitioner.

PLAGIARISM: CASE STUDY 3

In the case of *Re Legal Profession Act 2004; re OG, a lawyer* [2007] VSC 520 (14 December 2007) two students, OG and GL, enrolled in a combined business and law degree program engaged in plagiarism. In submitting an assignment in a marketing unit OG and GL used significantly similar, or the same, material throughout papers that were meant to reflect the students' individual work. The Court noted that there were 26 instances of similarities within the papers of OG and GL. When applying for admission to the profession (to the Board of Examiners) OG indicated that he had been given zero marks for an assignment in the marketing unit because of a misunderstanding. Specifically, OG stated:

> I received a zero grade for an assessment component in a Marketing subject at University for a misunderstanding that occurred. I had a clash in my Law and Marketing subjects and as a result the Strategic Marketing & Management subject coordinator exempted me from

> attending tutorials. I undertook an assessment component that was worth 15% of the total assessment for that subject, which was to be conducted as a group task for both the research component and the writing up of the assignment. However, I misunderstood this as a result of my non attendance at the tutorials, and whilst I conducted the research process in a group I mistakenly wrote up the assignment individually. As a result of my misunderstanding the topic coordinator awarded me a zero mark for that assessment component. I subsequently still, successfully passed the subject. No record of the event was recorded and at no time was it suggested to be plagiarism or the like. I did not go before the University Board, nor did I fail the subject for my misunderstanding.

When applying for admission to the profession GL disclosed that he had been found guilty of collusion and stated:

> ... I was accused of colluding with another student on an assignment for the subject of Marketing Planning and Strategy. I spoke to the Topic Co-ordinator and Head Lecturer and stated that I did not collude with the other student. They did not accept my reasoning for why the assignments were similar. My reasoning for why the assignments were similar was that it was a mere coincidence. The assignment was based on the findings of a group project completed a few weeks earlier, I was in the same group as the other student. The assignment called for developing a marketing strategy based on the product research in our group subject. There were only two possible strategies that could be used. They advised that I could go the University Board to defend the matter but based on my reasoning, they were of the opinion that our appeal would be rejected. They also said that if I went to the University Board there would be a mark of [sic] my record. If the matter was dealt with by the Topic Co-ordinator and Head Lecturer, they would not put a mark on my record. I decided to take the penalty of receiving a zero for the assignment and they said that the matter would not be taken further.

OG was admitted to the profession, as his letter suggested simple error, not plagiarism. Upon application for admission to the profession GL was asked to provide further and better information about the 'collusion'. In so doing GL, across several changing affidavits and oral testimony, indicated that he and OG had sat down and mapped out how each was going to complete the assignment, which they each knew had to be done individually. Despite GL eventually disclosing the truth about the academic misconduct he was not admitted to the profession on the basis that he had not been fully candid when required to be at the point of admission—specifically, GL had attempted to hide the extent of the collusion. OG denied the collusion, but was found to not be truthful during the course of testimony during the case. The Court determined found that:

> [OG] deliberately or recklessly misrepresented to the Board of Examiners the circumstances in which he came to be awarded a zero grade or mark for his second assignment. His actions, therefore, were the antithesis of a 'realization ... of his obligation of candour to the court in which he desire[s] to serve as an agent of justice'.

A sobering conclusion

The net effect of ineffectively referencing work used, or deliberately engaging in plagiarism, or if relevant, of failing to declare that one has engaged in plagiarism, is that a person who has invested time and money in their studies—sometimes many years and tens of thousands of dollars—will be precluded from practising law.

13

EXAMINATIONS

In examinations those who do not wish to know ask questions of those who cannot tell.

Walter Raleigh[1]

1 Walter Raleigh, 'Laughter from a Cloud', 1923.

Introduction

The use of examinations is very popular throughout Australian law schools. In fact, it would be rare for a law student attending any of the Australian law schools to not encounter examinations as part of the assessment regime for most compulsory law units. But why are examinations so popular?

Examinations are popular at Australian law schools

The answer is because examinations are cost efficient where there is a large cohort of students. At most universities exam papers can be marked quickly as there is no requirement for individual feedback unlike an essay or other formative piece of assessment designed more to give you feedback than purely a mark. While there are many creative ways to assess your learning, universities have to consider cost efficiency and an exam ticks all the boxes on efficiencies. We are not convinced it ticks all the boxes on having a clear picture of your learning though.

One of the great follies in university examinations is the temptation of academics to simply test knowledge. Examinations should not be designed just to test knowledge. Just testing knowledge in law is reasonably useless. As previously discussed in this book, your lecturers need to see that you can analyse a problem and the relevant law then synthesise an argument.

In the case of legal problems academics need to see that you can analyse legal concepts in a way that will enable you to match those legal concepts to fact patterns, make an argument and reach a conclusion that is sound in law. Regurgitating legislation and excerpts from judgments is of little use unless you can link it all together in a persuasive argument. In the case of theoretical questions, your lecturers need to see that you understand the various arguments raised in any given theoretical question and that you can proffer an educated opinion that seeks to address the question in a scholarly evidenced-based way. Again, simply quoting the view of a well-known jurist is of little use unless you can articulate why that view is relevant to the question and you provide your own analysis of that view in answering the question.

Examinations test your ability to analyse and synthesise and to understand theoretical concepts

Given that law examinations examine your ability to analyse and synthesise, coming up with what your lecturers think is the right answer is not necessarily the ultimate goal. The aim of a law examination should be to demonstrate an understanding of the legal concepts and how those legal concepts support a plausible and

The aim of law exams is to present an argument based on the law

legally sound argument. Therefore, an answer that is wrong in terms of the outcome may still warrant a pass if the argument is sound in its application of the legal principles. In other words, depending on your lecturer, you will not always fail just because you came to the wrong conclusion—it depends on how well you employed the law to argue an answer that leads to a sound conclusion!

The next question on your mind may well be, 'Why discuss examination technique?' The answer is fourfold. First, academics are often disappointed to see students who display an understanding of legal concepts throughout the semester fall in a heap come exam time. Often a student's failure to do well in an exam is a matter of technique and not lack of understanding—and that is a shame. With better technique, students can generally do better and their marks will reflect their true ability.

A student's failure to do well in an exam may be because of poor technique

Second, while students may finish law school having mastered the technique of sitting law examinations, many of them do not commence their studies with any great proficiency. Working on your exam technique early in your studies may help you to do better at law exams earlier rather than later when it may be too late.

Developing a good exam technique will help you achieve better marks earlier on in your degree

Third, law is unlike some other disciplines in that it is not necessarily a precise or 'black-and-white' discipline. The successful study of law requires analysis not rote learning. Law requires an understanding of the law, but further, it requires a persuasive argument based on the law and the facts. After all, litigation lawyers know the law before they arrive at court—otherwise clients would not pay them! However, it is when they get to court that they display their ability in analysis and synthesis by arguing 'the grey area' of the law. By this, we mean they argue that the facts before the court are the same or different to precedent, and therefore the court should apply the precedent similarly or differently. Or they argue that the current law is wrong and that the court should create new law. Either way, they know the law, but their analysis and synthesis of the law mean that the court should apply the law in the way the lawyer is suggesting. A law exam will assist you to display your skills in analysis and synthesis.

The successful study of the law requires analysis not rote learning

Finally, you need to do well in your studies. The legal profession is very competitive and if you wish to secure employment as a lawyer you will need good marks. As a matter of personal achievement, you should set your sights on achieving the best marks possible.

You need to achieve good marks in order to secure employment in the law

If you have invested the time and effort in understanding the law, it would be a shame not to perform to the best of your ability merely because of poor exam technique.

One final but very important point. Exams are not designed to trick you or to set you up to fail. Academics write exams to ensure that you discuss certain material and that you can display an understanding of the law and its application or the theoretical or philosophical underpinnings of the law. They exist to allow you to display the intellectual skills of analysis and synthesis. Treat them as an opportunity to showcase your ability to make an educated argument, not as an evil foisted upon you by the unfeeling and uncaring academic staff of your law school. Most academics take great pride in your doing well. It proves that they were able to teach you effectively and that the learning goals set for the subject were realistic and achievable.

Exams are an opportunity to showcase your ability to make an argument

Preparing for exams

Prior to commencing your preparation for an exam reread your subject outline or learning guide. Look for any guidance on how the lecturer wants the exam written. Different academics have different rules in relation to how exams are to be written. For example, some insist on correct and full citations for cases and secondary source references. Others are more relaxed about referencing in exams. Read the rest of this chapter with the strict proviso that your subject conveners may have specific requirements about how exams are to be written and you should check each of the issues below with them to ensure you are complying with their wishes and therefore maximising your chances of good marks.

Check with your lecturer as to how the exam should be written

Procedural issues

Most universities publish their exam timetable on the internet or display the exam timetable at various places around the university. Either way, ensure you check and double check the date, time, and venue. Turning up on the wrong day or time or at the wrong venue is no excuse and usually does not qualify you for a supplementary exam (if offered at all by your university). If your university does offer

It is your responsibility to ensure you attend the exam

supplementary exams, the threshold for qualifying for them is usually quite stringent and involves serious illness or misadventure. You should check your university rules for the threshold of sickness and misadventure prior to the examination period just in case you have to rely on such provisions.

Make sure you have the right items with you for the examination. This may mean creating an exam checklist for use during your time at university. Such items could include:

An exam checklist can help avoid a last-minute panic about what to take into the exam

- several working pens;
- several sharpened pencils (for use on uniscan/multiple choice answer papers);
- a blank A4 pad (if allowed under your university's exam rules);
- subject notes (if an open book exam);
- case notes (if an open book exam);
- subject textbook(s) (if an open book exam);
- a legal dictionary (if an open book exam); and
- a bottle of water (if allowed under your university's exam rules).

Intellectual issues

Be positive! It never ceases to amaze us how law students can be such pessimists. If you have kept up to date with your weekly readings and preparation and have understood the basic concepts being discussed in lectures and tutorials, then you should comfortably pass the subject no matter what the assessment regime is. Do not take a defeatist attitude when it comes to examinations, otherwise you risk failing the exam or at the very least dropping a grade or two for the subject. Remind yourself of how much you have learnt in the unit and how you have the right technique to express your knowledge in a persuasive way to the examiner. Try to avoid students who seem to wear poor preparation as a badge of honour—quite frankly you can do without negative influences just prior to sitting an exam.

Be positive—if you have worked during the semester you will pass

Have a plan

Like anything successfully accomplished in life, succeeding in law exams requires planning. If you are a full-time student you may have four or more exams per semester. If you are a part-time student you may have two or more exams per semester. These exams, added to your family, work, and social life, mean that life is probably very busy for you around exam time, so planning is vital. Decide how much time you need to devote to exam preparation for each subject. Then decide what topics you want to cover and how much time you will need to devote to each topic. Do not think that each subject, and each topic within a subject, should be allocated the same amount of time. Some subjects, and topics within subjects, you will have understood more easily than other subjects and topics. You should recognise this and devote more time to the subjects and topics you struggled with throughout the semester.

Decide how much time you will need to devote to exam preparation for each subject and topic within a subject

Hopefully you have kept reasonably good class notes during the semester. If you have been writing case notes you should have those in good and accessible order. As a general rule, it is too late to start learning material between the end of the teaching semester and the examination period. Most universities give students around one week of study time between the end of teaching and the commencement of the exam period. Notwithstanding this, it is too late to be learning new material during your exam preparation time.

It is too late to be learning new material during the preparation period

Exam notes

Preparing exam notes is one of the hardest tasks you face as a law student. But if done properly, they can reap the greatest reward. If you have drafted them properly, they will be able to assist you to answer every question appearing in the exam paper. Hopefully the notes you have taken throughout the teaching period are detailed, because you do not have time to create new detailed lecture and tutorial notes between the end of semester and the commencement of the exam period. An example of how to take notes was given in Chapter 6. You now have to consolidate those notes into exam notes.

Drafting exam notes is hard but can reap great reward

Exam notes should achieve at least three things. First, they should identify all of the legal issues surrounding each topic covered in the subject. This usually means identifying the general proposition or rule of law established by general and statute law and then the qualifications and exceptions to the general rule. Second, exam notes should direct the reader to be able to argue an answer to the legal issues raised in the questions. That is, either how the general rule covering the topic adequately

Exam notes should achieve three things

deals with the problem presented in the exam or how the qualifications and exceptions to the general rule adequately deal with the problem presented in the exam. Third, exam notes should supply the relevant legal authority for the general rule and the qualifications and exceptions to the general rule.

Exam notes are a summary of the important concepts discussed throughout the semester. They do not reflect every single issue discussed during the semester. In other words you need to decide what information should be included in your exam notes because not every item raised in discussion will be appropriate for inclusion in your exam notes. Remember these are notes that will be referred to quickly in a formal open book or informal take-home exam or are being used as study notes in a closed book formal examination. Therefore, in either case you must write them in a form that is: easy to navigate; able to be committed to memory (in a closed book exam); and, allows you to access the right information quickly (in an open book exam).

Exam notes are a summary of matters discussed throughout the semester

You should develop your own template for drafting exam notes. The following format may be of assistance in this process:

- Topic heading.
- State the general rule.
- List cases and statutes illustrating the general rule.
- State any qualifications of the general rule.
- List cases and statutes illustrating the qualifications to the general rule.
- State any exceptions to the general rule.
- List cases and statutes illustrating the exceptions to the general rule.
- State any test set down by superior courts that can help establish or refute the general rule, qualifications and exceptions.
- List any cases relevant to any test or tests.
- List secondary materials providing a critical or a philosophical slant on the topic.

When drafting your exam notes use as many headings and sub-headings as necessary to provide a clear roadmap of the document. Cases should not be the trigger for a new heading or sub-heading and are not 'topics' on their own. Cases fit in to support the general rule and its qualifications and exceptions. It is the legal issues that are the subject of headings and sub-headings. If you have written case

Use headings and sub-headings to help you navigate the document

notes throughout the semester, they should be easy to incorporate into the exam notes or be freestanding with a reference from the exam notes to the case notes.

If you are going to use the legal problem-solving model, as discussed in Chapter 5, you should revise its use. Imagine yourself answering an exam question using the model as your template. What information will you need? The information you need should be in an easy-to-access format via your exam notes. If you are answering a theoretical question, your exam notes will need to set out the various pieces of commentary you have read and the central thrust of the arguments presented in those papers.

Think carefully about what should be in your exam notes

The following is an example of exam notes for a common topic in the study of contract law.

TOPIC—CONSIDERATION

SUB-TOPIC—THE RULE IN PINNEL'S CASE

GENERAL PROPOSITION:

- Part payment of a debt does not discharge the debt as there is no consideration to support the new promise to discharge the debt.

EXCEPTION TO THE GENERAL RULE:

- If you agree to accept a lesser sum of money, plus something to which there was no existing entitlement, that 'something' will be good consideration and discharge the debt.
- *Pinnel's Case* (1602) 77 ER 237—**Facts:** Mr Cole owed Pinnel £8 10s and this sum was due on 11 November. On 1 October, Pinnel agreed to accept £5 2s 2d in complete satisfaction of the debt. Cole paid and Pinnel later sued. **Held:** (Pinnel won on a technical point of pleading) In terms of the rule surrounding consideration, Cole would have won, because he did something that he was not contractually bound to do. That is, Cole paid Pinnel earlier than what was required, and that acted as good consideration for Pinnel's promise to discharge the debt.
- *Foakes v Beer* (1884) 9 App Cas 605—**Facts:** John Foakes owed Julia Beer approximately £3,000. Beer was granted judgment in court and the two parties entered a contract whereby Foakes would pay £500 immediately and the balance of the money due by annual instalments of £150. In return

Beer would not institute enforcement proceedings. After Foakes had paid all the money back Beer commenced proceedings against Foakes for interest on the original £3,000. **Held:** The House of Lords found in favour of Beer on the basis that the agreement was to pay back an amount already owed. There was no consideration for the promise made by Beer not to commence proceedings against Foakes for the interest. Consistent with *Pinnel*'s case, a promise by Foakes to pay back an amount less than that due to Beer, was not considered good consideration for a promise by Beer not to sue Foakes for the interest on the debt.

- *D & C Builders v Rees* [1966] 2 QB 617—**Facts:** Rees owed D & C Builders £482 for building work they had done. The account was overdue for several months after which Rees offered D & C a cheque for £300 on the basis that if they did not accept it they would get nothing. D & C Builders were experiencing a cash flow crisis at the time and accepted the payment of £300 by way of a cheque in full settlement of the debt. They then sued for the balance. **Held:** The court found for D & C Builders on the basis that the payment of the £300 was not a material consideration for the promise to accept a lesser sum. Lord Denning was of the view that there was no distinction between payment by cash or cheque. Neither method of payment was more beneficial than the other (no extra 'something' as in *Pinnel*'s case).

The above treatment of a topic in contract law shows a simple way to set out exam notes. It quickly gives you: the general rule related to the topic; the exception to the general rule; and, the supporting case law. That is all exam notes need to give you—you do not have time to read sophisticated arguments and theories as your job in an exam is to draft a persuasive argument using the current law in a short space of time. As stated in Chapter 5, the creative part for which you will earn numerous marks is how you use the current law to build a persuasive legal argument. Exam notes simply provide assistance for you to structure an argument.

Now that your exam notes are in order, you should tab them for easy reference. Tabbing exam notes is no substitute for reviewing them—a matter to be discussed next. Tabbing your exam notes serves two purposes. First, it helps you find a topic you have identified as being important in the subject. Second, it helps if you have forgotten something important such as a relevant case or statute or even a general rule. Here are some hints on the final drafting of your exam notes:

- Number all the pages.
- Bind them so they cannot fall apart.
- Bind them so that they sit flat when open on your desk.
- Tab them by topic.
- Ensure you have appropriately used headings and sub-headings (in bold and underlined text) to allow the eye to move quickly to a topic and a particular point within a topic.
- Use bold lettering and underlining sparingly, otherwise it becomes too much for the eye to follow.

Once drafted, your exam notes should only need to be read about three times for you to have enough recall to spot the issues in an exam question and to answer most questions. This includes being able to refer to the right cases and statutes and knowing the qualifications and exceptions to the general rule of law that covers any particular topic.

Read your exam notes three times before the exam

One final important point: exam notes are no substitute for understanding the legal concepts and arguments. You should approach any style of exam on the basis of knowing the subject thoroughly before you commence writing the exam. Your exam notes should only be relied upon to jolt your memory. In other words, exam notes are there to help you learn the legal concepts and arguments before you commence the exam and then, in the case of open book exams, to provide a reminder during the exam. Learning the legal concepts and arguments by reading your exam notes during the exam is too late.

Exam notes are no substitute for understanding the legal arguments and concepts

Exam preparation

Once your notes are drafted and tabbed you are ready to begin your final preparation. Read your exam notes at least twice before attempting some practice exam questions. Get hold of some old exam papers. Some law schools bind their previous exams and hold them in their law library or have them available electronically through the library databases. You can even find plenty of exam questions on various university websites. Some publishers have tutorial questions and answers in their textbooks—for example,

Answer previous exam questions or tutorial questions under simulated exam conditions

LexisNexis Q&A series has questions with suggested answers. Always prefer your own university's practice exam questions particularly when the same subject convener has set the previous few exams as you will instantly feel comfortable with the style of the exam when you sit it.

However you obtain some previous exam papers, sit these practice questions under exam conditions as a test run for the actual exam. That is, sit down in a quiet room, and answer the same number of questions as will be in the exam allowing the right amount of time for each question and answering the entire number of questions without interruption. You need to experience the pressure of having to answer a question in a set period of time and the resulting intellectual and physical strain (yes, your hand will be sore after writing for three to four hours without a break). If you cannot find previous exam papers, then use the tutorial questions that you have answered throughout the semester as test questions.

If you used a study group throughout the semester, you can have other students mark them in a group and discuss the areas of difficulty in each question. You can even have the group discuss preparation strategies and exam notes and any contentious areas of the subject or areas that can lead to common mistakes. The use of small discussion groups for exam preparation is highly recommended.

Small groups can assist in the preparation stage for an exam

Exam technique

If you have worked hard during the semester by keeping up to date with the readings and preparing each week for classes and have drafted good case notes and exam notes, you should be in a good position to do well in the exam. However, success in exams depends not only on your preparation but also on good exam technique.

Success in exams depends on good technique

Understand the instructions

The exam venue for formal exams can be daunting in itself. For core units at law school there may be 200 to 500 students sitting the exam at the one time. This means that an assembly hall or gymnasium may be used as the venue of the exam. Rows and rows of individual desks will be set up with the exam booklets and the examination paper upside down on the desk. Usually you will have to show your student

Prepare yourself for a large exam venue and do not forget your student card identity card to the exam supervisors before you enter the exam room. Do not leave it at home as some universities will make you go to the Student Centre and produce identification so that they can give you an authority to sit the exam. You do not need this sort of last-minute stress just prior to sitting an exam.

Some universities have very strict rules about what you may bring into a formal examination. Some will not allow library books, water bottles, calculators, and dictionaries. You should check the rules before bringing some items into the exam. Almost all universities will not allow mobile phones to be brought into an exam room. Most will insist you leave them out of the room or place them on a table at the front of the room. These rules usually apply no matter whether the exam be open or closed book. Do not argue with the exam supervisors as they are only following the rules set by more senior members of the university. Also, arguing a few minutes before an exam will not get you anywhere and will only increase your anxiety level.

Know what you can and cannot bring into an exam before arriving

Once seated at your table, take a deep breath (or two) and if instructed to do so, fill in any exam attendance slips that may be required. Most importantly, listen to the exam supervisors' instructions. They have been trained to conduct exams according to the university rules. Most formal exam procedures include the following:

- instructions from the exam supervisors;
- completion of attendance slips;
- entering your name, student identification, and subject code and name on the front of each of the exam booklets used for answering the questions;
- a period of reading time in which you may or may not be allowed to write on the exam paper or on a separate sheet of paper, but not in the exam answer books;
- compliance with the 'pens down' request at the end of the exam; and
- leaving the exam paper on the desk at the conclusion of the exam.

When the reading time commences, read the front page of the exam containing the instructions and ask the exam supervisors if you do not understand the instructions. Understanding the instructions could be very important where, for example, there is an internal choice that requires only answers from certain sections of the exam paper (for example, answer one question from part A and two questions from part B of the exam).

Read the instructions on the front of the exam paper

Plan your time and your answers

During any reading time allowed for the exam, you should check if you are allowed to write on a blank sheet of paper (some universities do not allow you to write at all during the reading time). If you are allowed to write during the reading time or if you are not given any reading time once the exam commences, you should plan your time. In essence, plan how many minutes you will need to answer each question. For example, a common requirement in a three-hour law exam is to answer three questions. This means about 60 minutes per question. Sometimes your lecturer will tell you prior to the exam how many questions you will need to answer so that you can make this calculation prior to sitting down in the exam room.

Plan how many minutes you have to answer each question

After you have calculated the time you will spend answering each question you should note any issues that you immediately detect when you read each question. If there is a choice of questions to answer, decide which ones to answer. This decision is usually based on an early identification of the issues and the fact that you will have understood some concepts more easily than others.

Read the questions and note any issues you immediately detect

Do not be worried if when you first read the exam paper you do not understand one or two questions (if you do not understand any of the questions, check with the exam supervisors that you are sitting the right exam!). Often while you may not see the issues upon first reading, you will see them when the time comes to answer the question. This is because your mind is working more fluidly during the exam and after answering the questions you easily understand, you have already addressed several topics of the unit. This narrows the field in terms of potential topics for the remaining questions that you were maybe having difficulty with after a first reading.

Often it takes a second reading to spot the issues

At the commencement of the exam, spend five minutes of the allocated time to answer each question writing an outline answer. This is the best five minutes you can spend. An outline answer will ensure you stay focused and will prevent you from discussing irrelevant issues. If the question is a theoretical question, draft a short essay plan that flows logically and contains an argument—see Chapter 11 regarding tips on how to write theoretical essays. If the question is a legal problem then consider using the legal problem-solving model as discussed in Chapter 5. Even if you choose

Spend five minutes writing an outline answer

not to use the legal problem-solving model when answering the question in full, try using the model as a way to draft an outline. The legal problem-solving model provides an excellent basis for a draft answer as it focuses your mind on the essential elements of an answer to a legal problem-style question.

During this important planning stage of the exam, use your exam notes to fill in gaps and note the relevant cases and/or commentary. Write your outline answer in dot point not narrative form—you do not have time for a long-winded outline answer. Chances are there will be more than one issue in each question. Use headings and sub-headings to focus you and the marker on the point you are arguing. There is nothing worse than a rambling answer that is not on point—it shows the marker that you do not know what you are talking about!

Use your exam notes to fill in the gaps

Writing the exam

The following could be the most important tip of all. Answer every question you are asked to answer! Despite popular belief, markers try to allocate marks for any sign of an effort by a student. If the marker is staring at a blank page, the marker has no choice but to ascribe a zero next to the blank page. Any attempt at a question may yield some marks. Even if you have no idea about a question, have a guess. Chances are you are at least partly correct and will earn some marks. Further, experience has shown that the extra time you spend on one question at the expense of another question will not gain you enough marks to justify the extra time spent. Approaching exam technique in this fashion yields a result of diminishing returns. In other words spending an extra 20 per cent of the time allocated on any given exam question will not yield you an extra 20 per cent in marks. Therefore, give yourself ample time to answer all the questions on the paper. You should stick rigidly to the amount of time you have given yourself to answer any given question thereby ensuring you will have time to answer each question. You are doing yourself a disservice to do otherwise.

Answer every question you are asked to answer

Answer the questions you are confident with. That is, the questions whose subject matter you were comfortable with throughout the semester. This process will build confidence and relax you so that you are in a good position to answer what in your opinion are the more difficult questions.

Prioritise the questions

Do not use the 'scattergun' approach. That is, do not write down everything you know about a topic in the hope that some of it is correct and you will do enough to pass. The first thing this approach tells a marker is that you do not know the answer and that you do not have a structured approach to answering the question. Second, it is a waste of time to write down irrelevant information. Remember, even if an answer is wrong as to its conclusion, providing it is argued well, chances are that marks will still be awarded.

The 'scattergun' approach to answers does not allow you to maximise marks

Do not draft your answer in dot point form. Use the narrative form to answer exam questions. As already stated, use headings and sub-headings to direct your attention to the exact point you wish to make, but write your answer in narrative or essay form. In this respect make sure you write using clear expression and correct English grammar. Also, write in plain legal English and do not use legalese. Most importantly, write legibly! There is nothing worse than not being able to read a student's handwriting. Some academics have been known to call the offending student in to university and have her or him transcribe the entire exam paper into a hand-printed or computer-generated copy. Another method of solving this problem is to have the student sit in front of the lecturer and slowly read out the entire exam paper. Do not put yourself through this ordeal—write neatly and clearly.

Write in the narrative form using plain legal English

The Twenty Commandments of exam technique (a guide of biblical proportions!):

i) You shall prepare yourself adequately for the exam.
ii) You shall make your exam notes user-friendly.
iii) You shall double and triple check the day, time, and venue of the exam.
iv) You shall read the entire exam paper.
v) You shall use the reading time constructively.
vi) You shall plan the answer to each question.
vii) You shall avoid repeating the question in your answer. The people who write the exam know the question—they do not need to be reminded. It is just a waste of your time when you could be writing something important called 'the answer'.
viii) You shall avoid repeating sections of statutes for the same reason as the previous commandment.

ix) You shall fully cite cases unless your lecturer states otherwise.

x) You shall avoid citing legal authorities or commentaries without applying them to the actual answer as you leave the marker wondering why you raised them in the first place.

xi) You shall cut to the chase and not pad out your answer by long-winded introductions. You have a short time to draft a great answer—treat each minute as if it is your last in the exam.

xii) You shall not use the scattergun approach.

xiii) You shall reach a conclusion. There are marks available for a decisive conclusion so make sure you weigh up the options that the law or the commentary has provided and write a strong conclusion listing your reasons.

xiv) You shall use plain legal English not legalese.

xv) You shall avoid using secondary sources when answering legal problems. Use primary sources of law for legal problems and both primary and secondary sources of law for theoretical questions where appropriate.

xvi) You shall express yourself clearly and correctly.

xvii) You shall employ good spelling and grammar. This is important in the law and poor spelling and grammar detract from the force of your answer.

xviii) You shall write legibly. If you have terrible handwriting, print. Again, poor handwriting detracts from what it is you are trying to say.

xix) You shall not covet a definitive answer. There is usually not a single answer in the law. Every day lawyers in court seek to overturn the established law by exploiting the grey area of the law. Exam questions are designed for you to argue the grey area of the law.

xx) You shall stay calm and not panic!

What to do if you panic

In relation to the last commandment, sometimes upon reading the exam paper you do not immediately understand parts of it or all of it. The best strategy is to deal with the parts of the paper you do understand first and come back to the more difficult areas. If you find yourself panicking, stop—momentarily withdraw from the exam mentally and take several deep breaths. Calm yourself down then pick up the paper and start again. Panic is one of those destructive emotions. It is not going to help you answer the exam to the best of your ability.

Types of exams

There are many permutations and combinations of exams used by law schools. The following is an explanation of the different styles of exams you may encounter during your time at law school.

Formal and informal

A formal exam is a sit-down exam that takes place usually in a university venue at a set date and time. Generally the exam will be conducted by the exams department of the university and will be moderated by that department. On occasions exams may be moderated by the teaching staff themselves. The hallmark of the formal exam is that it is the same date and time for all students studying the subject and is conducted under conditions that monitor you sitting the exam. Formal exams may be closed or open book, a matter to be discussed below.

Formal exams are monitored

An informal exam is an exam that lacks formal monitoring by the university. Also, informal exams usually allow you to consider your answers over a longer period of time whereas formal exams usually require an instantaneous response. Further, informal exams can usually be taken home and completed over a number of days or over a week or more.

Informal exams usually do not require an instantaneous response

In terms of preparation, you should prepare for both types of exams in much the same way. However, given the lack of an instantaneous response required in informal exams, you have the opportunity to cast your research net a little wider and therefore you may consider preparing additional material in comparison to your preparation for a formal exam. However, at the end of the day your preparation is dependent on how well prepared you are prior to the examination period and ultimately how much time you have to prepare for the examination.

Informal exams may allow you to include additional material in your preparation

In terms of writing these two types of papers, it is logical to assume that lecturers have a higher expectation of students sitting an informal exam compared to a formal exam where there is slightly more pressure to perform. However, a good rule of thumb is to try to achieve the highest level of answer in both kinds of exam. The point is that no matter which style of exam you are sitting, you should be prepared to the point of being able to

You must be able to write the same quality answer in either a formal or informal exam

write answers to any questions in any type of exam. You should not be setting out to learn new information during the exam—it is too late for that!

Closed book

Closed book exams are generally conducted by way of a formal exam, otherwise there is no way to monitor the closed book policy. Closed book exams mean that you may not refer to any material such as textbooks or exam notes. In other words, you sit the exam armed only with your brain! Success in these sorts of exams is dependent on your memory. The ability to memorise cases, legislation, and legal concepts means success at this sort of an exam. Law schools are gradually moving away from closed book exams because the legal profession does not require lawyers to have instant recall. Lawyers generally always have time to research the law and take account of changes before having to tender advice. However, some law schools still run closed book exams.

Closed book exams mean you sit the exam armed only with your memory

In terms of preparation, closed book exams require very concise exam notes that are easy to memorise. In this respect, some system for memorising your exam notes may be of assistance. Some students mind map their notes, which means drawing diagrams that link the general rule of any given topic with the exceptions and qualifications of the rule with the cases and statutes attached at strategic points to illustrate the particular point being made. A similar effect can be achieved through the use of flow charts that disclose the logical progression of the topic.

Closed book exams require some method to efficiently memorise information

In terms of writing the exam, closed book exams are challenging. Under the pressure of a formal exam your brain is required to deliver the right knowledge of the law and its legal authorities and then allow you to draft a persuasive argument using the skills of analysis and synthesis. The most important thing is to write down an outline answer for each question and try and raise all of the relevant law during your drafting of the plan. Once you have started drafting an outline answer, you should be able to summon from your mind the relevant law to provide authority for your argument. Once you commence answering the question, do not allow your mind to wander from the task at hand and your outline answer. Keep focus and ensure you write as persuasive an answer as is

You must draft an outline answer so as to stay focused

possible. Again, the legal problem-solving model discussed in Chapter 5 can help you remain on point and ensure you have included all the relevant components of a good answer.

Open book

Open book exams usually allow you to refer to any material you choose such as textbooks, exam notes, and case notes. However, some universities have a rule that you may not take library books from your home university into the exam because of the disadvantage suffered by those students not quick enough to borrow the right books. You should always check for any rules that prevent material being brought into an exam before you commence the preparation phase of an open book exam. It is too late once you are just about to walk into the exam to have some material that you were relying on excluded from the exam venue.

Check the university rules as to what you can bring to an open book exam

Open book exams should not be treated as being easier than closed book exams. The same rule of thumb applies—be prepared to tender good quality answers without reference to materials. Too great a reliance on materials taken in to the exam room means too much wasted time looking up the materials at the expense of writing a quality answer. The materials you take into the exam should be treated as a way to jolt your memory only, that is a reminder should you forget something in the exam.

Materials should only be relied upon as an aide-mémoire

In terms of preparation nothing should change from your preparation for a closed book exam. Your notes, which will only be used as a reminder should you forget something, need to be concise and user-friendly. Even in an open book exam you do not have the luxury of time to be learning new material.

Preparation for an open book exam is the same as for a closed book exam

In terms of writing an open book exam, the only significant difference is that, unlike a closed book exam, there is no excuse for misspelling case and statute names or the name of a piece of significant commentary or forgetting case citations or the year of legislation and its jurisdiction. In other words, the quality of the answer should be the same in terms of its substance but given you have certain resources at your fingertips you should not make errors that come down to a failure of memory.

In an open book exam there are no excuses for the sorts of errors that occur due to memory failure

Take-home

Take-home exams generally must be completed within a certain timeframe. For example, the exam is issued on a certain day and time and must be returned on a certain day and time. Because there is no pressure as with a formal exam, there is usually a higher expectation as to the quality of the answer. Therefore, you should consider planning the answers a lot more thoroughly and develop a more thorough argument within the prescribed word limit (if there is a prescribed limit).

Take-home exams imply a higher expectation as to the quality of answer

In terms of preparation, nothing changes from what has already been discussed. You should know the issues and their authorities before picking up the take-home exam. It is too late to start learning the law after picking up the exam as you are wasting time when you should be writing persuasive answers.

Preparation is the same as for an open book formal exam

In terms of writing the exam, the temptation in take-home exams is to include 'everything' in them. This is a fatal mistake. You should continue to be disciplined about the structure of your answers and use an essay-planning model or a legal problem-solving model to structure your answers to ensure only relevant material is raised. Like any prepared piece of work, read each answer carefully after you have written it and then reread it. Ensure it flows well and makes sense. Be fastidious about quoting relevant law and ensure each point is persuasive to your argument or clearly flagged as a counter-argument.

In a take-home exam still be conscious of what is relevant and irrelevant

Viva voce

A viva voce is a face-to-face discussion with your lecturer. Usually the viva voce will be in the form of direct questions asked of you by your lecturer and you will be assessed on the answers. Usually such sessions do not allow you to refer to materials but some do. From an academic's point of view it is singularly unimpressive to wait five minutes while a student looks up material that will help them answer the question. Sometimes a viva voce will be held in a group, say five students in a room with the lecturer who is asking different questions of each student individually. Because of time restrictions and the large number of law students, these sessions will generally be relatively short compared to a formal exam. So your answers will carry significant weight in the overall mark. Always make

A viva voce is a face-to-face oral examination

sure you understand the question properly before answering. If necessary, ask for a moment to craft your answer in your mind or by jotting down some dot points so that you achieve the best possible mark.

In terms of preparation, you should prepare the same way that you would prepare for a formal closed book exam. To a certain extent your memory is being tested in a viva voce. However, like a formal exam you are also being tested on your understanding of legal concepts and sometimes it is easier to explain a concept orally rather than in writing. So for some students, a viva voce is an easier form of assessment. As already stated, you must be able to identify the legal issues and know the relevant law that assists you to answer the question posed by the academic. Further, you need to be able to argue persuasively for the interpretation of the facts and the law that you favour. This is challenging when you are under pressure.

A viva voce draws on your ability to memorise the law and articulate an argument

When answering questions in a viva voce, you should take time to think about the question. Do not rush into an answer that you may later regret. You will need to think quickly and decide how you will approach the answer to the question. Try to map it out in your mind, but do not go into overload! Just try to raise one, two, or at the most three points that you will argue and try to remember the relevant law surrounding those points. Do not try to use overly sophisticated language—keep your message as simple as possible. Use plain legal English and try to draw simple examples from the relevant precedents. Stay calm and keep your wits about you. Do not be worried if the lecturer interrupts you to clarify a point—treat this sort of an interruption as being helpful rather than as a hindrance. The academic is simply suggesting you narrow in on a particular element of your argument. This is a good sign and you should listen and go down the path the lecturer wants you to take because that is obviously where the answer lies.

Keep it simple—just try to make one, two, or no more than three points

Multiple choice

Multiple choice questions are not often used by law schools to examine students, the reason being that multiple choice does not allow you to analyse the facts and the relevant law and synthesise an argument. Multiple choice just forces you to choose a single usually unqualified answer. However, should you encounter multiple choice questions in your course of study, beware—they can be one of the hardest forms of examination depending on how the questions are constructed.

Multiple choice questions are not often used at law school

Some multiple choice questions are drafted so that there are four or more similar answers with only a small difference between the suggested answers. Other multiple choice questions are drafted so that there are four or more answers with interchangeable components and your job is to select the right component. On rare occasions you may come across the multiple choice question that gives four or more totally different responses. This last type of question is the easiest to answer given the stark difference between the suggested answers.

Be conscious of the different structure of multiple choice questions

In terms of preparation, you should prepare in the same way as you would prepare for a formal exam. Chances are that such questions would be set in a formal open book style exam. So the same rules for preparation apply. The only additional preparation you should consider is obtaining some practice questions so that you can be comfortable with the style of questions. Hopefully your lecturer will be able to point you in the right direction in order to find some examples.

Find some multiple choice questions to practise on before the exam

In terms of writing the exam, there is one very important point to consider. One of the problems with multiple choice questions is that if you reread the question too many times, the answers start to blur together. The process of successfully answering these types of questions is to read the question carefully once, then read the question again. Make sure you understand exactly what your lecturer is seeking from the answer. Then read the answers once. Usually the correct answer will be apparent. However, you will want to reread the answers to make sure. If you are still not sure, reread the answers a third time. However, do not reread them a fourth time as the blurring process will commence and confusion will set in. If you cannot decide on the right answer after you have read them a third time then move on to the next question and come back to the question or questions you have missed.

Do not read the answers more than three times

One final point, stick to the time you have allocated for the set of multiple choice questions. Multiple choice questions are likely to be worth anything between half a mark and two marks each; therefore, wasting too much time on any one question is counter-productive when you consider the marks available for the rest of the exam. When answering exams you must apportion your time to achieve the best possible marks. This means weighing the value of the question in the context of the entire exam.

Stick to the time you have allocated to answer the questions

Legal problems

Legal problems consist of a fact pattern featuring people or organisations conducting themselves in a way that leads to a potential legal problem. The legal problem then directs you to advise one or more parties involved in the fact pattern. It is suggested that you should use the legal problem-solving model discussed in Chapter 5 of this book to answer legal problems.

Use the legal problem-solving model to answer problems in an exam

For preparation, you should adopt the same procedure as described above for formal/informal and open or closed book exams depending on which type of exam you are going to sit. The only extra work you need do is to be familiar with the model prior to sitting the exam. If you have not used the model in tutorials then you should go over Chapter 5 again and ensure you understand how to answer questions using the model. You should obtain some legal problems, which are commonly found in law school libraries where previous exams are kept, and practise on them under mock exam conditions. If possible, have a tutor or fellow law student mark them not only for legal content and the correct application of the law but also to assess the structure of your answer using the legal problem-solving model.

Practise some legal problems to prepare yourself for using the model

Essays

Essay-style questions are very challenging as they raise the potential for an endless amount of writing. Clearly this is not so in an exam as the time allowed will limit how much you can write. It is this criterion alone that forces you to plan an exam essay very carefully. Most questions will require you to refer to certain theories or philosophies or substantive law (cases and statutes) or a combination of any of these referred to in the subject throughout the semester. You should reread Chapter 11 regarding drafting an essay plan. However, in a formal exam, you do not have the time to spend too long on drafting such a plan—so always keep in mind the time limitations.

Draft an essay plan when answering an essay question in an exam

You should prepare as you would for a formal/informal and an open/closed book exam. As discussed earlier in this chapter, summarise the relevant theories and philosophies referred to throughout the semester and be clear on what each theorist

Dot point the views of theorists in your exam notes for easy reference

and philosopher had to say about the relevant areas of the law they have provided commentary on. Note their views in dot point form in your exam notes for easy reference. Be familiar with their point of view and be prepared to argue your understanding of the various theories and philosophies as well as your own view on whether those theories and philosophies accurately reflect how the law operates within society.

In terms of writing an exam essay the rule of thumb, particularly in formal exams, is to stick to your essay plan and the time you have allocated to complete the essay. Too many students spend too much time on essays thinking the extra time will translate into extra marks. Chances are it will not. The only exception may be if you have not had time to make a major point in the essay. This is a result of bad planning and should be avoided in the process of drafting your essay plan. Some students have great success in breaking the essay up into topics and allocating a time period to complete each topic. Whichever system you use, just ensure you do not waste time chasing extra marks that generally you will not earn by spending an extra fifteen minutes on the essay question.

Stick to your essay plan and the time you have allocated to write the essay

One final point

It does not matter what kind of examination that you are completing, there is one golden rule. Answer the question! It is worthwhile reading the question several times then referring to it several times throughout the process of writing a draft answer or essay plan. It is even worthwhile referring to the question again throughout the process of writing the assessed piece. If it is a prepared piece of work you should certainly reread the question prior to handing in the piece of work. The point is simply this—sometimes when you have conducted some research or you have read some exam notes your mind becomes diverted from the actual question. It is surprising the frequency of students who refer to good authorities in their writing but do not actually answer the question. From a marker's point of view it is very frustrating reading a paper where the student has skirted around the issues using the right authorities and not actually answered the question.

Make sure you actually answer the question

Our final tip is to read the last sentence or paragraph of a large problem or theoretical question first. This will allow you to subconsciously look out for elements of the question that

Read the instructional words first

will lead you to the issues being raised and possible ways to answer the issues raised. For example, the following style of final questions often appears in legal problem-based exam questions:

(a) Has the client entered a contract?
(b) Advise the client on what remedies are available?

It would be easy to draft one fact pattern where both these questions are asked. If you know what the actual question is asking while you are reading the fact pattern, your mind will be looking for words and facts that will help answer the actual question. In other words, know what you are being asked and what you are looking for before you start reading the fact pattern.

14

GAINING CONFIDENCE AND DEVELOPING PROFESSIONAL HABITS

I hope I pass my exams and get a degree but, in any case, I'm going to enjoy myself.

Mary Robinson[1]

1 Mary Robinson, Chancellor, University of Dublin, former President of the Republic of Ireland and UN High Commissioner for Human Rights, explaining how she was intending to approach her studies at Harvard Law School: O'Leary, O. & Burke, H., 'Mary Robinson: The Authorised Biography' (London: Sceptre/Lir, 1998).

Introduction

In this chapter we close with some ideas about how to develop confidence in yourself as an adult learner, what to do when you need help, and how to begin your development as a future professional. At the outset, we believe that your obvious interest in becoming a lawyer and succeeding at law school means that you are best able to determine when you need help, what resource to use to assist you, and how to get it. Our experience of law students is that you will know:

- when you need help, because as an independent and self-motivated learner you will recognise when you are finding something confusing or difficult;
- that when a question or problem arises that you cannot answer there is usually someone who knows the answer, or somewhere you can go to help find the answer; and,
- that if you simply ask the question to the relevant person, or actively look for the answer in a book, library, or computer database, you will normally find it.

If what we say is true then you should have confidence in your own judgment to decide when things have become too confusing or difficult and you should therefore actively and confidently seek help. We acknowledge that there is a real sense of isolation for many new to university or law school. This comes about as a result of grappling with a new discipline, its jargon and processes. Our experience is that many law students in their first year struggle to come to grips with how the law should be read and what is expected by law school lecturers. It also comes from the fact that most of your student colleagues are clearly quite intelligent and may have the veneer of confidence and success. We urge you not to be so fooled. Our advice is twofold. First you need to develop confidence in your own learning abilities by becoming active in your studies. Do not avoid the hard readings and activities but relish the intellectual challenge. Second, think about what you hope to achieve from your degree program and consider that if part of those hopes includes becoming a legal practitioner then you need to instil or develop certain personal characteristics to properly represent the interests of your clients.

Developing courage

One of the little discussed components of studying and practising law is courage. Courage arises in many contexts but is essential to professional survival and ethical decision-making. In the following section we note the necessity to be courageous in order to successfully negotiate your way through law school. We also note the necessity for courage in legal practice and how courage is an underestimated quality of ethical legal practice.

Courage in your studies

You need to be brave and confident to respond to adversity and interact with many strange, and sometimes aggressive and adversarial people. If you intend to do this for others, as a professional advocate or adviser, then you may as well start by becoming a good advocate for yourself and learn to interact with others professionally and with confidence. In particular, you will need to develop your ability to understand when you are unable to do something and know that there is no shame in asking for help. We are aware of students who have felt very intimidated by their studies at the beginning of their degree program but who sought advice and achieved personal success. In one example a student failed a mid-semester assessment task in his first semester but sought help and consequently developed a study plan suitable for his lifestyle (as a working man with a young family). This student completed his law degree with honours, wrote a textbook for use by professional law colleagues and has a successful career at the Bar. Another student came from a non-English speaking background, and was recently divorced with a small child. This student sought advice in relation to improving her reading and writing skills as well as her legal and philosophical analysis skills. This single mother studied full-time and achieved her honours degree, and then a postgraduate degree, by research, in minimum time. These are but two examples of many where students have been determined to work through their initial sense of isolation or confusion and flourished.

If you feel intimidated ask for help

FACING FEARS

Another form of courage in law school studies is the ability to face your fears. One of the biggest fears many people have is the fear of public speaking. This is an understandable fear as by making comments in a public forum one places oneself in a position of immediate criticism, if not ridicule. Most, if not all, law courses require students to make some form of public presentation. Whether it be answering a question, presenting to a class, being an advocate in a moot or mock trial, or undergoing a viva voce examination, almost all law students will need to 'perform' at least once during their studies. Some students enjoy the challenge of testing their limits and others are wracked with panic. If you sense that you might be in the latter category then you will need to undertake certain preparations to give yourself the best chance of success.

So what can you do? The first stage of preparation is to understand the fact that public speaking does not kill. That might seem trite and condescending, but the truth is that many people, who have felt the deepest dread at speaking in public, have managed to overcome that fear, even if only for the limited purpose of successfully completing university studies. On a rational basis one is simply being asked to stand up and utter some words. We stand up and talk every day. The difference is that the words you will speak have usually been created, refined and produced many days in advance of the date of the assessment event. Simply, you will normally always have time to prepare what you need to say and all you are being asked to do, in a public speaking exercise, is speak those words, or speak a form of those well-rehearsed words in certain fashion.

The second stage of preparation is doing it. This requires time management. You simply cannot leave your preparation to the last minute. In the same way that an essay produced on the morning it is due is vastly inferior to one you have spent several weeks preparing, so your confidence in the words of an oral presentation will be stronger if you have spent time researching and developing those words carefully.

The third stage of preparation involves articulating those words you have prepared. You must practice physically enunciating the words you think you might say. Begin by talking to yourself—in front of a mirror can help—then in front of family and friends. The real benefit of rehearsing a speech in front of a family member or friend, particularly one who is not conversant with the law, is that you will be called upon to explain things that may not make sense more frequently than if you rehearse in front of someone who is aware of your topic and may be able to fill in the gaps if you have omitted something. In rehearsing, you should be conscious of the natural cadence of the words, your normal manner of speaking and any time limit you need to comply with. In addition to physically practising the words of an oral presentation, we recommend that you consider the 'uniform' that you will wear to undertake your task. If you are to speak in a court setting there may be a suggestion, or compulsion, to wear business attire. Like any sporting, industrial or artistic activity, there are real benefits—here psychological and physical—to practising what you are being assessed to do in the outfit you will wear on the relevant day. You would not take to the hockey field without shin-pads or a mouthguard; you would not enter a building site without a safety helmet, nor jump on a motorbike without appropriate protective clothing. Similarly, you would not feel that you are performing like a lawyer if you were not suitably attired.

Fourth, if you believe you just cannot engage in the activity, if you have experienced 'freezing' in a public speaking forum before, then you have other forms of assistance. The counselling service at your university will offer guidance and classes to assist in overcoming this fear. There are books that are specifically devoted to this topic. And there are exercises you can perform that will show you that you can speak in public, you can look and feel foolish, but you will not suffer long-term embarrassment or worse. One exercise we are familiar with is that used for those suffering a form of social phobia involving public speaking. The exercise simply requires the suffering person to board a bus, tram, or non-quiet train carriage, and several stops from the end of a journey to stand up and announce to the bus that 'The next stop is … (whatever the stop is).' The reason for the activity is to show the person who is suffering that they can: say something in public; say something that is not anything offensive or necessary but is perhaps a little unusual; feel embarrassment or other feelings; but realise that it is possible to have those feelings and still speak to others.

We acknowledge that speaking before a law school examiner includes more than just public speaking. It includes fear of possible failure, fear of possible loss of prestige in front of law school colleagues and more. However, many of these fears may be overcome if you properly prepare your work and practise that natural ability you have to speak.

The necessity of courage in legal practice

Every day legal practitioners are required to be courageous. Whether it be facing the displeasure of a senior member of a law firm or judicial officer, dealing with a disgruntled client, or responding to an aggressive opposing practitioner, legal practitioners must be able to stand up and argue on behalf of their clients and themselves. Sometimes the courage is to put forward arguments on behalf of a client in circumstances where you feel pressure not to do so. In others it may be speaking out in a forum where you are a lone voice and speaking against the desires of many others. In other circumstances it may be simply giving bad news to a client, or partner. In all these situations there is a level of bravery required to deal with the potential reactions of others. But perhaps the area where courage is paramount is in relation to a practitioner's ethical decision-making. One example would be where a practitioner has made an error. A number of responses by the individual who errs are possible, including blaming another or avoiding the issue. However, a practitioner who rightly accepts responsibility for an error and makes attempts to mitigate the damage from the error will be respected more than those who are subsequently found to be responsible but did not accept that responsibility. Being candid with a court, employer or client is essential.

A second example is one experienced by a student who had graduated and obtained a position in a small firm. This practitioner was asked to sign a form by her boss. The practitioner knew that by signing the form, not only would she be misleading a court, but she would be financially harming the relevant client. The practitioner was aware that her boss would be very unhappy if she did not sign the form and so she sought advice before acting. After thinking through her options the practitioner did not sign the form and, consequently, was dismissed from the firm for not having complied with that order. Leaving aside the disgraceful behaviour of the boss it is important to reflect on the courage of the practitioner here. She knew what the legal and ethically correct thing to do was, as she had spoken with an advisor in addition to researching the law. She had made the decision to comply with the law and professional and personal ethics. And importantly, she had the courage to implement her ethically correct decision in practice. You must note the point we are making here. There is a significant difference between knowing what the correct thing to do is and actually doing it. The latter takes real courage and sometimes, unfortunately, may result in negative ramifications.

The three components of the student's decision in the above example neatly mirror the broad decision-making model suggested by Parker and Evans.[2]

2 Christine Parker & Adrian Evans, 'Inside Lawyers' Ethics' (Cambridge University Press, 2007).

DECISION-MAKING MODEL

1 Be aware of the ethical issues that arise in practice, and of our own values and predispositions.
2 Take into account a range of standards and values that are available to help resolve those ethical issues and make a choice between them.
3 Implement the resolution in practice.

Your law school experience begins as soon as you enrol

If you are new to university studies you should understand that being a successful and confident student begins on your first day—usually enrolment or orientation day. On your first day it is understandable if you are nervous or shy. It is also understandable if you do not talk too much and get through the day by filling in some forms, getting your library card (usually your student identification card), and answering a few simple administrative questions. But what if you walk away not knowing when the first classes begin, or whether you should buy a textbook or two, when borrowed library books are due back, what to read for your first classes, or where those classes are to be held? Such a level of confusion will only make you anxious when it comes to returning to university for orientation or your first lecture.

On day one at university you must clearly understand three things. First, most people you meet in official capacities (whether at university or in the legal profession) are willing to help you if you ask. Unless the person you ask is stressed by issues unknown to you, or you have approached them in a discourteous fashion, then you will generally find that people will not be rude or unhelpful but will try to assist you if they can. Second, whether the person you approach for help is the vice-chancellor of the university or a fellow student or the person who empties the campus garbage bins they are all human beings. As such everyone should be approached respectfully but without fear. The point we make here is that universities are, or should be, egalitarian places of higher learning. Just because a person has a certain title (like 'the Dean') or has a tough reputation (as some lecturers do) does not mean that they are unable to be approached and asked for advice. The fear of those high in the hierarchy causes a lot of students to remain silent when they have valid concerns or questions that could be solved simply by speaking up. Third, you must be confident enough to ask for help if you need it. If you remain silent, no one, not even those who are keen to assist you, will be able to help. We also note the oft-used command in tutorials: 'If you have a question then most of the time most of the rest of the class will have the same question too—so ask it!'

To conclude we urge you to develop confident personal communication skills. If you are someone who already has very good skills—you may have been a debater at school, or the best writer of essays in your last degree—then you are better placed than many others. However, we can confidently say that as good a communicator as you are you will have room for improvement and law school can help you with that. If you are someone who is less confident about your skills then becoming confident will be a requirement of your law program, if not your subsequent career. Regardless of your current skill level, bear in mind that if you need help, you must communicate it.

Approaching your lecturers

In earlier chapters we discussed how you should approach your lecturers when you have academic questions. Here we revisit the topic and add some ideas about what to do when you need help with non-academic issues.

Demeanour

It might seem odd that we need to discuss this term when applied to student interactions with lecturers, particularly as many law students are already quite mature or working in professional environments. But our experience is that some students really do not understand how they present themselves to the world and how that presentation might be perceived by others they come onto contact with. This is very important when you are approaching a lecturer, because in the context we are speaking of here, you are usually communicating with your lecturer for some form of favour—either advice, clarification, or help—whether in class or not. It also goes to the development of a professional approach in your communications.

Most people you ask for help will help you

Good communication skills are essential, especially if you are seeking help

Consider how your manner will be perceived by your lecturers

Perhaps the best way to begin is to state that we are not attempting to place lecturers on some sort of higher status that requires students to treat them especially carefully or preciously. We are not saying that students should act in a fawning or grovelling way in order to gain favour. What we are suggesting is that your lecturers should be approached respectfully and courteously, because it is very difficult to develop a rapport with someone if you have been treated rudely, and your lecturers are no different from anyone else. A good way to illustrate our concerns about demeanour is to provide a few examples of behaviours in various contexts that are simply unacceptable.

TABLE 14.1 Maintaining a Courteous Demeanour

Please remember	Do not
Sometimes your lecturer may be on the telephone, conducting a test, out of the office, speaking with someone about confidential matters, and to interrupt may be perceived as quite invasive.	Enter your lecturer's office until you are invited to do so.
	Ignore any reasonable directions given to you in a class situation.
	Speak over the top of your lecturer (or any other member of class) unless for a very important reason.
Always ask politely with reasons because one 'attracts more with honey than vinegar'.	Write to your lecturer 'demanding' a re-mark of a paper, extension on an assignment, other assistance, etc.
Some lecturers demand full courtesies such as being called Professor, Doctor, Mister, or Ms as appropriate and they will, or should, reciprocate when so referring to you. Many lecturers in law today are less formal than in times past when many judges and barristers ran law schools and treated class in the same way as they would a court. Indeed many lecturers insist on being referred to by their first name only. But you will only find out by experience, so begin formally in case your lecturer is of the 'old school'.	Improperly address your lecturer.
When first communicating in writing, never communicate by first name, or worse still, no name!	Fail to use a lecturer's full title (even if only Mr/Ms) when first communicating in writing.

Please remember	Do not
	Consider that colloquial or risqué email communications, which may be acceptable to your friends, will be acceptable to your lecturer.
Always consider email to be 'exactly' the same as a formal letter and avoid ambiguities and poorly expressed comments that, on paper, look insulting, damaging or reflect poorly upon you.	Use email as though it is an alternative form of speech.
Frequently lecturers receive email correspondence from students where the email address gives no idea as to who has sent the message. If a lecturer receives an email that ends 'Yours sincerely, your favourite student' and the reply email address is <highcourtjudge@sick.com.au> it hardly gives the lecturer a genuine clue as to whom she or he is communicating with. Most universities insist that students correspond with university staff via their official university email account.	Fail to provide your full name and contact details in all communications.
	Come into class late without offering an apology.
	Come back from a break late.
Lecturers would prefer that you ask for permission to have your telephone on for good reason—such as a potential emergency—than for you to miss such a call or miss your class.	Fail to turn off your mobile telephone when in class, or in a meeting with your lecturer unless you have prior approval to leave it on.
If your mobile telephone rings, at worst, you should immediately leave the room; at best, you should not answer the call but simply turn your telephone off. We know of lecturers who will take a bucket of water to their first lecture to emphasise the potentially drastic consequences for your mobile telephone if it rings in their class!	Compound the mobile telephone taboo and answer it and then have a conversation in class.
Lecturers are not stupid and will resent having their time and that of your colleagues interrupted. Lecturers may also deduct participation marks if you are not constantly engaged in the class or physically present.	Run your personal life or business from class by having your mobile telephone vibrate with the result that you spend a lot of time leaving and returning to class.

(continued)

TABLE 14.1 Maintaining a Courteous Demeanour (*continued*)

Please remember	Do not
	Take up class time complaining about a personal grade on an assignment, or discussing personal issues relating to your studies, when a more appropriate forum is after class or during a break.
Part of the professional development of law students is the recognition that honesty is a crucial part of any lawyer's makeup. Never fall into the trap of trying to lie your way out of a problem. Frequently the truth will serve you better than any lie would. Further, if you are caught out as a liar you may suffer professional consequences. (See Chapter 12 and our discussion of academic misconduct and admission to the legal profession.)	Fail to be candid if you have done something wrong.

Non-academic issues

Many students will experience times when they find that their student workload is too much for them and feel they are compelled to hand things in late, or produce sub-standard work. This may be because of employment pressures, family commitments, medical or other personal conditions, or some alternative form of misadventure. Some students will suffer in silence and submit late or sub-standard work. Other students will approach their lecturers and seek advice about how they might be able to avoid academic penalty because of their non-university commitments or problems. We recommend that you speak with your lecturers about such issues if they are truly matters that are unexpected or out of your control. Your lecturers will usually be able to help if you have certain family or personal problems that are unforeseen. For instance, it is clear that most people will find difficulty completing their studies in a timely fashion if a close family relation suddenly dies, or they become very ill for an extended period of time. Be aware: most lecturers will not usually be interested in assisting you if you ask for an extension on assignments simply because you let your university work build up, or you made a miscalculation about how long an assignment might take to complete. Equally your lecturers will probably not be terribly approachable if you indicate that your difficulties revolve around you voluntarily taking on too much work (such as undertaking a full-time job while engaged in a full-time degree program) or study (for instance by accelerating your course beyond the normal progression pattern). Having said that, we recognise that it can be easy to miscalculate the demands of your legal studies, particularly when you first begin law school. It is better to approach your lecturers if you encounter a time-management problem and seek advice about how to resolve it, rather than submitting sub-standard, or late, work. However, you cannot abuse the trust that your lecturers expect from you. Should you become known as someone who is always requiring an extension or assistance you can be sure that the same reputation will follow you into practice. On this last point judges and magistrates are much less forgiving.

If balancing your work and life commitments with your legal studies ends up becoming a serious problem you should consider one of the following:

- seek advice from a university counsellor about how to better manage your commitments
- withdraw from one or more units of study until you have made the adjustments necessary to successfully pursue your law studies
- defer your studies for a semester or a year, subject to your university rules
- re-evaluate where and how you live while you study. If, for example, you have moved out of the family home, it may be worth considering moving back in with your parents
- finding another job that allows you more time to study

Importantly, if you choose to withdraw from any units, or defer your studies, always do so according to your university's rules and BEFORE the relevant HECS census date.

Be proactive if you perceive a problem

Where you know that a problem may arise you should always be proactive and approach your lecturer, or perhaps a counsellor or disability adviser (see below), to work out a solution that works for you. The following are a few examples of situations that may call for leniency in deadlines, or alternative assessment arrangements. For instance, if you are a person who has a known business commitment that will take you away from university for a few weeks you might be able to undertake other sorts of work to make up for class attendances. Alternatively, you might be permitted to submit your tutorial notes electronically instead of the usual face-to-face. Equally you should approach your lecturer, counsellor, or disability adviser, if you are someone who has a disability that might cause you to be disadvantaged relative to other students when it comes to some of your assessments. If you are dealing with a family member who has a long-term illness, or you have peculiar childcare arrangements then you should also bring these things to your lecturer's attention. There is nothing worse for lecturers than to be presented with such information and requests for help after a deadline. Usually nothing can be done and the student has suffered where, had they acted in a more timely way, such suffering need not have occurred.

A FEW NOTES OF CAUTION

- Whatever your situation is, make sure that you are realistic about its effect upon you so that your lecturer is in a better position to gauge what the best solution is. To say that you need a two-week extension on an essay because you became ill the night before it was due is unrealistic in terms of the amount of time requested.
- Never make a dishonest claim. While lecturers respect your need for confidentiality in these sorts of matters there are times when they become aware that someone's great Aunt Bessie has passed away for the fourth time. If a law student is caught fabricating such claims for the purpose of gaining some academic advantage then professional repercussions may ensue (see Chapter 12).
- Always be prepared to provide evidence of your claim—if you can take it with you when you first approach your lecturer then that can be quite helpful. This may be personally uncomfortable to deal with—particularly if you have suffered a death in the family—but many lecturers, or other university officers, will require written proof of something beyond what you state, no matter what the claim is. Normally this will simply be a personal medical certificate, or a note from an employer, but may also be a copy of a death certificate.

Frequently asked questions

TABLE 14.2 FAQs

Whom do I ask about enrolment issues?	Sometimes your lecturer, or law school, will be responsible but usually you need to direct all such enquiries to the student administration section of your university.
Whom could I speak with about my disability and its effect on my studies?	Universities have policies and procedures specifically designed to assist students with disabilities. You should become familiar with your university's policy and contact the relevant officer to discuss your situation. The university will, without breaching your confidence, inform the law school and your lecturers of the need to implement different procedures to assist your learning. Most lecturers are very interested to know that what they do in the classroom is effective for all students, and so if your learning may suffer under the standard teaching arrangements you should avail yourself of any assistance that the policy can provide. Some lecturers may ask their students to complete a disability survey at the beginning of semester so that they are able to plan their teaching approaches. If you feel uncomfortable disclosing such personal information to your lecturer check your university's disability policy and see if there is a disability officer to whom you can speak instead.
I cannot hand my assignment in on time. What do I do?	Always speak with your lecturer after examining the school's policy on assignment submission. If there is good reason for that lateness then you might be able to obtain an extension.
I feel uncomfortable with the behaviour of a fellow student. What do I do?	Always have a confidential conversation with your lecturer. Most lecturers are experienced in dealing with these issues and, providing your concern is genuine, your lecturer can usually discreetly cause changes in behaviour. If more direct options—such as moving students to different classes—are required then your lecturer can do that too.
I have real concerns with my lecturer and am uncomfortable in the class.	Most lecturers are reasonable people and if they are doing something that is of concern to you they would want to know about it so that they can do something about it (if required) or explain why their behaviour is the way it is (there may be pedagogical reasons for it). Most law schools would want you to speak to the lecturer first. In the event that you think such a conversation is not in your best interests then you should proceed up the 'food chain' to the unit coordinator, program coordinator, or head of school/Dean.
I have a timetable clash. Who do I speak with?	Unless the system is an automated system normally your School's administrative staff or unit coordinator will be the person who knows the answer. If they cannot help, they will know who to direct you to.

(continued)

TABLE 14.2 FAQs (*continued*)

I have two major assignments due on the same day. What can I do?	If there is a clash within your law units then you should politely complain to your lecturers. Most programs endeavour to avoid such clashes within year cohorts, and if enough of your fellow students are affected then you might find that one of the submission dates can be changed.
What do I do when I cannot 'log-on' to the unit materials as made available on the school's intranet?	In the first instance you should see your lecturer as there may be some difficulties at the university end. However, if you are informed that the unit site is operational then you might need to speak to student administration about your enrolment status—some universities preclude access to the library and other services until certain fees are paid.
What should I do when the campus bookshop tells me they have sold out of the textbook for one of my law units?	Tell your lecturer because the lecturer might have alternative materials, or know that a new order for books has been made. Generally speaking most capital cities have law bookstores that sell most of the law textbooks. You should ring a few of those.
Whom should I speak to about a personal issue that is affecting, or may affect, my studies?	Most lecturers are empathetic and will strive to assist you through personal problems to the extent that they affect your studies. However, lecturers are usually not qualified counsellors. If you need counselling advice, or feel uncomfortable disclosing certain matters to your lecturer, then see the counselling service within your university.

What to do if you feel you have been treated unfairly

We noted above the need for law students to develop confidence and personal communication skills. If you genuinely feel aggrieved about an assessment event or other treatment associated with your academic studies then you should approach your lecturer in the first instance. You should do so politely but assuredly and explain how you feel you have been unfairly treated. If your lecturer agrees with you then you might obtain a more favourable result. If your lecturer disagrees with you then you should politely request an explanation. Frequently the answer you receive clarifies a misunderstanding thus allowing you to change your thoughts about mistreatment. Sometimes you and your lecturer will simply disagree about a point that involves academic discretion or judgment. If, however, you do not receive an explanation at all, or the answer you get is inadequate then you would be entitled to complain to your lecturer's supervisor, usually a program coordinator. We are not trying to make life difficult for our colleagues when we suggest this, but we would prefer that a genuine concern be properly dealt with. On the odd occasion academic practices have been changed because a student was courageous enough to call certain behaviours into question. This form of courage is an important quality in law students as well as in professional lawyers.

Appeals or reviews of grade

By following the advice in this book we hope that you will not have to use the appeal or result review mechanisms that your university has installed. Appeals and result reviews are available for students who fail a unit and/or feel that they have been unfairly treated and received a grade lower than they expected. In some universities this appeal mechanism applies to all grade boundaries. Usually, a student is able to use the appeal or review mechanism only if they fall within certain 'grounds' specified in the university calendar or regulations. These grounds typically include: an arguable belief that your marks have not been properly calculated; that you suffered some form of misadventure that was not taken into account at the time your grades were calculated; that you were disadvantaged by something your lecturer did or did not do. Students who use the appeal or review mechanism usually need to provide the university with an application, in writing, sometimes on a special form, within a specified period after results are published. Should you ever need to be involved in this process please be sure to read your university's calendar or regulations very carefully as strict time limits and other restrictions might apply.

Counsellors and disabilities

All universities have some form of counselling service available to students. Counsellors are trained psychologists with expertise in student matters. The student counselling service will typically be able to provide you with advice, care, and information on a vast range of topics. Some of the matters that counsellors deal with include:

- learning difficulties (although your university may also have learning specialists, such as student skills support officers, who complement the counsellors);
- advocacy and support for students—helping students contact their lecturers about confidential matters;

- bereavement counselling;
- management of personal disputes with university staff or fellow students;
- time management;
- misadventure; and
- harassment (your university may have an EEO or discrimination officer dedicated to these matters).

Studying law is not a simple task. It is challenging and the drop-out rate can be high due to the complexity of the material and the level of application you are required to give to your studies. The sorts of marks required of school leavers to gain entry into law school are high (usually in the top decile) and the calibre of student creates competition within the student body. There is competition for certain jobs in the profession—this in turn creates further pressure to achieve high marks at law school. Whether you are a graduate student studying law over three years or an undergraduate student studying a combined law degree over five or six years, it is likely that your life will change over the period that you are a law student. This means that you may be subjected to any number of different types of family and relationship pressures and breakdowns. Like death or serious illness in the family or of a close friend, these pressures can often divert your attention away from your studies.

The most common issues before counsellors tend to be personal issues that impact on your ability to cope with the workload of your degree program. If you find that you are struggling to cope with life, work and study then you should see a counsellor for two reasons. First, chances are that you are worried about the problem that is affecting your ability to study. Worrying over such matters is detrimental to your health, so you are doing yourself no good intellectually and physically by allowing the problem to 'fester'. It is better to talk through the problem with a trained counsellor who may be able to assist you to solve the problem. Second, counsellors can usually help you remove or shift the pressure created by the university workload. In most cases, the university counsellor will, in conjunction with you and your lecturers, put in place a study plan to assist you to successfully get through the unit or units you are currently struggling with. You should never feel defeated by going to see a counsellor—they are trained professionals who can assist you to deal with personal problems or an excessive workload during your life at law school. They are there to work with you, and the academics teaching you, to assist you in successfully learning the law and learning life skills.

Disability officers

Disability officers exist within universities or law schools. These people have specialist interest or training in the development of disability programs for students who are identified as having a disability. Students who are eligible for a disability program may have assessment arrangements different from those of their colleagues. This difference is not to advantage the disabled student, but rather to place the disabled student in a position such that they are not disadvantaged relative to their colleagues. A disability program may allow for automatic extensions on submissions for assignments, more time in examinations, the adoption of different teaching practices by the lecturer, or the use of other devices not normally used in classrooms. In this day and age there is no reason why a disability should prevent you from successfully studying law. There are many law students who have been sight-disabled, or restricted to a wheelchair, and their disability has not stopped them from being high achievers in government and academia. Likewise there have been judges and senior solicitors and barristers who have risen to the highest levels of the profession carrying a disability of some description. Disability officers are there to ensure that, as far as possible, your disability does not prevent you from achieving your learning objectives. Disability officers are there to assist you to achieve your learning objectives and have the expertise to assist you in formulating an integration plan that will see your disability become less significant in your attempt to attain a law degree. They will coordinate with your lecturers and tutors to ensure that account is taken of your disability and any extra facilities are available to ensure you are studying on a level playing field with other students. Should you have a disability, you should make yourself known to the disability officer in your law school or university and discuss any potential for the development of an integration plan.

Further resources

You should become familiar with what your student union or law students' association can provide. In addition to social activities and functions, your student union or law students' association can provide:

- support in academic disputes;
- opportunities for entering regional, national, and international mooting, witness examination, paper presentation, client interviewing and other law related competitions;

- summer clerkship advice;
- career development seminars;
- peer mentoring;
- a forum for the sale of second-hand textbooks;
- facilities and resources not available elsewhere in your law school or university;
- help in forming study groups; and
- advice on a range of matters—economic, student fees, enrolment, housing, etc.

Finally

Studying law is intellectually challenging and may result in a very rewarding career. You should look back on your days at law school with fond memories and perhaps you will still see friends socially and/or professionally that you met at law school. We hope this book will help make your law school experience more satisfying and academically rewarding.

Remember, be proactive! Seek out the answers and take responsibility for your learning. In this way you will successfully negotiate becoming a lawyer.

Index